THE BUDDHIST TANTRAS

BUDDHIST TRADITIONS

Edited by
ALEX WAYMAN

VOLUME IX

The Buddhist Tantras

LIGHT ON INDO-TIBETAN ESOTERICISM

by Alex Wayman

Motilal Banarsidass
Publishers Pvt. Ltd.
Delhi

First Edition: New York, 1973
Reprinted: Delhi, 1990

ISBN: 81-208-0699-9

Also available at:
MOTILAL BANARSIDASS
Bungalow Road, Jawahar Nagar, Delhi 110 007
Chowk, Varanasi 221 001
Ashok Rajpath, Patna 800 004
24 Race Course Road, Bangalore 560 001
120 Royapettah High Road, Mylapore, Madras 600 004

PRINTED IN INDIA
BY JAINENDRA PRAKASH JAIN AT SHRI JAINENDRA PRESS, A-45 NARAINA INDUSTRIAL AREA, PHASE I, NEW DELHI 110 028 AND PUBLISHED BY NARENDRA PRAKASH JAIN FOR MOTILAL BANARSIDASS PUBLISHERS PVT. LTD., BUNGALOW ROAD, JAWAHAR NAGAR, DELHI 110007.

The author, Alex Wayman, in front of the OM MANI PADME HUM stone, Upper Dharamsala, H.P., Spring 1970.

FOREWARD

The author, Alex Wayman, here reprints a number of his published Tantra essays, and writes some others to fill out this work, *The Buddhist Tantras.* It has much material not readily available elsewhere in Western language sources. This new material includes such matters as the tantric theory of divinity, classification of offering materials, authoritative symbolism of the mandala-palace, an explanation of tantric ritual, the tantric teaching about the body's nine orifices, and the theory of female energy in the Buddhist Tantras. It concludes with a correlation of the two Tantra collections of the Tibetan Buddhist canon, which are the revealed Tantra in the Kanjur, and exegetical works in the Tanjur. The work is leavened with illustrations and drawings. The author demonstrates here, as he does in his other works on the Tantra, an "at-homeness" with the tantric literature; and shares with the reader his sympathetic burrowing in these recondite texts.

The edition is the same as the original one, except for a new frontispiece and minor changes at the outset for the Indian edition.

ALEX WAYMAN

CONTENTS

TABLES

PLATES

DRAWINGS

PREFACE

This work is prepared from my previously published articles in the field of the Buddhist Tantra plus new studies especially made to round out the material for a reasonably integrated volume. It has particular contact with two previous books in the tantric field, *Mkhas grub rje's Fundamentals of the Buddhist Tantras*, translated by F. D. Lessing and Alex Wayman (Mouton, 1968)—which I refer to as *Mkhas grub rje's*; and my *Yoga of the Guhyasamājatantra; the Arcane Lore of Forty Verses* (the publication of which is going forward in Calcutta)—which I refer to as *Yoga of the Guhyasamājatantra*. *Mkhas grub rje's* is written by a Tibetan proficient in the Tantra on behalf of his Tibetan disciples. The *Yoga of the Guhyasamājatantra* is a synthetic commentary on forty verses written by myself as a Westerner and is almost completely based on the *Guhyasamājatantra* and commentarial literature in that lineage. In contrast, the present work goes further than the last one named in communicating varied aspects of the Buddhist Tantra to Westerners by researches based on texts sometimes using the *Guhyasamājatantra* lineage, but with special reliance on what are called the lower Tantras; and in the case of the fourth or highest class of Tantra with frequent utilization of the Mother Tantra (*Śrī-Cakrasaṃvara*, *Hevajra*, and *Kālacakra*); besides by more contact with the living tradition. That is why the present work is mainly different, both in content and in organization, from my two previous book engagements with the vast Buddhist Tantra literature. I also have under active preparation two other works in this field: Tibetan Miniature Paintings based on the Lessing manuscripts, which deals with the Buddhist Tantras principally in terms of individual deities; and Minor Buddhist Tantra Texts, with relatively brief but important texts in full translation. All those works, whether published or in press or preparation, have a common method which is the subordination of personal opinion about the Tantra to authoritative explanations by the proficients of this cult.

I am pleased to express appreciation to the following journals, publishers, or agents for permission to reprint in whole or part certain articles of mine: Bhandarkar Oriental Research Institute (Poona) (Golden Jubilee Volume) for "Early Literary History of the Buddhist Tantras . ." *Oriens Extremus* (Lessing Memorial issue) for "Buddhist Genesis and the Tantric Tradition." The Tibet Society Bulletin (Bloomington) for "Preparation of Disciples for Evocation of Deities." Adrien Maisonneuve, 11 rue St Sulpice Paris (Etudes tibétaines dédiées à la mémoire de Marcelle Lalou) for "Symbolism of the Maṇḍala Palace." Institut de Civilisation Indienne, Université de Paris (Mélanges d'Indianisme à la mémoire de Louis Renou) for "Concerning *saṃdhā-bhāṣā / saṃdhi-bhāṣā / saṃdhyā bhāṣā*." University of Chicago Press (which holds the copyright) for "Female Energy and Symbolism in the Buddhist Tantras" and portions of "Totemic Beliefs in the Buddhist Tantras" (*History of Religions*). Koyasan University (Japan) (Studies of Esoteric Buddhism and Tantrism) for "The Fivefold Ritual Symbolism of Passion." Lokesh Chandra, International Academy of Indian Culture (New Delhi) for "Outline of the Thob Yig Gsal baḥi Me Loṅ . . ." I have made corrections according to my present knowledge and minor changes for mutual consistency as well as some additions.

It is with deep gratitude that I express my indebtedness to Mrs. Margaret Lessing of Berkeley, California, for making available to me the manuscripts of the late Professor Ferdinand D. Lessing, which have furnished some invaluable materials for the present book, especially the photographs and texts he collected for his researches in the iconography and cult of the Lamaist temple of Peking, the Yung-Ho-Kung. These materials account for all the Plates, except for 1, 5, and 11. They also furnished models after which the Dharmodaya, Green Tārā, and Buddhaḍākinī drawings were executed by Mr. Osamu Yoshida.

The American Philosophical Society deserves thanks for its support of my travel to India in Spring 1970, which, while not for the express purpose of this book, fortuitously coincided with the Kālacakra ceremony in Dharmsala. My attendance at this important ritual occasion provided some of the living touches which secure a contemporary relevance for ancient texts. Plates 1, 5, and 11, are after photographs taken by my wife and myself during that ceremony.

There are varied text sources for the studies herein reproduced. Since so much is derived from Tibetan works—the overwhelming extant corpus for the Buddhist Tantra—I should be explicit. There are a number of references here to the Derge Kanjur and Tanjur and native Tibetan works at the University of California, Berkeley, from studies beginning in the early 1950's. The Tohoku catalogs to which I refer in connection with notes from these sources are described in my article "Female Energy . . ." (note 1). There are also many references by 'PTT' (with volume, page, and page folio number) to the Japanese photographic edition of the Peking Tibetan Buddhist canon (Kanjur and Tanjur) and including Tsoṅ-kha-pa's works. I used this edition after it was purchased by The University of Wisconsin, and eventually assembled a large collection of reproduced texts from this edition by the kind access to an excellent duplicating machine of the University-Industry Research Program Madison, Wisconsin. I still make much use of these duplicated texts with the added convenience of being able to make notes on the pages. Moreover, I use some texts of my own—preeminently for this book, Tsoṅ-kha-pa's *Sṅags rim chen mo* (which I often refer to as the *Sṅags rim*) in the Peking popular blockprint; this is his great compendium on the Buddhist Tantras. Besides, it was necessary to consult some further canonical works to complete the present book, and I have accordingly made some use of the Narthang edition of the Kanjur and Tanjur, now conveniently accessible at Columbia University.

For ease of combining the various published essays with further studies in the present form, I usually omit the original texts, Sanskrit and Tibetan, such as face the translation of *Mkhas grub rje's* and are abundant in *Yoga of the Guhyasamājatantra* as well as in my various published articles over the past twelve years. These omissions not only facilitate the reading of this book but also allow my transition from a former transcription of Tibetan to the Library of Congress transcription system. In all cases, references are given so that persons who wish may consult the original texts.

Finally, for the mechanics of issuance, I must thank Mr. Donald Weiser for his interest in publishing this book and the expeditious manner of his handling it.

I

INTRODUCTIONS

The great goddess located in the heart,
Causing the yogin's yoga -
The Mother of all the Buddhas -
Is called Queen of the Diamond Realm.

Sarvarahasya-tantra, verse 45.

1

PERFECTION OF INSIGHT: BUDDHIST TANTRA WITHIN MAHĀYĀNA BUDDHISM

"Perfection of Insight" is the translation of the term *prajñāpāramitā*, but not here employed in its sense of a certain body of Buddhist literature, namely the Prajñāpāramitā scriptures. The present discussion of *prajñāpāramitā* will show that it is through misunderstanding the role of this faculty that the status of Buddhist Tantra has been falsely explained, as though Mahāyāna Buddhism and Tantra under the name of Mantrayāna are two distinct and different things.

This is not to deny that if one takes tantric practices historically, in the sense of obscure cults which probably existed in India before even the rise of early Buddhism, those are essentially different from Mahāyāna. But also such obscure cults are different from what we now have as Buddhist Tantra, in terms of Tantric literature and associated practices. That is to say, both the Hindu Tantras and the Buddhist Tantras have thoroughly integrated those obscure cults into sectarian forms. The Buddhist Tantras are so imbued with Buddhist terminology, mainly of Mahāyāna Buddhist variety, that it is necessary to first study Mahāyāna Buddhism, especially in its formal presentation in the Mādhyamika and Yogācāra schools; otherwise one would be trying to find some mystical tantric meaning in an obscure phrase which in fact is clear enough when recognized as a Buddhist tenet from the Abhidharma literature or from those two Mahāyāna schools. Therefore, it is completely pointless to say, as some critics do, that the Buddhist Tantra is based on degenerate cults but that in some works the monks cleaned and tidied them up to give them a respectable form. Since the Tantra is essentially a practice, with incantations, breath control, and so forth, one must evaluate it by the way it is, as set forth in its principal "revealed" scriptures, authoritative commentaries, and actual practice as can still be observed (for example, among the Tibetans in India).

According to passages cited by Tsoṅ-kha-pa in the introductory section of his work on the stages of Tantra called *Sṅags rim chen mo*, the Mahāyāna (Great Vehicle) has two divisions—the prajñā pāramitā method (that part of Mahāyāna which is not tantric) and the mantra method (the strictly tantric part of the Mahāyāna). In his quotation (folio 12b-4) from the (Kālacakra work) *Vimalaprabhā*, these two wings of the Mahāyāna are termed "cause" and "effect". But also the Diamond Vehicle (Vajrayāna)—so called because the diamond is unsplittable and unbreakable—can be considered the Vehicle that incorporates both the *prajñāpāramitā* side (the "cause") and the *mantra* side (the "effect"). Therefore, the vehicle of the Bodhisattvas (who are the Mahāyāna saints) has two degrees, first the perfection of insight (*prajñāpāramitā*) and then the practice of mantras, initiation in the *maṇḍala*, etc. To observe this in a textual way, the reader may refer to the final section of this work for the "Outline of the Thob Yig Gsal Baḥi Me Loṅ," and notice how this compendium first gives the non-tantric background for the Tantras, and then the Tantras. Tsoṅ-kha-pa introduces further terminology (folio 12b-6) with a passage from the *Sekoddeśa:*

> Holding the form of the void is the cause;
> The fruit is the adherence to incessant compassion.
> The indissoluble union of voidness (*śūnyatā*) and compassion (*karuṇā*) is called "mind of enlightenment" (*bodhicitta*).

At 17a-1, he quotes the Tantra called *Vajrapañjarā* (Chap. One), as follows (my numbers):

(1) If the void were the means (*upāya*), then there would be no Buddhahood, because the fruit would not be different from the cause. The means is not voidness.

(2) Voidness has been taught by the Buddhas to ward off the adherence to a self on the part of those who have gone astray through views and of those who seek the view of self.

(3) Hence the binding as the means of ecstasy is called the *maṇḍala*-circle. The yogin with pride of a Buddha is close to Buddhahood.

(4) So he would accomplish with the means the thirty-two characteristics of the Teacher, along with the eighty minor marks of the Lord (*prabhu*). The means has the form of the Teacher.

Tsoṅ-kha-pa gives the key ideas of those four verses in their order: (1) rejecting the claim that exclusive contemplation of voidness is the means; (2) the requirement to teach voidness; (3) accompaniment of the great means which is not shared (with the Prajñāpāramitā way); (4) teaching reasons for requiring accomplishment with that means. The meaning of the *maṇḍala* as the unshared means is that in the Prajñāpāramitā way, the means is the first five perfections, of giving, morality, forbearance, striving, and meditation; with the perfection of insight as the sixth. At folio 18b-5,6, he points out that the five perfections go with accomplishing enlightenment in three incalculable eons. When the *maṇḍala*-circle (of deities) is taken as the means, with ecstasy due to "binding" of the male and female deities, this shows *devatā-yoga* (yoga of the deities) and produces divine pride (free from ordinary pride) which is the quick path to Buddhahood, that is to say, to acquirement of the two kinds of formal body (*rūpa-kāya*), the Sambhogakāya and the Nirmāṇakāya in the present life. Therefore, those four verses from the *Vajra-pañjarā* are important for elucidating this fundamental position of the Buddhist Tantra—the quick path. According to Tsoṅ-kha-pa, the same ideas can be garnered from other Tantras.

But while the Mantra way differs from the Prajñāpāramitā way as concerns the means, and therefore differs as regards fastness and slowness in attaining the goal of Buddhahood, Tsoṅ-kha-pa points out at folio 9a-2 and by subsequent citation of Mahāyāna sūtras, that there is no difference in terms of Prajñāpāramitā (perfection of insight) itself. He says (perhaps referring to Tibetan polyandry):

> A mother is the shared cause of the sons. A father is the cause of diversifying their lineages. In the same way, the Mother Perfection of Insight is the shared cause of the four Sons; while the cause of diversifying the great and lesser lineages of their vehicles is the means consisting in generating the mind (of enlightenment), and so forth.

That is to say, a difference in means (considered to be the father) diversifies the Hīnayāna into the Śrāvakayāna and the Pratyekabuddhayāna; while another difference in means diversifies the Mahāyāna into Mādhyamika and Yogācāra. But the Perfection of Insight (considered to be the mother) is the same for all the four Sons; and in consideration of this Mother of the Buddhas and Bodhisattvas, such a scripture as the *Saddharmapuṇḍarīka* (The Lotus of the Illustrious Law) sets forth the thesis of One Vehicle.

This insistence that the Prajñāpāramitā of the "Prajñāpāramitā vehicle" and of the "Mantra vehicle" is the common Mother lets us conclude that even when Prajñāpāramitā is personified as a goddess and represented in tantric iconography in union with the Buddha, that in fact it is still the same Prajñāpāramitā as is mentioned in the Prajñāpāramitā scriptures and in the various non-tantric Mahāyāna scriptures. But saying this will undoubtedly not satisfy the critics—both within and without the fold of Buddhism—who denounce the Buddhist Tantra as a degenerate development within late Buddhism. They will surely retort that it is a fine thing to extract this from a book, but that in practice Tantras has a worship of the female element in its concrete form of the woman. The ready answer of course is that one cannot deny such practices in some lineages of the Tantra, and that the same Tantra, by reason of metaphorical employment of words, can be understood differently. But, to be practical, it is passing strange that anyone would bother with the Tantra to justify his "degenerate" practice, for who so bent among worldly persons would divert his energies by muttering a *mantra* a hundred thousand times at dawn, noon, sunset, and midnight, with fasting and other inhibitions, to engage in a "degenerate" practice, when, as we know so well, people at large engage in degenerate practices without bothering to mortify themselves at dawn, noon, sunset, and midnight!

As one who over a long time has seen much sexual symbolism in these tantric books, I must insist that the Tantras containing such symbolism will never be understood if the reader simply extracts one sentence and judges the whole work thereby. In short, to appreciate what the Tantra amounts to, one must take it through an extended corpus, consult commentaries, and so on. This means spending some time with it, but the usual critic is too impatient. He makes his snap judgment on the basis that among all subjects the Tantra is the most easy to judge. That while one must study any recognized human discipline, such as chemistry, for years to talk responsibly about it, one does not have to work at Tantra for a whole day to speak authoritatively about it!

So I shall repeat what Tsoṅ-kha-pa said: that Prajñāpāramitā is the common Mother, and invite the reader to determine for himself if certain studies contained in the present work bear out this contention. And for the meaning of Mother, let it be understood that Prajñā is by no means a virgin, since from time immemorial, according to Buddhist teachings, mankind has been defiling this *prajñā* which is their own insight. Thus the course of *prajñā* is not, as in ordinary human terms, from innocence to loss of a pristine state, but rather from original defilement to the pure goddess state. The Buddhist *prajñā* is not like the Hindu Śakti, the new power created by the gods to wreak havoc on their opponents, the Asuras; but the old passive faculty become powerful for helping some beings over the opposition to be godlike. That is to say, the Hindu Śakti has a mythological base, whereas the Buddhist *prajñā* is rooted in man's psyche as the ordinary ingredient of every-day thinking. In the Hindu theory, the gods have to come up with a new plan; in the Buddhist conception, man must

PLATE 2. The glorious Conch Shell, depicting Queen Māyā (she gave birth to Gautama Buddha while holding the branch) surrounded by deities. Original in the Berner Historisches Museum.

find a new role for his capacities. In this light, the Hindu Śakti and the Buddhist tantric *prajñā* do have something in common, but it is not proper to identify them.

The thirty-seven natures accessory to enlightenment as goddesses

Perhaps there is no clearer example of the tantric goddess as accessory to enlightenment than the personification in the *Śrīcakrasaṃvara* tradition of the thirty-seven *bodhipakṣyā dharmāḥ* as goddesses. This identification is found in Lui-pā's *Śrī-Bhagavadabhisamaya-nāma* (Toh. 1427), and there could be no higher authority for this, since Lui-pā is among the most famous of the masters of the Mother Tantra. In utilizing his text as preserved in Tibetan translation in the Tanjur, it was helpful to take advantage of Abhayākaragupta's *Niṣpannayogāvalī* (as edited by B. Bhattacharyya), wherein is presented the Sambara-maṇḍala containing all the Sanskrit names of the principal deities of the *Śrīcakrasaṃvara-tantra*. It is of interest that the central deity, under the name Śrī-Heruka, is given the correspondence to "right samādhi" instead of his consort, but the obvious meaning is that he is here present with his female side, usually called Vajravārāhī (the Diamond Sow). The thirty-seven natures accessory to enlightenment (*bodhipakṣya-dharma*) is an important feature of the path both for early and later non-tantric Buddhism. The identifications follow:

1. Station of mindfulness on bodies — Ḍākinī
2. Station of mindfulness on feelings — Lāmā
3. Station of mindfulness on natures — Khaṇḍarohā
4. Station of mindfulness on thoughts — Rūpiṇī
5. Base of magical power in longing — Pracaṇḍā
6. Base of magical power in striving — Pracaṇḍākṣā
7. Base of magical power in analysis — Prabhāvatī
8. Base of magical power in thought — Mahānāsā
9. Faculty of faith — Vīramatī
10. Faculty of striving — Kharvaryī
11. Faculty of mindfulness — Laṅkeśvaryī
12. Faculty of samādhi — Drumacchāyā
13. Faculty of insight — Airāvatī
14. Power of faith — Mahābhairava
15. Power of striving — Vāyuvegā
16. Power of mindfulness — Surābhakṣī
17. Power of samādhi — Śyāmādevī
18. Power of insight — Subhadrā

19. Samādhi limb of enlightenment	— Hayakarṇī
20. Striving limb of enlightenment	— Khagānanā
21. Joy limb of enlightenment	— Cakravegā
22. Cathartic limb of enlightenment	— Khaṇḍarohā
23. Analysis-of-the-doctrine limb of enlightenment	— Śauṇḍinī
24. Mindfulness limb of enlightenment	— Cakravarmiṇī
25. Equanimity limb of enlightenment	— Suvirā
26. Right understanding	— Mahābalā
27. Right conception	— Cakravartiṇī
28. Right speech	— Mahāvīryā
29. Right bodily action	— Kākāsyā
30. Right livelihood	— Ulūkāsyā
31. Right effort	— Śvānāsyā
32. Right mindfulness	— Śūkarāsyā
33. Right samādhi	— Śrī-Heruka
34. Generation of the virtuous natures so far not arisen	— Yamadāhī
35. Protection of the virtuous natures that have arisen	— Yamadūtī
36. Elimination of the sinful natures that have arisen	— Yamadaṇṣṭrī
37. Avoidance of the sinful natures so far not arisen	— Yamamathanī

That takes account of all the goddesses of the Sambara-maṇḍala, if we accept that Vajravārāhī is included in Śrī-Heruka, which of course is the meaning of their mystic union. Besides, all the goddesses have parental Buddhas. Nos. 1-4 are the *ḍākinī*-s under Ratneśa (=Ratnasaṃbhava). 5-12 are the Circle of Mind (*citta-cakra*) under Akṣobhya, and they range in the sky. 13-20 are the Circle of Speech (*vāk-cakra*) under Amitābha, and they range upon earth. 21-28 are the Circle of Body (*kāya-cakra*) under Śāśvata (=Vairocana), and they range beneath the earth. 29-32 and 34-37 are the Pledge Circle (*samaya-cakra*) under Amoghasiddhi; and 33 (the maṇḍala-lord) is under Akṣobhya; his Diamond Ṣow side is under Vairocana.

Tsoṅ-kha-pa (Lhasa Collected Works, Ta, *'dod 'jo*, 112a-4) explains Nos. 26-33 (the Eightfold Noble Path) in this context:

"Right understanding": Great devotion to the Word of the Buddha.
"Right conception": The errorless comprehension of its meaning, and not casting aside a project which is good to do.
"Right speech": Having words that do not deceive the sentient beings, and free from lies.

Plate 3. Śrī-Heruka, or Sambara (Previously published in Lessing, *Yung-Ho-Kung*).

"Right bodily action": Not transgressing the ten virtues in all that is done.
"Right livelihood": Living in a way that does not harm the sentient beings.
"Right effort": Performing the virtuous acts of bowing, circumambulating, etc.
"Right mindfulness": Being mindful of the Word of the Victor.
"Right samādhi": With object of consciousness in the manner of Heruka.

But we cannot leave this subject without alerting the reader to the multiple roles of these goddesses. For example, the *Abhidhāna-uttara-tantra* (PTT. Vol. 2, p. 66-3) identifies the last four Bodhisattva Stages, for which see Table 18 in the present work, with the four *ḍākinīs* of the above list (Nos. 1-4) in respective order, which is their standard order. The same Tantra identifies the first six Bodhisattva Stages with other *ḍākinīs*. Furthermore, reference to my Table 5 will show that four doorkeepers of the *Śrī-Cakrasaṃvara maṇḍala*, namely Nos. 29-32, constitute in this given order with translation of names (Kākāsyā, She the Crow-Faced; and so on) the first four of the six members of the Stage of Completion. Nos. 34-35 (Yamadāhī and Yamadūtī) are reversed as the last two of the six members. Right after Table 5 there is a different explanation for the remaining two Yama goddesses (Nos. 36-37). But *prajñā* herself appears in many roles and guises—the cleverness of the market place, the science of the laboratory, the wisdom of the sage; a sword, a fire; a nymph.

2

EARLY LITERARY HISTORY OF THE BUDDHIST TANTRAS, ESPECIALLY THE GUHYASAMĀJA-TANTRA*

There are several reasons for discussing literary history of the Buddhist Tantras in general, while taking main evidence from the *Guhyasamāja* cycle. For one thing, the texts and commentaries of Tantric nature are replete with remarkable matters, intriguing to any scholar with the philological background to read them. Besides the inevitable "tantric secrets", there are numerous problems of Indian textual history to be solved to the extent these texts can be reliably dated in terms of centuries. Such an investigation is undoubtedly challenging, because the cult of Tantra, whether Hindu or Buddhist, has something of an anti-historical tone to it, by the very nature of esotericism.

When it is seen that these Buddhist Tantras are composed by taking a previous lore reaching back into the Vedic literature and amalgamating this tradition with various Buddhist tenets, it appears that one should be able to assign a definite period of time for such synthesizing. And then there is a problem comparable to the dating of Upaniṣads and Purāṇas, because we hear a specious argument that it is possible to write such books at any time! Possible, yes; but not possible to furnish the feature of authority, as when the Tantra is represented as a revelation of the supreme Buddha in the form of Vajradhara; not possible at any arbitrary time to have a text

* This article first appeared in *Annals, Bhandarkar Oriental Research Institute*, Vols. XLVIII-XLIX (Poona, 1968), which may be consulted for the Tibetan and Sanskrit texts omitted here.

be the main communication of religious leaders and geniuses, part of a creative ebb, capable of arousing the faith, the concordant practice, and commentarial labor of great thinkers, as were the Upaniṣads in the sense in which we speak of the great Upaniṣads and the Upaniṣad literature. And while the group of Upaniṣads called the Yoga Upaniṣads[1] are not the greatest of their class, they too bear the imprint of creative thinking of *some* period, whatever it may be, only prior to the composition of the "revealed" Buddhist Tantras, because those particular "sectarian Upaniṣads" have many remarks about centers in the body, mystic veins, and other materials, in typical Upaniṣad disorganization, that are noteworthy as constituting ideas incorporated in the Buddhist Tantras in more organized and *śāstra*-like form.

But, then, why "especially the Guhyasamāja-tantra"? Any searching examination of this Tantric literature, mainly extant in the Tibetan language, leads the reader to notice a compatibility of style of writing, repetition of certain incantations (*mantra*), overlapping descriptions of ritual practices; although it is true that certain groups of texts display much more of similar matter, a fact which led to the classification of Tantras, eventually into the standard classes of Kriyā-, Caryā-, Yoga-, and Anuttarayoga-tantras, by which the Tibetan Tantric canon is arranged.[2] Now, I concern myself mainly with the *Guhyasamāja-tantra* simply because it is necessary to follow through at least one current in its various connections to see the picture with some clarity, and I happen to have done so with the *Guhyasamāja-tantra* through my researches in writing a still unpublished work, *The Arcane Lore of Forty Verses*; *A Buddhist Tantra Commentary on the Guhyasamāja-nidāna-kārikā.* In a literary history introduction to this work I have argued that an Explanatory Tantra (*vyākhyā-tantra*) of the *Guhyasamāja* called *Vajramālā* was composed in the fifth century A.D., and the basic tantra *Guhyasamāia* probably in the fourth century A.D.

350 AD →

I. Dating of the Guhyasamāja

It would be well to summarize here the kind of reasoning I have employed in that manuscript to arrive at the approximate dating, as well as to add further considerations. First we notice that scholars are fairly well agreed about the dating of the named commentators on the *Guhyasamāja* cycle and the Tantra Siddhas generally. Leaving out the references, we observe that Saraha is a contemporary of King Dharmapāla (769-809). In

1. *The Yoga Upaniṣads*, tr. by T. R. Srinivasa Ayyangar and ed. by G. Srinivasa Murti, The Adyar Library, 1952.

2. Cf. Alex Wayman, "Analysis of the Tantric Section of the Kanjur Correlated to Tanjur Exegesis". Part II of Chap. 16, below.

the second half of the eighth century we must place both the tantric Nāgārjuna of the "Ārya School' and Buddhaśrījñāna of the "Jñānapāda School". In the ninth century—probably first half—comes the tantric Candrakīrti, author of the *Pradīpoddyotana*, as well as King Indrabhūti and his sister Lakṣmīnkarā, who is probably not the same person as Śrī Lakṣmī, author of a beautiful commentary on Nāgārjuna's *Pañcakrama*. Various tantric masters such as Śabara and Nāropā lived in the tenth century, while Tilopā, Nāropā's *guru*, must be placed around the end of the ninth and beginning of the tenth centuries. In the second half of the ninth I would also place the tantric Āryadeva. Translations into Tibetan show that Guhyasamāja commentarial and *sādhana* literature continued to be written through the twelfth century. In short, the Tanjur *Guhyasamāja* cycle of commentarial literature is composed from eighth to twelfth centuries. The same inclusive dates roughly cover the commentarial cycles of other Buddhist Tantra literature.

Given that general period of commentarial composition, there remains the problem of dating the "revealed" scripture, the *mūla-tantra Guhyasamāja* (first 17 chapters of the Sanskrit text) and its *uttara-tantra* (the 18th chapter) along with their cluster of Explanatory Tantras available only in Tibetan except for a few quotations of Sanskrit in Nāgārjuna's *Pañcakrama* and Candrakīrti's *Pradīpoddyotana*. The Explanatory Tantras in question are the three cited in the *Pañcakrama: Caturdevīparipṛcchā*, *Saṃdhivyākaraṇa* and *Vajramālā*; the one cited in Āryadeva's *Caryāmelāpakapradīpa: Jñānavajrasamuccaya*—all four of which are in Tibetan; and the one cited in the *Pradīpoddyotana: Devendraparipṛcchā*, which was not translated into Tibetan. The Explanatory Tantras represent further "revelations" which have varying authority for the subsequent commentarial traditions.

A. *The date of the Explanatory Tantra Vajramālā*. In that manuscript on the *nidāna-kārikā* which was quoted in Candrakīrti's *Pradīpoddyotana* from the *Vajramālā*, I arrived at a direct reason and an indirect reason for dating the *Vajramālā*. Here there is no room to provide the extensive data on which the following reasoning is based: (1) *The direct reason:* This work contains the ten Viṣṇu avatāras in a kind of esoteric embryology theory, and these ten are precisely the standard list for which there is epigraphic evidence (from Bengal) of the fifth century onwards. I have presumed that at the time this standard list became publicized it went hand-in-hand with an esoteric tradition of syncretized Vaiṣṇavism and Buddhism. *The indirect reason:* In that manuscript on the *nidāna-kārikā* I have set forth my hypothesis that the *Pañcakrama* set of 33 female *prakṛtis* and 40 male *prakṛtis* can be subdivided without change of order into five groups in each set, the first set (of female *prakṛtis*) especially going with the five stages of the Vaiṣṇava path to union with the Lord Kṛṣṇa. This adds more weight to the presumed Vaiṣṇava-Buddhist syncretism which I attribute to the fifth century A.D. However, the term "*pañcakrama*" as in Nāgārjuna's title does not seem compatible with that Vaiṣṇava path. (2) There is a further reason stemming from the interesting tie-ups between the *Vajramālā* and later commentary on the one hand, and the *Laṅkāvatāra-sūtra* on the other hand. I refer here (a) to Yogācāra-type vocabulary, such as the "eight-*vijñana* set"; (b) to the stress on winds, in the *Vajramālā* as the esoteric doctrine of winds by the word *vāyu*, and in the *Laṅkāvatāra-sūtra* to the exoteric doctrine of winds by the word *pavana;* and (c) by occasional quotation of the *Laṅkāvatāra* in the *Guhyasamāja* commentaries, such as those of the tantric Āryadeva. This *sūtra* was first translated into Chinese in 443 A.D. and apparently enjoyed much popularity among Indian Buddhists to justify Bodhidharma's exclusive stress on this work when he brought it to China in the 520's of the Christian era.

B. *The date of the Guhyasamāja-tantra.* Of course, the tentative dating of the Explanatory Tantra *Vajramālā* in the fifth century A.D. has a firm implication for the latest date of the *Guhyasamāja*, but our approach to the latter will be as independent as possible from the *Vajramālā* consideration.

There is a tradition reported from Tārānātha that the Tantras were transmitted in utmost secrecy for 300 years before being rendered somewhat more public by the Siddhas. This tradition was accepted by B. Bhattacharyya in the Introduction, xxxv, to his edition of the *Guhyasamāja-tantra* in the Gaekwad Oriental Series. However, Bhattacharyya associated the *Guhyasamāja* with Asaṅga. Having studied this problem through the works of Asaṅga I concluded that while Asaṅga lived at the "right time" (circa 375-430 A.D.), he could not reasonably be credited with the *Guhyasamāja-tantra.*[3] On the other hand, Japanese scholars in general, and Shoun Toganoo in particular, who worked with the Tantra decided on an historical sequence of Buddhist Tantras with approximate centuries, to wit: *Mahāvairocana* (sixth century), *Tattvasaṃgraha* (seventh century), and *Guhyasamāja*, which they considered degenerate Tantra (eighth century). This dating forces the *Guhyasamāja* to be composed contemporaneously with the first commentaries by named persons. To understand this position, one should note that the Japanese have been pre-eminent in modern-day Buddhist scholarship in wonderfully encyclopædic scope. But the Japanese Buddhist scholars almost always prefer to work with Sanskrit or Tibetan texts that have Sino-Japanese translations. The Tibetan texts were only aids in comparative text study; and so few Japanese scholars have learned to move easily in those Tibetan texts which have neither Sanskrit nor Sino-Japanese parallel versions, as is the case with the bulk of the Tantric literature. Matsunaga is perhaps alone

3. Alex Wayman, *Analysis of the Śrāvakabhūmi Manuscript*, University of California Publications in Classical Philology Vol. 17 (Berkeley, 1961), pp. 25-41.

in examining one of the *Guhyasamāja* Explanatory Tantras, the *Jñānavajrasamuccaya*, and deciding that Candrakīrti may have had some hand in composing or in expanding it.[4] Naturally his conclusions about the *Jñānavajrasamuccaya* carry no material implication for other Explanatory Tantras, each of which has to be judged by its own content. I think Matsunaga proved his point that the tantric Candrakīrti had something to do with that Explanatory Tantra, but this does not mean that he had more to do with it than revising or filling in a text which already existed in more than one recension. Generally speaking, though, the late dating of the *Guhyasamāja* by Japanese scholars rests on the same tenuous, unexamined grounds, as did the early dating accepted uncritically by B. Bhattacharyya. I hold that only by the procedure of facing up to the content of the *Guhyasamāja* literature can one begin to approximate the historical context.

If one does just that, he must take account of two basic commentarial traditions of the *Guhyasamāja*. One of these, "the Ārya School" (of those adopting Mādhyamika-famous names, Nāgārjuna, Candrakīrti, Āryadeva), writes its commentaries on the basic Tantra by citing the 18th chapter (the *uttara-tantra*), the various Explanatory Tantras, while incorporating what is presumably oral tradition. The other, the "Jñānapāda School" (headed by Buddhaśrījñāna) cites the 18th chapter and also the other chapters of the basic Tantra, generally refrains from quoting the Explanatory Tantras, and frequently cites other Tantras, especially those of the Yoga-tantra cycle, while also incorporating what is presumably oral tradition. There is of course some overlapping of these commentarial stresses; for example, Āryadeva also is prone to quote other Tantras, and also non-tantric works such as the Prajñā-pāramitā Scriptures. But the approaches are probably a matter of temperament, and interestingly parallel to the well-known two traditions of Buddhist Abhidharma called the Sautrāntika and the Vaibhāṣika. Here the "Jñānapāda School", more literary as well as literal, is like the Sautrāntika which takes its stand on the scriptural texts. The "Ārya School", less literary and more interpretative as well as pedantic, is like the Vaibhāṣika which takes its stand on the monumental commentaries. Therefore it is difficult to use the mere difference of the two traditions to conclude anything about the status and history of the Explanatory Tantras. Also, this use of Yoga-tantra texts may well rest on the tradition mentioned in the *Blue Annals* that the Yoga-tantra is "Outer" as compared with the Anuttarayoga-tantra (including the *Guhyasamāja*) which is "Inner".[5] In fact, the Yoga-tantras such as the *Tattvasaṃgraha*, *Vajraśekhara*, and *Śrī-Paramādya* have much in common with what is

4. Yūkei Matsunaga, "A Doubt to Authority of the Guhyasamāja-Ākhyāna-tantras", *Journal of Indian and Buddhist Studies*, XIII:2 (Mar., 1964), pp. (16) to (25).

5. George N. Roerich, *The Blue Annals*, Part one (Calcutta, 1949), pp. 351, ff.

called the Stage of Generation or Production (*utpattikrama*) of the Anuttarayoga-tantra, especially in the terminology of three *samādhis*, of Initial Praxis (*prathama-prayoga*), Triumphant Maṇḍala (*vijayamaṇḍala*), and Victory of the Rite (*karma-vijaya*).

What is significant about the two commentarial traditions is precisely that there are two, with many differences within each of these traditions. Just as the Sautrāntika and Vaibhāṣika of non-tantric Buddhism could not have arisen fully-grown, in the form in which we know them, in the century immediately following the passing of the Buddha, so also the "Ārya School" and the "Jñānapāda School" could not have arisen in the century immediately following the composition of the *Guhyasamāja*, let alone the very same century! Indeed, any one who even partially surveys the *Guhyasamāja* literature as extant in Tibetan and notes the remarkable variance in explanation of a given passage of the basic Tantra, would experience at least a mild shock at the flimsy reasons given for a late dating of the *Guhyasamāja*. One example will be given to show what is meant, and this case is particularly chosen for a context where one would expect minimal variation between the commentaries because the expression to be explained is merely the "three kinds" of each sense object as mentioned without explanation in the basic tantra of *Guhyasamāja*, Chap. 7:

Ārya School:

Nāgārjuna's *Tantraṭīkā* on *Guhyasamāja* (Derge ed., Sa, f. 105b-7): (form, the object of sight) "has the nature of outer, inner, and both".

Candrakīrti's *Pradīpoddyotana* on *Guhyasamāja* (Derge ed., Ha, f. 49a-5): (form, the object of sight) "should be perceived and comprehended as inferior, intermediate, and superior"; in Tsoṅ-kha-pa's *Mchan-ḥgrel* on the *Pradīpoddyotana* (PTT, Vol. 158, p. 55-3), we learn that the superior kind is the Buddha going with that sense object, e.g. Vairocana as form; (p. 56-1, form is also of three kinds, pleasurable, repulsive or displeasing, and neutral).

Jñānapāda School:

Praśāntajñāna's *Upadeśā-niścaya* on *Guhyasamāja* (PTT, Vol. 63, p. 64-5): the three kinds are superior (lust), intermediate (delusion), and inferior (hatred).

Celu-pā's *Ratnavṛkṣa-nāma-rahasya-samāja-vṛtti* (PṬT, Vol. 63, p. 183-5): inferior, intermediate, and superior.

Jinadatta's *Pañjikā-nāma* on *Guhyasamāja* (PTT, Vol. 63, p. 259-1): "Because one discerns it as having the nature of superior, and so on, there are three kinds; having the nature of outer, inner, and both, means "non-apprehension" (*anupalabdhi*), so one should understand it by the nature of three gates to liberation, of voidness, etc."

Ratnākaraśānti's *Kusumāñjali-guhyasamāja-nibandha-nāma* (Vol. 64, p. 127-1): the three kinds mean the respective offerings by the three kinds of yogins, the one of lust, of delusion, and of hatred.

Smṛtijñānakīrti's *Srīguhyasamāja-tantrarāja-vṛtti* (PTT, Vol. 66, p. 132-3): "The "three kinds" means that one knows (the object) as the three gates to liberation, the signless, etc."

Ānandagarbha's *Srī-guhyasamāja-mahātantrarāja-ṭīkā* (PTT, Vol. 84, p. 127-4, 5): "The three kinds are outer, inner, and secret. That was explained by Ārya-Jñānapāda to mean fifteen in an external set, fifteen in a personal set, and fifteen in a secret set. Having cited his words, I should here explain clearly his meaning." He goes on to take the outer as three, which multiplied by the five sense objects yields the number fifteen, and does the same for the inner or personal, and for the secret which involves the *prajñā-upāya* union. In each case, the three are the Buddha, the Bodhisattva, and the Devī associated with that object by the triad of perception, sense organ and sense object, i.e. for form, the three are the Buddha Vairocana, the Bodhisattva Kṣitigarbha, and the Devī Rūpavajrā.

There are three main sources for the various comments cited above. One is the Explanatory Tantra *Saṃdhivyākaraṇa*, which is a verse paraphrase, with slight enlargement, of the first twelve chapters of the *Guhyasamāja-tantra*. In its treatment of Chap. 7, it states (PTT, Vol. 3, p. 240-3):

> The three kinds of form and other sense objects are the non-apprehension of inner, outer, and both; one should offer those to the gods.

The next source is the Explanatory Tantra *Vajramālā*, which states in what I call the "*nidāna-kārikā*", no. 19:

> Afterwards the *yogin* who sees the non-duality should be dwelling upon sense objects "inferior", "intermediate", and "superior" by seeing the triple gnosis.

The third source is the *uttara-tantra* (18th chap. of the Sanskrit text, p. 158):

> The "desires" (i.e. the 5 strands of desire, *pañcakāmaguṇa*) "form", "sound", etc.—pleasurable, painful, and neutral—continually

generate in the heart, (respectively), the source of "lust", "hatred", and "delusion".

With all that information at hand, it is easy to see that some commentators relied especially on the *Vajramālā*, some especially on the *Saṃdhivyākaraṇa*, some especially on the *uttara-tantra*; and then some commentators tried to harmonize two different terminologies of "three kinds" by taking it as "three times three", i.e. three each of each three. The *Saṃdhivyākaraṇa* expression "non-apprehension" suggested to some commentators the non-tantric doctrines of "Perfection of Insight" (*prajñā-pāramitā*) with its stress on voidness (*śūnyatā*), so they saw an opportunity to make contact with non-tantric Buddhism by the well-known set of Buddhism, the three gates to liberation (*trīṇi vimokṣa-mukhāni*), that is, the voidness (*śūnyatā-*), the wishless (*apraṇihita-*), and the signless (*ānimitta-*) gates.[6] When one takes into account that these commentaries vary much more in most other places, where the *Guhyasamāja* passages are not restricted by such concrete objects as the sense objects, it is difficult to avoid the conclusion that some centuries of oral tradition have intervened between the basic *Guhyasamāja-tantra* and the eighth century when the "historical" writers began to appear on the scene. Of course, if the basic Tantra had been concocted by the first commentator, or had been composed just prior to his writing activity, there should not have been any question of what the "three kinds" were. Instead the commentators might have differed only in their metaphorical interpretation of the standard "three kinds".

The above chain of reasoning shows we must set the *Guhyasamāja-tantra* sufficiently early that even the *Vajramālā* Explanatory Tantra, if my fifth century date be accepted, would be one of several ways of interpreting that Tantra, and so the *Guhyasamāja* basic Tantra must be assigned at least a century earlier. But I conventionally place it in the fourth century A.D., with possible authorship of Indrabhūti the Great, who should not be confused with the later King Indrabhūti.

II. Possible Greco-Roman concepts in the Buddhist Tantras

At the annual meeting of the American Oriental Society in Chicago, April 1965, I first called attention to Greco-Roman attributions of func-

6. As I explained in the article, "The Buddhist 'Not This, Not This'," *Philosophy East and West*, XI: 3 (Oct., 1961), pp. 99-114, the three gateways to liberation are understood in the Yogācāra school (headed by Āryāsaṅga) to be based on the conditioned (*saṃskṛta*) as the five personality aggregates—the wishless gateway; on the unconditioned (*asaṃskṛta*) as *nirvāṇa*—the signless gateway; and on both (reality and unreality)—the voidness gateway.

tions to corporeal centers as closely paralleled by doctrines of the Buddhist Tantras. This report was incorporated in a larger study "The Five-fold Ritual Symbolism of Passion", published in the anniversary volume of Koyasan University,[7] and based especially on Tibetan sources. Later I noticed that the tantric Nāgārjuna's *Piṇḍīkramasādhana*, which was published by L. de la Vallée Poussin,[8] contains a Sanskrit passage that identifies the five *skandhas* with five corporeal centers. To save space, I shall omit the Sanskrit original, and give my translation of those verses (Nos. 56-60) as follows:

> The knower of *mantras* will place on his head Vairocana's germ syllable Oṃ of white color, because it is the intrinsic nature of the personality aggregate of form (*rūpa-skandha*).
> Having contemplated in the throat Amitābha's red Āḥ, pertaining to the intrinsic nature of the aggregate of ideas (*saṃjñā-skandha*), he attains lordliness of speech.
> The *mantrin* should deposit in his heart Akṣobhya's Hūṃ, shining like the deep blue gem, as the form of the aggregate of perceptions (*vijñāna-skandha*).
> He should place at the navel a yellow Svā belonging to the Jewel Lord (=Ratnasaṃbhava) and the cause of purifying feelings, because it is the form of the aggregate of feelings (*vedanāskandha*).
> The *mantrin* then deposits in both feet a Hā of green light, as the reality of the Karma Lord (=Amoghasiddhi), because it is the nature of the personality aggregate of motivations (*saṃskāra-skandha*).

In that published paper I identified the five corporeal locations of the five personality aggregates (*skandha*) with the five spots constituting targets for five arrows as in *Guhyasamāja-tantra*, Chap. XVI (Bhattacharyya ed., p. 121):

> The "knower of mantras" should contemplate in the middle of the Diamond Sky (=Clear Light) an adamantine Mañjuśrī of great power; he should recollect his projecting point with the praxis of five arrows, and make them fall, in the manner of the formidable thunderbolt, in five spots.

Thus, two Buddhist Tantra texts available in Sanskrit—the *Guhyasamāja-tantra* and its associated *Piṇḍīkramasādhana*—refer respectively to

7. Alex Wayman, "The five-fold ritual symbolism of passion," this work (Chap. 15).
8. Louis de la Vallée Poussin, ed., *Pañcakrama* (Gand, 1896); (the editor has included the *Piṇḍīkṛta-sādhana*=*Piṇḍīkrama-sādhana* as Part I of the edition).

five spots in the body and to five corporeal locations of the five personality aggregates.

The particular passage which first enabled me to compare with some Greco-Roman concepts was a Tibetan quotation or paraphrase by Tsoṅ-kha-pa of a work he cited as *Khyad par gsal byed*, which I later traced as the *Viśeṣadyota* (Toh. 1510), a work by Tathāgatavajra, with full title *Lūyipābhisamayavṛttiṭīkāviśeṣadyota-nāma*. I shall repeat here only the explanation for the placement of the "aggregate of form" (*rūpa-skandha*), because this was the foundation for making the comparison. Here the text: "explains that since the aggregate of forms is the basis of seeds, the chief place of the *rūpa-skandha* is the middle of the head; and explains that the forehead is the place of the *bindu:* hence one contemplates it (i.e. the aggregate of forms) there."[9] Therefore, it was easy to see a connection with the Greek *psyche* and the Roman *genius*—considered to be located in the head which was supposed to be the source of seed. Again, Greek thought associates the liver with deep emotions, so also the aggregate of feelings is the navel. There was also a close parallel between the location of perception (*vijñāna*) in the heart as the wind basis of consciousness and the seat of breath. The locations of the two remaining personality aggregates—ideas (*saṃjñā*) and motivations (*saṃskāra*)—in the throat and feet respectively, are not obviously parallel to the Greek or Roman concepts, for which I especially used the book by Onians.[10]

Another implication of Greek influence arose through the collaborated translation by the late Ferdinand D. Lessing and myself of *Mkhas grub rje's Fundamentals of the Buddhist Tantras*, Indo-Iranian Monographs Vol. VIII (1968). In the section on Yoga-tantra, Mkhas-grub-rje mentions that for each of the four seals (*mudrā*) called "Symbolic Seal", "Law Seal", "Action Seal", and "Great Seal", there are four causes (T. *rgyu* = Skt. *hetu*). For a long time Dr. Lessing and I were at a loss as to how to translate the words for these four causes in the Tibetan text. The words used were not the standard causes well-known from Buddhist Abhidharma texts. Then it occurred to me that the Tibetan words reflected an attempt, presumably through Sanskrit words as intermediary, to render the well-known four Aristotelian causes, namely the efficient cause (T. *ḥbyuṅ baḥi rgyu*), the formal cause (*raṅ gi ṅo bo*, S. *svarūpa*), the material cause (*ḥgrub paḥi rgyu*), and the final cause (*grub pa dbaṅ du ḥgyur baḥi rgyu*). To illustrate the application of these terms, I shall briefly explain Mkhas-grub-rje's employment of them for the "Symbolic Seal" (*samaya-mudrā*). In this case, the "efficient cause" is the thunderbolt tie (*vajrabandha*), the necessary preliminary. The "formal cause" involves the rite of executing the

9. Cf. Wayman, "The five-fold ritual symbolism of passion," reprinted herein.

10. R. B. Onians, *The Origins of European Thought about the Body, the Mind, the Soul, the World, Time, and Fate* (Cambridge at The Univ. Press, 1954).

"Symbolic Seal" per se, amounting to executing the symbolic seal of a particular Buddha, e.g. Vairocana, while seeing that Buddha dwelling in front and then reaching non-duality with that Buddha. The "material cause" involves contemplating in the heart of the deity in front, a moon and on it a white five-pronged thunderbolt; dwelling upon it for a protracted period while muttering the general and special incantations results in a "materialization". Thereupon, one has the "final cause" by the contemplation which reduces the personality aggregates and so on to voidness (*śūnyatā*).

Of course, this is a different kind of evidence from the preceding data regarding corporeal placement of the five *skandhas*. In the present case, I suppose there might be some question as to whether the four Aristotelian causes are rightly applied. Let us, however, proceed on the supposition that the Aristotelian causes seem to fit in translating Mkhas-grub-rje's section on the Yoga-tantra. Then, the problem arises of how such Greco-Roman influence could be found in the Buddhist Tantras, which so often are dismissed as typical of the late and declining phase of Indian Buddhism in the latter part of the first millenium A.D., thus removed by many centuries from the presumed period of Greek influence.

In assessing Greek transmissions to India, these need not be attributed to Greeks alone, because around the beginning of the Christian era many Greco-Roman ideas circulated in Central Asia and were carried by miscellaneous peoples. One conclusion is reasonable: that Buddhism was more influenced by such foreign ideas than was Hinduism. This is obvious in the iconographic art types, especially the form of the Buddha image in Gandhāra. It has long been held that foreign elements have entered into the formation of certain Buddhist Mahāyāna scriptures, especially those centred around the Buddha Amitābha (of boundless light). It is therefore reasonable that Greco-Roman concepts should have entered more into the Buddhist Tantras than into Hindu ones, whether Śaiva or Vaiṣṇava, that is, if we agree further that the Buddhist Tantras came into being sufficiently close to the time of Greco-Roman prestige to adopt certain foreign modes of thinking where their usefulness was apparent and at that time perhaps commonplace, their origins forgotten.

The literary history of these Tantras and their forerunning literature might well run this way in order to account for inclusion of any Greco-Roman concepts: After the old Upaniṣads just before and around the time of the Buddha, there gradually arose the type of work now called the sectarian Yoga Upaniṣad, the bulk of which is composed during the "Hindu revival" after the Maurya Dynasty downfall and down to the rise of the Gupta era. These sectarian Upaniṣads were being written by the Hindus when many foreign ideas were circulating in North-West India from about 100 B.C. to 200 A.D., but this does not mean that such Upaniṣads were influenced by such foreign ideas. However, profane science appears to have been so influenced, because during this period two systems of Roman astronomy were circulated in India to be later included in the *Pañcasiddhāntikā* of Varāhamihira. Also there were esoteric cults borrowing freely from different sources, Buddhist, Hindu, and foreign elements. The eclectic character of such movements helped to bring in certain far-out ideas that neither orthodox Hinduism nor orthodox Buddhism could be expected to entertain. At that time the word "Tantra" may not yet have been applied to such cults. Also, at the university center of Taxila in far North-West India there was ample opportunity to learn various Greco-Roman concepts; and also, for that matter, for some typically Indian ideas to be transported to the West or to enter into the religious syncretisms of Central Asia.

Conclusion

In the early Gupta period there was a vast amount of collecting and rewriting of old legends, as well as the composition of formal treatises, political, philosophical, and so on—required by the new age which had turned to written-down religious texts beginning to compete with the memorized tradition. This remarkable outpouring of new works would make the fourth and fifth centuries the Golden Age, determining the form of Hinduism even up to modern times. These two centuries were also the creative age for the Buddhist Tantras, determining their pattern of rite and doctrine for subsequent centuries. Not only the *Guhyasamāja* but also the other "revealed Tantras" were composed mainly at that time, and by this we do not preclude the later addition of chapters as happened to the *Mañjuśrī-mūla-kalpa* or an expanded recension as apparently occurred to the *Jñānavajrasamuccaya*. In the eighth century tantrism entered a new phase with the emergence of the Siddhas or tantric masters and the beginning of tantric rationalization, that is, the enterprise of commentary by the tantric pandits, who tried to explain all sorts of obscure points in those "revealed texts". And despite the difficulty a few commentators would be eminently successful.

3

BUDDHIST GENESIS AND THE TANTRIC TRADITION*

The Buddhist genesis story is very ancient, being found in the Pāli scriptures besides the northern Buddhist accounts. It is mentioned in all three branches of Buddhist scriptures, Sūtra, Vinaya, and Abhidharma. A Sanskrit version entitled Rājavaṃśa (royal lineage) exists in the *Mahāvastu.* In the Abhidharma literature the account is given in the description of *vivarta* (differentiation of the beings due to evolution of the inferior worlds) as contrasted with *saṃvarta* (consubstantiation of the beings due to dissolution of the inferior worlds). At least in later Buddhist accounts, the legend does not have the importance that the Biblical Genesis has in the Judeo-Christian tradition. Our treatment suggests that in the earliest Buddhism it may well have had a much greater importance than it had later on.

In any case, Tsoṅ-kha-pa (1357-1419 A.D.), founder of the Gelugpa school of Tibetan Buddhism signals the importance of the legend in an elaborate discussion utilizing both non-Tantric and Tantric sources in the first part of his work *Dpal gsaṅ ba ḥdus paḥi gnad kyi don gsal ba*, "Elucidating the meaning of the essential points of the *Śrī-guhyasamāja* (*Tantra*)" (Lhasa ed., collected works, Vol. Cha), which has the abbreviated reference *Don gsal.* Tsoṅ-kha-pa uses this legend as a rationale for the

* This article first appeared in *Oriens Extremus*, 9:1 (1962), which may be consulted for the Tibetan and Sanskrit texts omitted here.

types of meditations found in the Anuttara-yoga-tantra, a literature which often mystifies and repels Western scholars because of its complicated ritualism and sexual symbolism. Here there is space for only the main ideas of Tsoṅ-kha-pa's discussion.

The non-Tantric Buddhist legend may be organized and summarized as follows:

There are three efficient causes of the periodical destruction of the world systems, viz., fire, water, and wind. According to the *Abhidharma-kośa* (III, 100c-d, and commentary), fire brings an eon of evolution to an end by destroying all of the realm of desire (*kāma-dhātu*) and the First Dhyāna Heaven of the realm of form (*rūpa-dhātu*). Water destroys all that as well as the Second Dhyāna Heaven; and wind destroys all the latter as well as the Third Dhyāna Heaven of the realm of form. Only the Fourth Dhyāna of this realm remains intact. The First Dhyāna is also referred to by its divine residents, such as the Brahmā retinue deities, the Second Dhyāna by its chief deities, the Ābhāsvaras, the Third Dhyāna by the Śubha deities.

I. In the next period of evolution, while the lower receptacle worlds are re-evolving, the sentient beings fall to lower planes in a process usually described as starting from the level of the Ābhāsvara deity class (after the destruction by fire). They fall from that divine world and come "here". "Here" is explained as Jambudvīpa (our world continent or specifically India). Buddhaghoṣa of the southern school and Vasubandhu of the northern school of Buddhism agree that these "men of the first eon" pass through each of the intermediate worlds by a type of birth called "transformation" (*upapāduka*)[1] after each successive death. The *Abhidharma-kośa* (II, 9b-c) says that the beings with this type of birth are the hell-beings, the beings of the intermediate state, and the gods. Hence the "men of the first eon" were in a condition rather comparable to the present (disembodied) intermediate state (*antarābhava*) between death and rebirth. Asaṅga explains that these "men of the first eon" (*prathamakalpa*) passed through these worlds with actions involved with desire (*kāmāvacara-karma*) that are superior, chief, best (*parama*, *agrya*, *śreṣṭha*), and whose fruitions are experienced immediately, not at another time. And these men have a beautiful form (*rūpin*) and are "made of mind" (*manomaya*)[2]. In addition, the *Mahāvastu* (I, 339) says that these men are self-luminous, feed on joy, and go where they wish.

II. Then, on the surface of the earth which at that time was in a fluidic

1. This is one of the four kinds of birth in Buddhism. Beings are also "born from a womb" (*jarāyu-ja*), "born from an egg" (*aṇḍa-ja*), "born from moist heat" (*saṃsveda-ja*).
2. V. Bhattacharya, editor, *The Yogācārabhūmi of Ācārya Asaṅga*, Part I (Calcutta, 1957), pp. 41-42.

state there appeared an earth essence[3] which some being disposed to greediness tasted with his finger. It pleased him, he came to eat mouthfuls, and other beings followed suit. Thus these beings became dependent on morsel food, still subtle. They lost their original qualities of feeding on joy, body made of mind, and so on, and their bodies became heavier and more substantial. The ones who least indulged, retained with pride their beautiful form. The sun, moon, and year became known. In the course of time this earth essence disappeared and a honey-like excrescence appeared on the surface of the earth. Asaṅga explains that hell beings, beings in the embryonic states, and the gods involved with desire (*kāmāvacara-deva*) have just the subtle kind of food, which does not give rise to excrement or urine.[4]

III. Then, in place of the honey-like earth excrescences, a rice-pap appeared and the beings subsisted on that coarse morsel food, described thus by the *Mahāvastu* (I, 341-2): "rice, not discrete, without chaff, fragrant grain" (*śāli akaṇo atuṣaḥ surabhitaṇḍulaḥ*). At that time, the distinguishing characteristics of male and female appeared, and the beings had mutual sexual desire with associated acts.

IV. The last phase of the legend shows the arising of the "private property" idea with individual rice plots, then stealing with consequent violence. Those beings decided to select someone to judge the disputes. He was called the great chosen one (*mahāsammata*), and the beings each gave him one-sixth of the rice crop for his royal services to provide security. Mahāsammata was the first king (*cakravartin*). According to the Buddhist *sūtra*, he inaugurated the lineage of the Śākya clan, in which Gautama Buddha was born. According to the latter's biography, Gautama was born with auspicious characteristics portending either a Cakravartin or a Buddha. In Hindu legend also, "People suffering from anarchy . . . first elected Manu, the Vaivasvata, to be their king; and allotted one-sixth of the grains grown and one-tenth of merchandise as sovereign dues".[5]

The Tantric account presented by Tsoṅ-kha-pa claims to have information about those beings beyond what non-Tantric Buddhism teaches. Thus he writes, "Moreover, the men of the first eon, i.e., the beings who have died and transferred from the Ābhāsvara god class, and so on, down to their birth as men of Jambudvīpa, agree with the merits (*guṇa*) of the [thirty-two] Characteristics and [eighty] Minor Marks, so they are adorned with the merits of a Buddha".[6] Also, "The description 'adorned with the

3. *Pṛthivīrasa* in the *Mahāvastu* (I, 339), *bhūmirasa* in Asaṅga's *Yogācārabhūmi*, p. 42.
4. *Yogācārabhūmi*, pp. 99-100.
5. Kautilya's *Arthaśāstra*, translated by R. Shamasastry (Book I, Chap. XIII), pp. 22-23.
6. *Doṅ gsal*, 19b-6.

merits of a Buddha' does not occur in the *Abhidharma* or in the *Vibhaṅga*".[7] But why did those beings become dominated subsequently by delusion, lust, and hatred? He says, "Thus, they had obtained possession of the 'knowledge body' (*jñāna-deha*)—the superior body like the body of a god of the 'realm of form', free from the coarse body which undergoes development; but then it was overcome by all the action (*karma*) and defilement (*kleśa*) arising from their own mind, and came into the power of those two".[8] He goes on to explain the reason as the habit-energy (T. *bag chags*, S. *vāsanā*) handed down from beginningless time, and continues, "Although they had a body comparable to the Illusory Body (*māyā-deha*) they did not know the Illusory Samādhi (*māyopama-samādhi*) through hearing (*śrutā*) and 'pondering' (*cintā*), and could not comprehend it through 'creative contemplation' (*bhāvanā*). Hence they wander in phenomenal existence".[9] In further additions to the standard account, Tsoṅ-kha-pa calls the earth essence also "ambrosia" (*amṛta*),[10] and he calls the separation into male and female the division of means (*upāya*) and insight (*prajñā*), respectively.[11]

The usual Buddhist formulations of the Path, such as the Eightfold Noble Path, are not obviously applicable to the legend, as classically stated. They aim to eliminate the domination of action and corruption. Why try to rebecome the first eon men? These men were pure only through lack of temptations, which had been removed by the dissolution of the inferior worlds and which would inevitably reappear with the new manifestation of those worlds. Yet even the old non-Tantric Buddhism can be interpreted with steps that inversely match the successive periods of the legend, especially with Tsoṅ-kha-pa's word "*amṛta*". (1) A devotee renounces his property to become a monk. He reverses the last period, characterized by private ownership of rice plots. (2) The monk is supposed to regulate his way of life, including moderation in food and adherence to celibacy (*brahmacarya*). He reverses the eon characterized by coarse morsel food and the division into sexes. Also, according to the Hindu epic *Mahābhārata*, the god Brahmā adopted the form of a swan and said: ". . . I know that self-restraint is the door of immortality (*amṛta*). I impart to you this

7. *Ibid.*, 20a-5,6. By "Abhidharma" Tsoṅ-kha-pa presumably means both the *Abhidharma-kośa* (both *kārikās* and auto-commentary by Vasubandhu) and the *Abhidharma-samuccaya* of Asaṅga. To this one should probably add the further commentary on the Vasubandhu work by Prince Yaśomitra. By "Vibhaṅga" Tsoṅ-kha-pa presumably means the *Vinaya-vibhaṅga* in the Tibetan Kanjur and its commentary by Vinītadeva. Tsoṅ-kha-pa by this remark indicates that such a teaching is not found in either the Abhidharma or Vinaya literature.

8. *Don gsal*, 20a-6, ff.

9. *Ibid.*, 20b-2,3.

10. *Ibid.*, 30b-4,5.

11. *Ibid.*, 31a-6 to 31b-1.

hallowed (*brahman*) secret: there is no state superior to the human".[12] (3) This man then practices *yoga* and various *samādhis* which develop certain inner resources and which are supposed to win a command over subtle elements.[13] He reverses the second period, characterized by subsistence on subtle morsel food, and comes to taste the "primeval earth", the "deathless" or "ambrosia" (*amṛta*)—while still a man of Jambudvīpa. (4) His mind separates from the "deathless" and is freed or liberated. He feeds on joy, as did the men of the first eon, but he has arrived at this comparable stage together with a discipline that eliminates the propensities of hatred, lust, and delusion. This stage is called Nirvāṇa by the Buddhists, Mokṣa by the Hindus.

However, Mahāyāna Buddhism claims to have a higher attainment than this liberation, the ideal of early Buddhism. Later the aim was to become a Complete Buddha, with the three bodies called the Dharmakāya, Saṃbhogakāya, and Nirmāṇakāya, who is restricted neither to the quiescent realm nor to the phenomenal world. In accordance with a passage cited above from Tsoṅ-kha-pa, one must reach by discipline a condition comparable to the first eon men and have in addition the Illusory Samādhi. In Tsoṅ-kha-pa's view, one must purify birth, death, and the intermediate state by *yogas* concordant with the way the men of the first eon experienced those three phases during the interval between when they were still "first eon men" and when they had the ordinary bodies of period no. 3. (Of course, in Indian belief the men of later periods are those very men.) He says, "Contemplation of the Dharmakāya is the purification of death, because, briefly speaking, the Dharmakāya is equivalent to the experience by the men of the first eon of the clear light of death".[14] Again, "contemplation of the Saṃbhogakāya is the purification of the intermediate state", and "contemplation of the Nirmāṇakāya is the purification of birth".[15]

Tsoṅ-kha-pa writes, "Also, the *Pañcakrama* states, 'The Saṃbhogakāya as well as the illusion of conventional truth—that is the Gandharva-sattva', making the Saṃbhogakāya equivalent to the intermediate state [body]; hence one should have no doubt that the generation of the Primeval Lord (**ādinatha*) is an element equivalent to the intermediate state".[16] The Dharmakāya is also associated with death and with comparable states such as coitus [union of *upāya* and *prajñā*] in a passage of the *Mukhāgama*

12. Critical Edition, Śānti P., 288.20.
13. For further information, one may refer to Mircea Eliade, *Yoga: Immortality and Freedom* (New York, 1958).
14. *Don gsal*, 25a-4.
15. *Ibid.*, 25b-1.
16. *Ibid.*, 26a-1,2. To understand Tsoṅ-kha-pa's remark one should know that in this literature a *gandharva-sattva* means a being of the intermediate state.

quoted in Tsoṅ-kha-pa's *Sṅags rim chen mo.*[17] The Nirmāṇakāya is illustrated in some Tantric *āgama* by the Avatars of Viṣṇu interpreted as intra-uterine stages.[18]

There are two phases of the Anuttara-yoga-tantra—the Stage of Generation (*utpatti-krama*) and the Stage of Completion (*saṃpanna-krama*), respectively the phase of the path (*mārga*) and the phase of the fruit (*phala*). Tsoṅ-kha-pa says, "Therefore, it is a mistake not to finish during the phase of the first Stage (*krama*) the part consisting in the various elements concordant with the three things, birth, death, and the intermediate state".[19] Hence, one must meditate consistently with the three bodies of the Buddha in the phase of the path; in the phase of the fruit one gains those bodies, called the "three bodies of the fruit".[20]

It would be difficult, perhaps impossible, to determine how old such teachings are. However, the above should indicate the profundity of that old Buddhist legend.

17. Cf. Alex Wayman, "Studies in Yama and Māra," *Indo-Iranian Journal* (1959), p. 57.
18. *Ibid.*, pp. 70-72.
19. *Don gsal*, 26a-4.
20. *Ibid.*, 26a-3.

4

ANALOGICAL THINKING IN THE BUDDHIST TANTRAS

The employment of systematic analogies is frequent in the Vedic literature, from the *Rig-Veda* itself, down to the Upaniṣads, the oldest of which (such as the *Chāndogya* and the *Bṛhadāraṇyaka*) precede the rise of Buddhism. A threefold symbolism is frequent in the Vedas, where all the gods were included in one or another of the three realms: heaven, atmosphere, and earth. A fourfold system had also become popular, with one of the four representing the perfect state. For example, of the four chief priests for the great Śrauta ceremonies, it was the Brahman or high priest who knew all three Vedas and protected the ceremony from hostile demons, while the other three priests each knew one Veda. In the case of the celebrated Puruṣa hymn of the *Rig-Veda*, this glorified Person is three-fourths outside our world and one-fourth in it. Of the four Ages, the Golden Age has four parts, the successive ones three, two, and one parts (or "fourths") and are correspondingly degenerate. In the *Māndukya-Upaniṣad*, the waking state is the first fourth; dream, the second fourth; deep sleep the third fourth, and the Self (*ātman*) the fourth and called "the fourth" (*turīya*). Of course, the examples of the threefold and fourfold systems could be multiplied at length. The fivefold system became popular in the Upaniṣads, for example, in the *Taittirīya-Upaniṣad*, where the microcosm-macrocosm analogy is presented in terms of the fivefoldness of the world and of the individual.

Both threefold and fivefold systems of analogy are prevalent in the Buddhist Tantras; and because early Buddhism does not go in for this kind of thinking—even though there are many numerical categories in

Buddhism—one may say that the Buddhist Tantras in this feature of systematic analogies constitute a development in Buddhism akin to Vedic formulations, especially of the later Upaniṣads. The threefold correspondences in the Buddhist Tantras are especially in terms of the Body, Speech, and Mind—the "three mysteries" of the Buddha:

Body	—	*mudrā* (gesture)
Speech	—	*mantra* (incantation)
Mind	—	*samādhi* (deep concentration)

The fivefold correspondences go with the set of five Buddhas. For example, the *Hevajratantra* associates the five Buddhas with the five candidates for training in accordance with their dominant vice:

Vairocana	—	Delusion
Akṣobhya	—	Hatred
Amitābha	—	Lust
Ratnasambhava	—	Slander (*paiśunya*)
Amoghasiddhi	—	Jealousy (*īrṣya*)

But the Buddhist Tantras do not lack the fourfold correspondences. They are especially used to correlate steps of training. For example, the Anuttarayoga Tantra has a division into the Stage of Generation (*utpatti-krama*) and Stage of Completion (*saṃpanna-krama*). Each of these has its own explanation of the four *mudrās*: *karma-mudrā*, *dharma-mudrā*, *samaya-mudrā*, and *mahā-mudrā*. Here the word "*mudrā*" is employed in its more abstract significance as a "seal".

In the classical period, the Indian philosophical schools debated the extent to which analogy is a valid source of knowledge, or authoritative; and the Realists (followers of the Nyāya school) accepted analogy as an independent valid source of knowledge. In agreement with them, Candrakīrti, the great Mādhyamika commentator of the Prāsaṅgika school, accepted in his *Prasannapadā* (Chap. One) all four sources of knowledge (*pramāṇa*) in practical life, namely, direct perception (*pratyakṣa*), inference (*anumāna*), testimony (*śabda*)—which is the lineage of trustworthy persons (*āptāgama*)—and analogy (*upamāna*). Now, in *Mkhas grub rje's*, the position is laid down that the philosophical viewpoint of all sections of the Tantras is the Prāsaṅgika. This means that all four Tantra divisions, the Kriyā, Caryā, Yoga, and Anuttarayoga, have the Prāsaṅgika-Mādhyamika for a philosophical base. One way Mkhas grub rje's statement can be understood is that the Tantras accept the Realist's position of analogy as an independent source of knowledge. If this is a basic reason, it would still be valid even for those tantric works that include much Yogācāra terminology, such as the "store consciousness" (*ālayavijñāna*); for in such a case this terminology from another school could be considered as part of the syncretic character of the Tantras.

Those four tantric classes themselves constitute systems of analogy, being explained in terms of the candidates for whom those Tantras are expressed as well as in terms of the deities which principally represent the particular class of Tantra. This is the orthodox Tibetan explanation derived here from Tsoṅ-kha-pa's *Sṅags rim chen mo*. There is an unorthodox Tibetan explanation found in Smṛti's *Vajravidāraṇā-nāma-dhāraṇī-vṛtti* in the Tibetan Tanjur, Rgyud section, which relates the candidates in the four Buddhist systems of exegesis to kinds of washing.

In an article "Totemic Beliefs in the Buddhist Tantras,"[1] I prepared a table for classification in clans, consisting of a number of such analogical correspondences which I selected from my reading in this literature, especially the Anuttarayoga Tantra, over a number of years.[2]

The rationale for the correspondences on a given line of the table is

1. *History of Religions*, Vol. 1, No. 1 (Summer 1961), pp. 81, ff.

2. Many such textual correspondences are presented by way of identification with the five winds, *prāṇa*, *apāna*, *udāna*, *samāna*, and *vyāna*, which in the given order are the natures of the five Buddhas, Akṣobhya, and so on, of the Table. This is the order in which they are explained in the collected works, Kloṅ rdol bla ma, sec. Ga (Peking ed.), 29*a*-4 ff., identified with the Buddhas, elements, and bodily locations. The correspondence of Buddhas to knowledges is that given in the *Advayavajra-Saṃgraha* ("Gaekwad Oriental Series," Vol. XC), p. 36; this is consistent with *Mkhas grub rje's*. I gave a reference for the Buddha-skandha equation in my article "Contributions Regarding the Thirty-two Characteristics of the Great Person," *Liebenthal Festschrift*, p. 245, n. 10. The identification with the ambrosias is cited in a later subsection, "The Five Ambrosias." The identification of Buddhas with vortices of elements is in a Sanskrit passage of the *Vajramālā*, as quoted in the Vajrajāpakrama of the *Pañcakrama*, ed. de La Vallée Poussin. For the clan names cf. Snellgrove, *Hevajra-tantra*, Part I, p. 128. The correspondence with sensory domains is part of a passage in Tsoṅ-kha-pa's collected works, Vol. Ca (Lhasa ed.), "Dkaḥ gnad," 4*b*-1 ff. While I explained the purity of the sensory domains as female appearances of the Buddhas, strictly speaking, according to the latter text, this viewpoint falls in the category "purity of insight (*prajñā*)" (T. *śes rab kyi rnam dag*); while this purity can be treated also as the five Buddhas themselves through the category "purity of means (*upāya*)" (T. *thabs kyi rnam dag*). In some contexts the correspondences with "Body" (last line in Table) are localized in the crown of the head rather than throughout the body. This is the case with the column "Superintendence," where the normal order would be (1) body, (2) speech, (3) mind, (4) acts, and (5) merits, co-ordinated with crown of the head, and so on down to privities, associated respectively with the five germ syllables Oṃ, Āḥ, Hūṃ, Svā-Hā. This set of correspondences is found in a Tantra (Tohoku Catalog No. 453), the *Advayasamatāvijaya*, Derge Kanjur, *Rgyud ḥbum*, Cha, 240*a*-2 and 241*a*-1. While some of the above references are made to native Tibetan texts, there is no doubt that all these correspondences are drawn ultimately from the Tantras and Tantric commentaries originally in Sanskrit and translated into Tibetan as available in the Kanjur and Tanjur. For example, the correspondences of Buddhas to winds and bodily locations is found in Ratnarakṣita's commentary called the *Padminī* (Tohoku Catalog No. 1420), Derge Tanjur, *Rgyud*, Wa, fol. 26. However, the native Tibetan works are sometimes more convenient sources for utilizing and understanding these materials. When correspondences found in these or other tests are inconsistent with the Table, this situation frequently

TABLE 1

TANTRIC PATHS

Orthodox Explanation

TANTRA	CANDIDATES	DEITIES
Kriyā	Those who delight mainly in external ritual over inner samādhi.	Laughing
Caryā	Those who delight in external ritual and inner samādhi equally.	Mutually gazing
Yoga	Those who delight predominantly in inner samādhi over external ritual.	Holding hands
Anuttarayoga	Those who delight in inner samādhi completely.	United

Unorthodox Explanation

TANTRA	CANDIDATES	WASHING WITH VOIDNESS
Kriyā	Śrāvakas (auditors)	External washing purifies body.
Caryā	Pratyekabuddhas (=ṛṣis, seers)	Inner washing purifies speech.
Yoga	Yogācārins (mind-only school)	Secret washing purifies mind.
Anuttarayoga	Mādhyamikas	Reality washing by diamond-like samādhi unifies body, speech, and mind.

harder to establish. There is obviously some arbitrariness; yet there do seem to be parallels. For example, in the case of Akṣobhya's clan, water when untroubled (*akṣobhya*) serves as a mirror, hence the mirror-like knowledge. Regarding the association of perception (*vijñāna*) or mind (*citta*) with water, these are compared with the ocean or its waves and with a mirror in the *Laṅkāvatāra-sūtra*. Later we shall see that initiation (*abhiṣeka*) attended with "sprinkling" is performed under the auspices of the Buddha Akṣobhya, who is also the "ambrosia" urine. As to association with purity of sounds, this may be due to the fact that the water disk is located in the heart, where, in the Hindu terminology, is found the *cakra* Anāhata (the unstruck sound), that is to say, the place where sound is self-originated. For the corresponding candidate of hatred, this association is clarified in my work in press, *Yoga of the Guhyasamājatantra*. This has to do with the uninterrupted character of the stream of consciousness,

results from positing a Buddha other than Vairocana for the "center of the *maṇḍala*" and thus according that other Buddha the "Knowledge of the Natural Realm (*dharma-dhātu*)." Furthermore, a yogic attainment involving the movement of a "wind" from one center to another naturally changes the correspondences to bodily locations.

TABLE 2

CLASSIFICATION IN CLANS

CLAN NAME	BUDDHA	PERSONALITY AGGREGATE (SKANDHA)	KNOWLEDGE (JÑĀNA)	AMBROSIA (AMṚTA)	SUPERINTENDENCE (ADHIṢṬHĀNA)	PURITY OF ELEMENT AND ITS BASE	PURITY OF SENSORY DOMAIN
Vajra (thunderbolt or diamond)	Akṣobhya "The untroubled one"	Perceptions (*vijñāna*)	Mirror-like	Urine	Mind (*citta*)	Water disk in heart	Sounds
Ratna (jewel)	Ratnasambhava "Source of jewels"	Feelings (*vedanā*)	Of equality	Blood	Merits (*guṇa*)	Earth disk in privities	Odors
Padma (lotus)	Amitābha "Boundless light"	Ideas (*saṃjñā*)	Discriminative	Semen	Speech (*vāk*)	Fire disk in throat	Tastes
Khaḍga (sword), Karma (ritual action), or Samaya (pledge)	Amoghasiddhi "Unfailing success"	Motivations (*samskāra*)	Of the procedure of duty	Human flesh	Acts (*karma*)	Wind disk in navel	Tangibles
Cakra (wheel), or Tathāgata (thus-come)	Vairocana "The illuminator"	Form (*rūpa*)	Of the natural realm (*dharmadhātu*)	Excrement	Body (*kāya*)	Space (*ākāśa*) throughout body	Forms

mystically called "hatred" by hostility to cause and effect. Another interpretation is found in Buddhaguhya's commentary (extant in Tibetan) on the *Mahāvairocana-sūtra* (Chap. One), which among a long list of mentalities includes the "stream mentality" (*chu bo'i sems*). Buddhaguhya explains this one as independent of the two extremes, where the two are nihilism and eternalism, and that this mentality takes recourse to natures which avoid those two extremes. In this sense, the middle path of Buddhism is a "hatred" toward the extremes of nihilism or eternalism, of existence or non-existence. But Buddhaguhya also points out that the stream flows with dependence on the two extremes of eternalism and nihilism (in the sense of two banks). Further down the list, he comments on the "water mentality" (*chu'i sems*) as the one which adheres to washing off all unvirtuous thoughts. This water mentality is consistent with Akṣobhya's initiatory water as well as with the mirror-like water that reflects the moon as it is.

5

THE NATURE OF BUDDHIST ESOTERICISM

Esotericism of the Buddhist Tantras begins with what are called the "three mysteries of the Buddha," but these could also be translated the "three secrets of the Buddha". As Padmavajra explains them in his *Tantrārthāvatāra* Commentary (Toh. 2502, Derge ed., 147a-2, ff.), the secret Body, Speech, and Mind of the Tathāgatas, are these:

> Secret of Body: Whatever form is necessary to tame the living beings.
> Secret of Speech: Speech exactly appropriate to the lineage of the creature, as in the language of the *yakṣa-s*, etc.
> Secret of Mind: Knowing all things as they really are.

Since the candidate aims to correlate his body, speech, and mind with those three of the Buddha, at once Padmavajra's simple explanation shows the limitation of some Western expositions of the Tantra. For example, S. B. Dasgupta, *An Introduction to Tantric Buddhism*, devotes Chap. V (The Element of Esoteric Yoga) to the tantric theory of the body, claiming that this is the fundamental stress of the Buddhist tantrists, that they seek to find the truth along with perfect bliss in the body, on the basis of its arrangement of *cakra-s* and so on. Then Agehananda Bharati, *The Tantric Tradition*, has his longest chapter (also No. 5) on *mantra*, claiming that this is "the chief instrument of tantrism." John Blofeld, *The Tantric Mysticism of Tibet* is on the right track with his brief section "The interplay of body, speech, and mind," where the body does prostrations, makes gestures (*mudrā*), etc.; speech utters *mantra-s*; and the mind visualizes the deity.

As to the classification "secret," I brought forth an explanation in the study included in this work, "Female Energy and Symbolism in the Buddhist Tantras." This is Ānandagarbha's point that a tantric teaching is labelled "secret" when there is a restriction on teaching it to others. This sense of the word is deeply impressed on those who take the tantric initiations, especially the Hierophant's Initiation (*vajrācārya-abhiṣeka*). It should be noted, as will be justified in my treatment of the meaning of initiation, that the mere assignment to a disciple of a single deity to meditate upon, along with praises of that deity to memorize and repeat—is not counted as "secret" in Ānandagarbha's sense.

So far my reading in tantric texts has found no clearer light on the esoteric than is in the extensive commentary by that same Ānandagarbha (a prolific commentator on the Yoga Tantra class) entitled *Śrī-Paramādi-ṭīkā* on the Tantra portion called *Śrī-Paramādya-mantrakalpakhaṇḍa-nāma.* Whereas D. L. Snellgrove, *The Hevajra Tantra*, Part I, pp. 42-43, thinks that the Tantra he worked on is symbolizing the sexual act (*maithuna*), we shall learn—at least from Ānandagarbha—that the vocabulary of the sexual act is used to symbolize the secret, which is not the same as physical sex. At issue is a certain verse found in the Tantra (Tibetan Kanjur, PTT, Vol. 5, p. 172-3), which that Tantra prefaces by saying this is "the Reality of the hand symbol of Śrī-Paramādya." I translate the verse as follows:

> The great weapon of the great lord who has the supreme success (*siddhi*) that is great, is said to be the five-pronged thunderbolt which is the great reality of the five secrets.

Ānandagarbha's extensive commentary on this verse (PTT. Vol. 73, p. 127-5 to p. 130), starts by explaining that the "supreme success" is the *siddhi* of Śrī-Vajrasattva (the glorious diamond being). The "great lord" is Mahāvajradhara. The great reality of the five secrets amounts to the (1) *bodhicitta* (mind of enlightenment), (2) understanding it, (3) its realization, (4) its non-abandonment, and (5) the knowledge characterized by attainment; and these are represented by five goddesses, who are "seals" (*mudrā*) arising from the Body, Speech, and Mind diamonds (*vajra*) of Mahāvajradhara. Observe that the source is again the "three mysteries of the Buddha."

Now, the intriguing feature of this classification is what the commentary refers to as the "five secrets" (*gsaṅ ba lṅa*). Why not call the goddesses "secret", or the subsequent commentarial explanations! But, no, it is precisely what non-tantric Buddhist texts would take as a topic of open discourse, that this commentary decides to label "secret"—such things as the mind of enlightenment, understanding it, and so on! But what do those five have in common to justify calling them "secret"? Only, that like the secret of female sex, they are inward, and so they can be represented by five goddesses.

Also, the commentary frequently speaks of the four goddesses, by leaving out Vajrasattva, who is ordinarily considered a male deity. However, his inclusion in the group of five can be justified by his dual nature of male-female, as will be shown by the explanation. I have made a tabulation from Ānandagarbha's data, showing the five secrets along with the five goddess group and initial commentarial explanations—which should begin to clarify this matter.

TABLE 3

THE GREAT REALITY OF FIVE SECRETS

THE FIVE SECRETS	FIVE "GODDESS" GROUP	EXPLANATION
1. Bodhicitta (mind of enlightenment)	Vajrasattva (Diamond being)	Who has both the great pleasure and the unwasted *vajra* (diamond).
2. Understanding it	Rāgavajrā (Diamond of passion)	Who pleases Vajrasattva's mind so he will not swerve from the Thought of Enlightenment.
3. Its realization	Vajrakilikilā (Diamond joyful utterance)	The basic pledge to arouse attachment to the great pleasure and unwasted *vajra*.
4. Its non-abandonment	Vajrasmṛti (Diamond memory)	She is "Diamond memory" because unshattered by victory over lust, etc.
5. The knowledge characterized by attainment	Vajrakāmeśvarī (Diamond queen of desires)	She, the "Diamond queen of desires" is the sensory objects that are materialized by the lord Vajrasattva.

It follows from the explanation of Vajrasattva that his inclusion in the five goddess group is simply because he has the "great pleasure" which must be counted as female in contrast with the "unwasted *vajra*" which is male. This is the closest this literature comes to the "passive-active" polarity. It is because Vajrasattva is androgyne that both men and women can practice the Tantras as yogins and yoginīs.

Furthermore, Ānandagarbha (*op. cit.* p. 129-3) identifies the set of four goddesses with Tathāgatas in the sense that each goddess confers the diadem initiation going with the family (or lineage) of that Tathāgata.

Rāgavajrā	—	Akṣobhya
Kilikilā	—	Ratnasambhava
Vajrasmṛti	—	Amitābha
Vajrakāmeśvarī	—	Amoghasiddhi

Subsequently Ānandagarbha (*op. cit.*, p. 130-2, 3) refers to this group of four as the "secret *maṇḍala*" (*gsaṅ ba'i dkyil 'khor*); calls this the "city of liberation"; and says the word "secret" in this *maṇḍala* context means that the body of the lord dwells amidst the set of diamond goddesses. He means that Vajrasattva is surrounded by the four goddesses. In this case, the word "secret" again has a sexual meaning, now referring to the privacy of the queen harem. But it is not the sexual language which is secret, rather what it symbolizes. The real secret is that the mind of enlightenment (the *bodhicitta*) has enticed the four lovers called "understanding it," "its realization," "its non-abandonment," and "the knowledge characterized by attainment." And a further secret is that the "mind of enlightenment" itself contains another lover called "great pleasure." This, then, is the spiritual orgy, along with the magical song and instrumental music, the flowers and incense (*op. cit.*, 130-1, 2).

The critic of the Tantras could now object, urging a uselessness of such sexual symbolism. He could say that it is a fine thing to have the mind of enlightenment, the understanding of it, and so on; but is it not a kind of charade to take each element of the unquestionably spiritual ascension and disguise it with the rich vocabulary of goddesses, offerings, and the like, so the commentarial discussion gets bogged down in the goddess discussion rather than in the more legitimate discourse on the understanding, etc. of the mind of enlightenment! The answer is that some Buddhist non-tantric books do exactly what this critic would enjoin. They treat the mind of enlightenment and further elements of the Bodhisattva path without any tantric terminology. A good example is the *Daśabhūmika-sūtra* (the scripture on the ten stages of the Bodhisattva). An intelligent scholar, Har Dayal, upon studying this kind of literature for a London doctoral thesis, wrote *The Bodhisattva Doctrine in Buddhist Sanskrit Literature*. This shows that one can also become bogged down in non-tantric terminology, because in the end the learned author labelled the Bodhisattva practice a "Doctrine". But the Tantras have a premise that the actual pursuance by the Bodhisattva of his enlightenment goal is akin to sex. That is to say, the understanding of the mind of enlightenment is a lover. And because this goddess loves Vajrasattva's mind of enlightenment, he, enchanted by her love, does not swerve from this Thought of Enlightenment.

In my forthcoming *Yoga of the Guhyasamājatantra* I have cited the explanation of Līlavajra (the teacher of Buddhaśrījñāna) about three kinds of "secrets": The first, the "self-existent", is a secret element located in the stream of consciousness, certainly by the commentarial indications to be identified with the "embryo of the Tathāgata", the potentiality of Buddhahood. The second is the "pregnant" (*sbas pa*), and this is the kind which is conferred by the guru when the disciple is initiated; that is, when the disciple is prepared through initiation, the tantric secrets become in the disciple the "pregnant". The third, the profound, is conferred by oneself. Here again the terminology of "secret" brings in the female element, first with the seed in her, next with her pregnancy, and last with the profundity of insight (the goddess).

Tsoṅ-kha-pa's *Sbas don* (p. 11-5 to 12-1) presents a list of seven topics which should not be made clear to persons who do not have lineage in this (tantric) vehicle. He says the list is taken from Łva-ba-pa's commentary (presumably Toh. No. 1401, the *Sādhananidāna-śrīcakrasaṃvara-nāma-pañjikā*) and is practically the same as the list in the *Saṃpuṭottara* (in fact, PTT. Vol. 2, p. 283-3,4). He slightly expands each item of the seven, as follows:

1. The secret domain of reality, i.e. the domain of the *prajñā* which is reality.
2. The secret circle of the Victor, i.e. the circle of deities.
3. The secret "pregnant" truth, i.e. as in the *Saṃpuṭottara*, the illustrious pregnant things.
4. The secret which is the secret lotus, i.e. the lotus in the *mūla-cakra* as well as the lotus of the *mudrā*.
5. The secret delight by the seed, i.e. the delight engendered from the dripping of *bodhicitta* from the HAṂ syllable at the crown of the head.
6. The secret which is combining all, i.e. combining the secrets of *vajra* and lotus, etc.
7. The secret uninterrupted bliss, i.e. entering the single uninterrupted taste of both the objective reality and the subjective.

This appears to be a comprehensive list of items which should not be made clear to immature, i.e. uninitiated persons, who do not have the vows and pledges going with the higher initiations. Explaining these items to such persons constitutes the seventh fundamental transgression among the fourteen (cf. *Mkhas grub rje's*, pp. 328-29)—the one which is called "mountains".

Tsoṅ-kha-pa (*Sbas don*, p. 12-1) goes on to set forth what is meant by explaining such secrets and says that there are two ways of explaining—one according to the "hinted meaning" (*neyārtha*, *draṅ ba'i don*), the other according to the "evident meaning" (*nītārtha*, *ṅes pa'i don*). For an example of how Nāro-pāda explains in both ways, see the later essay (chap. 10) on Tantric Ritual.

It should be clear from the above that a Buddhist Tantra is not just a series of secrets. In fact, most of those secret topics appertain to the body of tantric literature called the Anuttarayoga Tantra; and even in the works of this class one could find many statements that do not fit—at least on the surface—among these "secrets". Still, it is reasonable that the Anuttarayoga Tantra should contain so much material to be labelled "secret" because the foregoing chapter on Analogical Thinking shows that this Tantra division is meant for candidates "who delight in inner samādhi completely," and the "secrets" of this chapter are mainly those which are oriented inward and so have the secrecy, metaphorically, of the female sex.

With this new light on the "secrets" it would be profitable for the reader to have an evaluation of the book, S. B. Dasgupta, *An Introduction to Tantric Buddhism*. The author had utilized a number of Sanskrit manuscripts of Buddhist Tantras belonging to the Anuttarayoga class. Therefore, he found abundant information on such matters as the *cakra-s* in the body and what he calls the "sexo-yogic practice." In fact, he generally favored the kind of data which reminded him of the Hindu Tantra and which he could therefore relate to his previous knowledge. Naturally, all his extracts are valid passages, even though, as the present researches show, the continuous line of teachers provides a somewhat different approach than what one can obtain by unguided random selection. His work is mistitled, because it is certainly not "an introduction to Tantric Buddhism." But when he included much of the material of this book in his more mature work, *Obscure Religious Cults*, the material cannot be criticized that way, because now there is no misrepresentation of constituting an "introduction."

If not those tantric "secrets" themselves, one thing should be clear: the sexual symbolism is not intended to dismay the unworthy, or to throw anyone off the track in an effort to conceal a secret. Rather, as symbolism should be, it is intimately related, as a kind of metaphorical extension, to the very facts pointed to by the symbolism. In ordinary human terms, it is no secret to anyone that he or she is a sexual being in the sense of having sexual attributes; a person does not have to be told this. But a woman does not know the secret of her mysterious processes for bringing a new life into the world, simply by having them. Someone has to tell her about them. She could be told that in India the intrauterine processes were calculated by ten lunar months, which appear to have been the prototype of the ten Bodhisattva stages. More generally, to the extent something is concealed because it is internal, it is not known simply by reason of its possession. Here again, the sexual symbolism is not the secret. The disciple does not know the tantric secrets, even though they are within him; and so the guru is absolutely essential to guide the disciple to knowledge, the disciple's own insight (*prajñā*). The disciple develops this in the sequence of hearing, pondering, and cultivating, while becoming a "fit vessel" (*snod ruṅ*, in Tibetan). Such is the meaning of coordinating his body, speech, and mind to the "three mysteries of the Buddha."

However, it might be asked if it is not the case that the tantric texts themselves are secret. There is little doubt that the main texts in the revealed sense, now preserved in Tibetan translation in the Kanjur, were handed down for some centuries orally; and this sort of transmission ensured a restriction to an esoteric group. But the principal texts, usually in verse (*śloka*) form for memorizing purposes, were not strictly secret to the masses of people, but were unknown or inconsequential to them. Down the centuries, there would have been a relatively small number of persons who sought the tantric "secrets" and were turned down. These tantric texts were positively secret to the very persons who memorized them, if memorizing is all they did with those texts. The reason is that the Tantra is essentially a practice, for which directions are required. A text giving such directions is not sufficiently detailed when written in the traditional Indian form of summary verses. Therefore, the guru had to add commentarial explanations. He would fill in those necessary details omitted by the basic texts, and fill them in for the disciples who had been conferred the necessary initiations and taken the vows. His explanations were thus secret in the sense that they could be withheld, but the basic texts had the secrecy of obscurity, just as any manual, on whatever topic, would be obscure if written in too abbreviated a form to permit anyone to follow through with the necessary actions.

Of course, now certain Buddhist tantric texts have become more available to Westerners. The Sanskrit text of the *Guhyasamājatantra* was edited and published. The *Hevajratantra* was edited and translated into English. In this sense they are not secret in the sense of being withheld from the reader. But they are still secret, if one can believe the commentators, in that reading these Tantras still conveys little of what the tantrists themselves are doing in the drawn-out rites, with their multitude of details, chanting, and so on; and little to imagine of what the best commentaries have to say in amplification of the individual words. In the case of a tantric text, it will always be a mistake for any reader to think that his proven intelligence (by university degrees and the like) or his proven intuition (by life experience and the like) will enable him to penetrate the meaning of a basic Buddhist Tantra text, because the meaning is in the doing of it, and there is no substitute for someone showing how to do it. That someone of course is the guru.

II

FOUNDATIONS OF THE BUDDHIST TANTRA

Just as the milk of lioness
Is not to be put in a vessel of earth,
So also the Great Yoga Tantra is
Not to be given to unworthy vessels.

Abhayākara's *Vajrāvalī*, Sec. 50

6

DIVINITY ACCORDING TO THE BUDDHIST TANTRAS

For the numerous deities of the Buddhist Tantras, the best descriptive coverage is in Benoytosh Bhattacharyya, *The Indian Buddhist Iconography*. The luxurious growth of these cults is bewildering in complexity. Therefore, some general explanations of a unifying type are in order.

Nāro-pāda, in his *Vajrapada-sāra-saṃgraha-pañjikā* (PTT. Vol. 54, p. 11-2), inaugurates his deity chapter by two citations to explain the word "divinity" (*devatā*). The (*Kālacakra* work) *Vimalaprabhā* states: Because conventional ecstasy has arisen in the body's nature of five elements, one speaks of "divinity." And the *Śrī-Vajrāmṛta-tantra* states: Why does one speak of "divinity"? In the body is located the body possessor; in order to comprehend, there is the "comprehender"; in order to comprehend oneself, there is divinity. For that reason, one speaks of "divinity".

Nāro-pāda explains divinity in terms of the one who achieved ecstasy in the body (the co-natal joy) and who comprehended, i.e. was enlightened. He implies the Buddha under the title "Tathāgata", because this is the source of all the Buddhist Tantric deities, or the dominion in which they serve. Mkhas grub rje, in his commentary on the *Hevajratantra* called briefly the *Brtag 'grel* (Lhasa Collected Works, Vol. Ja, folio 104a-3, ff.), has a useful exposition, which I shall further summarize and partially paraphrase as follows:

(a) *Meaning of the expression "Tathāgata"*. The Tathāgata has the two collections, of Knowledge (*jñāna*) and of Merit (*puṇya*). Through Knowledge, i.e. the Insight (*prajñā*) indissoluble from Thusness (*tathatā*), he has gone into the single taste of Thusness. Through Merit, he has come (*āgata*), i.e. returned from Thusness, to the cycle of existence (*saṃsāra*) with the formal body (*rūpa-kāya*). Accordingly, he is called "tathāgata" ("thus-gone," "thus-come").

(b) *Families* (*kula*) *of the Tathāgata*. All the diverse appearances of the Tathāgata can be grouped in families, frequently spoken of as six kinds, namely, Vajra, Tathāgata, Ratna, Padma, Karma, and Vajrasattva families, because whatever the Buddhist deity, it can always be counted or included in these families. (Here the terminology "Tathāgata family" is differentiated from the over-all Tathāgata in the manner explained in *Mkhas grub rje's*). By incorporating the Vajrasattva into the Vajra family, there are five. If the Ratna family is incorporated into the Tathāgata family, the result is the "Thunderbolt of Body" (*kāya-vajra*). If the Karma family is incorporated into the Padma family, the result is the "Thunderbolt of Speech" (*vāg-vajra*). The Vajra family is separately taken as the "Thunderbolt of Mind" (*citta-vajra*). The deities are grouped into five families because they are the purity of the five elements of the body (cf. Nāro-pāda's above remark) and the purity of the five personality aggregates (*skandha*). They are also reduced to three families because the practitioner's stream of elements (*saṃtāna*) have the threefold grouping of body, speech, and mind, which the tantric path aims to coordinate with the Buddha's three mysteries of Body, Speech, and Mind.

(c) *The progenitors of the Buddha families*. The names of the Buddha progenitors common to the Buddhist Tantras are Vairocana, Akṣobhya, Amoghasiddhi, Ratnasaṃbhava, Amitābha, and Vajrasattva. Furthermore, certain Buddhist Tantras replace those names with others. For example, the *Hevajratantra* has the appellations Brahmā, etc. Mkhas grub rje explains the progenitors in terms of those names as follows:

> The Buddha Vairocana is called Brahmā. The Tibetan *saṅs rgyas* translates the Sanskrit "Buddha". Because he enters the elimination of defilement, he establishes the part of freedom from defilement. Moreover, the Tibetan *tshaṅs pa* (Brahmā) is equivalent to entrance into Nirvāṇa; hence the name is used with the meaning of "Nirvāṇa of no fixed abode" (*apratiṣṭhitanirvāṇa*).
>
> Akṣobhya is called Viṣṇu. The reason for using this term is that Akṣobhya establishes the "Dharmadhātu knowledge" and by means of this knowledge enters the reality of the intrinsic nature (*svabhāva*) which pervades all things.
>
> Amoghasiddhi is named Śiva, because through the nature of "knowledge of the procedure of duty" (*kṛtyānuṣṭhāna-jñāna*) he continually provides all sentient beings with mundane and supramundane goods.
>
> The term Sarva is used for Ratnasambhava because, through his "equality-knowledge" (*samatā-jñāna*), he establishes in this equality the full comprehension of the nature of all things.

Amitābha is referred to by Tattva, because he establishes the part of "discriminative knowledge" (*pratyavekṣaṇa-jñāna*) which comprehends reality (*tattva*), and with sublime joy is like the sky. Vajrasattva is termed Vibuddha ("expanded") because he has expanded to the states of the "great co-natal joy" (*sahajānanda*) while fully comprehending them.

Mkhas grub rje broadens this explanation of Vajrasattva to apply to all the other Buddha-progenitors as well. Of course, the term "co-natal" means "born in the body" (*dehe saṃbhavati*; cf. *Hevajratantra*, I, v. 14).

The meaning of the Buddhas as progenitors is further illustrated by placing various elements of the path under their respective dominion. For example, Tsoṅ-kha-pa's *Sṅags rim chen mo* (Peking blockprint, 365b-3, ff.) cites a number of works and explains the six members of the Stage of Generation (*utpatti-krama*) in the Anuttara-Yoga Tantra. In my summary:

TABLE 4

STAGE OF GENERATION

MEMBER	THROUGH WHICH FAMILY	ACTIVITY	REASON FOR THE FAMILY
1.	Vairocana	Contemplation of the palace which is the Buddhas' dwelling.	Because he is the nature of the material aggregate (*rūpa-skandha*) of the Tathāgatas.
2.	Vajrasattva	Passion towards the divine Father-Mother, after generating the symbolic circle (*samaya-cakra*) by means of the five Manifest Enlightenments (*abhisaṃbodhi*) and then generating the knowledge circle (*jñāna-cakra*).	Because that is the meaning of the lord who has passion in order to produce "materializations" (*nirmita*) from the *bodhicitta* of the Father-Mother pairs of the retinue deities.
3.	Akṣobhya	Initiation (*abhiṣeka*), conferred by the eight "wisdom goddesses" (*vidyā*)	Because he is the essence of the water initiation.
4.	Amitābha	Enjoyment of the ambrosia (*amṛta*).	Because he is the "Thunderbolt of Speech," which satiates.
5.	Amoghasiddhi	Offerings.	Because he is the progenitor of the Karma family, and hence has power over offerings to the Buddhas, and actions for the sake of the living beings.
6.	Ratnasambhava	Praises.	Because praise is the extolling of merits; and at the time of arising of merits of Body, Speech, and Mind, Ratnasambhava is those merits.

Besides identification with male deities, as in the *Hevajratantra* with the names Brahmā, etc., sometimes the Buddhas appear in the form of goddesses. Among these goddesses the ones (frequently in fierce form) that the Tibetans especially invoked for occult results (*siddhi*) are often called *ḍākinī*. Among these lines, Tsoṅ-kha-pa (*Sbas don*, PTT ed., p. 4-3,4) cites the Tantra "Ocean of Ḍākinīs" for an identification of the six stages of yoga of the Stage of Completion (*saṃpanna-krama*) in the Anuttarayoga Tantra, with six of the Ḍākinīs among the eight doorkeepers in the *Śrī-Cakrasaṃvara maṇḍala*. I shall complete the table with materials drawn from my forthcoming *Yoga of the Guhyasamājatantra*, which has full justification for this data, unavoidably given here in the most abbreviated form.

TABLE 5

STAGE OF COMPLETION

MEMBER	ḌĀKINĪ	NAME OF MEMBER	COMMENT
1.	She the Crow-Faced	pratyāhāra ("withdrawal")	Withdrawal, i.e. interiorization of the ten sense bases (five personal and five objective).
2.	She the Owl-Faced	dhyāna ("meditation")	Meditation on the nature of the five Tathāgatas
3.	She the Dog-Faced	prāṇāyāma ("control of the winds")	Control of the winds in five colors, with diamond muttering (*vajrajāpa*).
4.	She the Boar-Faced	dhāraṇā ("retention")	The five signs, mirage, etc., with purification of mind (*citta-viśuddhi*) and personal blessing (*svādhiṣṭhāna*).
5.	She, Yama's Messenger	anusmṛti ("recollection")	Recollection, so as to proceed in the reverse order, with Revelation-Enlightenment (*abhisaṃbodhi*).
6.	She, Yama's Cremation Ground	samādhi ("consummation")	The consummation of knowledge, with *yuganaddha*, the pair-united.

The passage from the "Ocean of Ḍākinīs" continues, taking care of the last two goddesses: "She, Yama's Tusk, achieves the wide-spread firmness; She, Yama's Annihilation, engenders the entire fruit and liberates from *saṃsāra*." (Yama is the Lord of the dead, in Indian mythology).

This deific identification of elements of the path is further demonstrated in my essay "Symbolism of the Maṇḍala-Palace" as well as in the essay "Five-fold ritual symbolism of passion."

The guru as a divinity

The identification with divinity is also performed in the case of the guru, for which the *Vajrapāṇyabhiṣeka-mahātantra* (as cited in Tsoṅ-kha-pa's *Lam rim chen mo*) provides the basic position:

> Master of the Secret Folk, how should a disciple look upon his preceptor? As though upon the Lord Buddha. The mind of him so disposed incessantly generates merits; he becomes a Buddha bringing benefit to all the worlds . . . One should hold to the preceptor's virtues, and never hold to his faults. If one holds to virtues, he attains success; if one holds to faults, he attains failure.

However, this brings up the problem of what constitutes the spiritual teacher. For example, the brief tantric scripture, *Śrī-Mahākha-tantrarāja* (Derge Kanjur, Rgyud 'bum, Ga, 203a-6) states: "It is said that there are two kinds of gurus—that external guru himself; and the inner guru, the presiding deity (*bdag po'i lha*)." The presiding deity is defined by Ānandagarbha in his great commentary, the *Śrī-Paramādiṭikā* (Toh. 2512, Derge Tanjur, Rgyud, I, 22a-3): "One's presiding deity is *kāmadeva.* The conviction that his diamonds of body, speech, and mind are one's own—with a praxis that it is really so—is the meaning of *yoga.*" The "presiding deity" appears to mean the same as the "tutelary deity" (*iṣṭa-devatā*), or the deity which the disciple serves with daily devotions and enshrines in the heart.

The inner guru is further differentiated in a suggestion of Buddhaśrījñānapāda's *Mukti-tilaka-nāma* (PTT, Vol. 65, p. 24-4) in the text line, "the superior three speakers who teach that way." Vitapāda's commentary on that line in the *Mukti-tilaka-nāma-vyākhyāna* (PTT, Vol. 65, p. 135-2,3) explains the words "who teach that way" as meaning: who teach the nature of the indestructible mark (*mi śigs pa'i thig le*; Skt., *amata-tilaka*, or *akṣata-bindu*) as co-natal (*sahaja*) (i.e. in the heart). The commentary explains the inner kind as three gurus: the great basic teacher (*rgyu'i slob dpon chen po*), the conditional teacher (*rkyen gyi slob dpon*), and the co-natal teacher (*lhan cig skyes pa'i slob dpon*). He quotes a work called the *Rin chen phreṅ ba źes bya ba'i de kho na ñid* in amplification of these terms:

> The one acting as the teacher purifying one's own stream of consciousness in the sequence of the shared (*sādhāraṇa*), unshared (*asādhāraṇa*), abiding in pledges (*samaya*), water, etc. is the great basic teacher.
>
> The great goddess who purifies the field in one's own stream of consciousness by sporting together with that (great basic teacher) and by sixteen parts—is explained to be the conditional teacher.

> One's own mind (*citta*) when given permission by that (conditional teacher) is the co-natal teacher because of the co-natal blessing and because of comprehending the co-natal joy.

The commentary goes on to explain that those are "superior" because they surpass other gurus. In further explanation, it appears that the first of the three is the tutelary deity serving as the focus for the disciple's adherence to practices shared with non-tantric Buddhism and other Tantras, practices not so shared but special to the cult of that deity, pledges along the way, initiations of water and so forth. That in time this service of the first kind of guru awakens the great goddess who takes the disciple through various yoga experiences, sometimes stated with sixteen parts (cf. my essay on the inner zodiac). Finally, that one's own mind is the third guru, comprising the union of the tutelary deity and the great goddess (often called yab-yum by the Tibetan term). This is a form of divine pride (*devatā-garva*), necessary for the quick path of Tantra.

Classifications of Divinity

Moreover, the multitude of minor deities are incorporated in the Buddha families by the manner of speaking that those deities are "seals" (*mudrā*) of the Buddha families. Thus, when the performer identifies himself with a deity, his hand gesture (*mudrā*) can be taken as the deity. In the evocation procedure, there is a developmental order of the deity as a syllable (*akṣara*), then as a hand symbol (*cihna*), and finally as a deific body. More fully, Buddhaguhya in his *Dhyānottara-paṭala-ṭīkā* (PTT. Vol. 78, p. 75-4) sets forth three main kinds of divinity to be contemplated, and he further breaks them down into varieties, which we tabulate as follows:

TABLE 6

NATURE OF DIVINITY

CONSISTING OF FORMAL BODY (*rūpa-kāya*)	CONSISTING OF SOUND	OF ABSOLUTE KIND (*pāramarthika*)
(1) Shaped with eye, etc. and corporeal members.	(1) Consisting of letters.	(1) Nature of *dharmadhātu*.
(2) Consisting of *mudrā*.	(2) Consisting of enunciation. (2-a) Consisting of expressed sound of whispered, etc. recitation that is generated by palate, lips, etc. (2-b) Consisting of mental recitation of general *mantras*. (2-c) Consisting of the imagination equivalent to beings (*sattva*) from respective *mantra* letters.	(2) Nature of nondiscursive knowledge with non-apperception of meditative object.

The 2-b category is also referred to as "diamond words" (*vajrapada*), described as soundless (lips shut), hence mental, for example, in Smṛtijñānakīrti's commentary on *Mañjuśrī-nāmasaṃgīti* (PTT. Vol. 75, p. 55-1).

Another type of classification, overlapping the foregoing one, is found in Padmavajra's work, the *Vāhikaṭīkā-nāma* (Derge Tanjur, Rgyud, Dza, 29b-1, ff.). Here the organization is in terms of the Bodies of the Buddha. In the oldest classification, these are the Dharmakāya and the Rūpakāya. Later the Rūpakāya further divides into the Saṃbhogakāya and the Nirmāṇakāya, which are standard in the Mahāyāna. Some Mahāyāna sects added a fourth one called the Mahāsukhakāya. This is Padmavajra's statement:

> Those deities who are born by transformation have a body belonging to the Nirmāṇakāya, on which account, among the four bodies, Dharma, Sambhoga, Nirmāṇa, and Mahāsukha, three have varieties.
>
> Among them, the Nirmāṇakāya is the gods born by transformation. The Dharmakāya is the set of planets, asterisms (*nakṣatra*), etc. The Sambhogakāya is the two-footed (divinities); and the Nirmāṇakāya is like the Sambhogakāya in this respect.
>
> The Nirmāṇakāya is the gods who range in the palace. The Sambhogakāya is those (yogins) with *samāpatti* in the initial *samādhi* (*prathamasamādhi*). The Dharmakāya is those who have transcended the ecstasy.
>
> Besides, it is explained by the Dharmakāya: Whatever the gods dwelling in the wind and *vijñāna* (i.e. *vijñāna* riding on the winds), their non-apperception is the Dharmakāya. Moreover, those with *samāpatti* (meditational equipoise) in the three samādhis are the Sambhogakāya. Those who mutually gaze by reason of habit-energy of adhering to the idea of "mine", are the Nirmāṇakāya.
>
> Likewise, it is explained by knowledge: The non-oozing ecstasy of dwelling in the Akaniṣṭha (heaven), is the Dharmakāya. Those with the ecstasy of frequently tasting the Dharma in introspection, are the Sambhogakāya. Those who are self-originated by reason of a former vow, but do not know it, are the Nirmāṇakāya.

All these can be taken as an explanation of Buddhaguhya's category of absolute deity, first kind: nature of *dharmadhātu*. These can also be discussed by the terminology of "three *sattvas*," for which see *Mkhas grub rje's*.

Besides, one can expand upon the absolute divinity of Buddhaguhya's variety referred to as "non-discursive knowledge." Tsoṅ-kha-pa's *Sṅags*

PLATE 4. Mahāvajradhara.

rim chen mo at folio 37b-2 cites the commentary on the *Saṃpuṭa* by Dpa' bo rdo rje (*Śūravajra) that there are three levels of non-discursive ecstasy. The first is based on sound (the sound of laughter), which in mystical experience is referred to as "hearing the Lord". The second is based on sight (seeing the form of the deity) therefore "seeing the Lord". The third is based on touch (as when the deity and consort hold hands or unite), and would be later described as "touching the Lord". In fact, this section of the *Sṅags rim chen mo* thereby establishes the division of four Tantras in terms of the role of the divinities of the Tantra. That is to say, the *Kriyā Tantra* has the deities laughing; the *Caryā Tantra*, the deities mutually gazing; the Yoga Tantra, the deities holding hands; the Anuttara-yoga Tantra, the deities in union.

The Ādi Buddha

Finally, there is the Primordial Buddha, or the final perfection of divinity, the composite of all Buddhas, called Vajradhara (Holder of the Diamond), and also Vajrasattva (Diamond Being), Samantabhadra (Entirely Auspicious—the Vow of Enlightenment), or Kālacakra (wheel of Time). Vajradhara is sometimes depicted in union with the Goddess, and sometimes by himself, as in the illustration.

In explanation of Mahāvajradhara, the *Guhyasamājatantra* (Chap. XVII, p. 135) has the verse:

> Then Vajradhara, the Teacher, who is bowed to by all the Buddhas, best of the three diamonds, best of the great best, supreme lord of the three diamonds . . .

And the Explanatory Tantra *Vajramālā* (PTT. Vol. 3, p. 229) states:

> Vajradhara is explained as endowed with the profound and far-reaching; the Diamond Being (vajrasattva), best of those with two (legs); who is master of destroying and benefitting.

As to the *Guhyasamāja* verse (XVII, 39), the *Pradīpoddyotana* (PTT. Vol. 158, p. 154-3) states in part that the three diamonds are the diamonds of Body, Speech, and Mind in the case of "supreme lord of the three diamonds". Tsoṅ-kha-pa's *Mchan-'grel* explains the "lord of body": displays simultaneously innumerable materializations of body; "lord of speech": teaches the Dharma simultaneously to boundless sentient beings each in his own language; "lord of mind": understands all the knowable which seems impossible. Hence, these are the "three mysteries" of the Buddha. The *Vajramālā* verse stresses Vajradhara in human form as Vajrasattva, the chief hierophant.

7

PREPARATION OF DISCIPLES; THE MEANING OF INITIATION

By "preparation of disciples" is meant their preparation to evoke deities—a process frequently called in Sanskrit *sādhana*; and this is to be distinguished from the initiation of disciples. Thus there are two parts to the present essay, exhibited textually toward the end of the present work with "Outline of the Thob Yig Gsal Baḥi Me Loṅ," because Chapter 4 of the outlined treatise treats the lineages of permission to evoke deities, and its subsequent Chapter 5 treats initiation and shows that Mantrayāna begins with initiation.

Preparation of Disciples for Evocation of Deities

It is well known that Tibetan monks meditate upon a wide variety of deities. Many of these gods and goddesses are depicted upon the temple banners called Tankas, of which a goodly number have found their way into Western museums as well as into private homes. The Sanskrit word for these evocations is *sādhana*, translated into Tibetan as *sgrub thabs* (pronounced *drewp top*). Westerners invariantly want to know the meaning of these deities and their accompanying incantations (*mantra*), in Tibetan *sngags*, pronounced *ngok*: and would be surprised to learn that they do not have such and such meanings in the Western sense of intellectual understanding. Their meanings arise through the regular practice and service of the deity. Nevertheless, there are some general remarks that can be made about such practices.

The Sanskrit books available on these subjects convey meager information. This is because the collection of *sādhanas* contain only the bare description of the deity. These tiny treatises may start out by saying that out of the void appears such and such a germ syllable, which changes into a such and such, upon which a certain deity is imagined with so many heads and arms, with certain symbols in the right hands and certain ones in the left hands, and so on. Separate books contain general instructions about such evocations, and of course the *guru* or master supplies all the instructions that were missing in the book. The Tibetan manuals are superior to the former Indian ones, in that all the literary instructions concerning a particular evocation are brought together into one book.

An essential ingredient of every evocation of a deity is that the candidate must get permission. Here the Sanskrit word is *anujñā*, Tibetan *rjes gnang* ("*je nang*"). The theory of "permission" is stated in *Mkhas grub rje's Fundamentals of the Buddhist Tantras*. Unavoidably, the permission to evoke a deity comes from the deity itself, especially in auspicious dreams. The master acts as an intermediary in conferring the permission. In practice, the way this is done is for the master to generate himself into the deity, and then, as the deity, to grant permission to the disciples. That is one reason why the disciple is supposed to look upon the *guru* as a Buddha, to never dwell upon his faults, but only on his virtues. This is not to imply that the *guru* is actually a Buddha, but only that by so regarding the *guru*, the latter is able to function in the role of conferring this all-essential permission and the consequent initiations.

The first Lcang skya Hutukhtu of Peking, Ngagdbang Blo-bzang-chos-ldan, wrote a little treatise entitled, *Spyi ḥgroḥi rjes gnang gi bśad pa* ("Explanation of the general permission"), meaning the mandatory preliminary attitude to be engendered. The disciples having bathed and approached respectfully the master, imploring him for the "permission", he tells them some of the basic Buddhist teachings. For example, how difficult it is to attain human birth among the various destinies, good and bad; and then the fortunate circumstances of finding the teacher. Thus, with aspiration for enlightenment and liberation, they must embrace the Illustrious Doctrine. Then, about the two vehicles, the non-tantric and the tantric. Having taken those precepts to heart, the candidates are convinced that by relying on such and such a tutelary deity or such and such a protector of the religion, they (the candidates) will keep a fortunate condition, free from the untoward states (of being born when or where there is no teacher, and so on). The candidates go on to imagine that in the sky in front of the offerings, it is as though a vast cloud of the tutelary deity, the Buddhas, Bodhisattvas, protectors of the religion, fairies, and so on, were condensing. Before that throng, the candidates take refuge in the Three Jewels, confess their sins long accumulated, rejoice in the virtues accumulated by themselves and others, and, for the sake of the sentient beings, pray for the "permission" of such and such a tutelary deity or protector of the religion. The master has the candidates repeat key sentences after him. Then, in order to reveal the *maṇḍala* and vivify the basis of the permission, the disciples are generated into deity.

The way in which this "permission" is granted is especially shown in the Tibetan ritual of the goddess Ushṇīshavijayā as found in the four-volume collection of *sādhanas* called the *Rin lhan*. I once studied this text in the East Asiatic Library, University of California. Here we find that the master first generates himself into the goddess Ushṇīshavijayā with her retinue of eight deities. This has the two phases of generation of self into deity and generation of deity in front, which are described extensively in *Mkhas grub rje's Fundamentals of the Buddhist Tantras*. The *Rin lhan* text first sets forth the "permission of body", which concerns the bodies, small, large, and infinite, of the Lordess Ushṇīshavijayā and of her retinue. Then it portrays the "permission of speech", which concerns the vow to hold the Lordess as the protective deity. Finally, it tells the "permission of mind," which concerns the installation of the Lordess's body, only the length of a finger, in the heart. Naturally, those three kinds of permission each have a well-defined ritual side too complex to go into now.

It is clear that the process of evocation and of granting permission is somewhat advanced, particularly in the demands upon the imaginative ability of the master and the disciples. From ancient times, Buddhism classified candidates in terms of keen faculty, medium faculty, and inferior faculty. Certainly, there is a preceding training for the disciple. Of this, the theory of Buddhist meditation has much to say.

For example, Mr. Norbu loaned me the first folios of a work entitled *Rgyal baḥi bstan skyong gYu Grags gnis kyi sgrub thabs dang ḥbrel baḥi rjes gnang bya tshul*. The title means: "Method of performing the evocation of the two protectors of the religion called (in short) gYu and Grags, along with the associated permission." The title suggests that this book will show the procedure by which the master evokes the two deities, first Rdo rje gYu sgron ma ("She the diamond turquoise lamp") and next, Rdo rje Grags rgyal ma ("She the diamond fame victory"); and then, how he confers the permission of those two deities upon the disciples, somewhat along the lines delineated above. We find at the outset an introductory statement that there are three parts to the method of performing the evocation and associated permission. All rituals are similarly divided, into (a) initial praxis, or preliminaries; (b) the main part of the rite; (c) concluding acts. The evocation and permission are counted as the main part of the rite.

Mr. Norbu called my attention to a word which occurs near the beginning of this work. It is written *tsa-ka-li*, and he explains that it means these certain miniature paintings, on which I am presently writing a book based on the manuscripts of the late Professor F. D. Lessing of Berkeley. Naturally, the master cannot be expected to carry around with him those large tankas which hang in the temples. For the purposes of permission and initiation of the disciple, the miniature serves handily. It must be carefully prepared to depict correctly the manner in which the particular deity is to be contemplated. Hence this kind of painting is made with especially fine details and with vivid coloring. In fact, the text in question mentions this word in connection with (a) the initial praxis. Here we find that on a platform in front, the performer arranges various offerings and adornments for the deity, including the *tsa-ka-li*, which, as I understand the sentence, is adorned with arrow and silk.[1]

After Mr. Norbu pointed out that word *tsa-ka-li*, I soon had the luck of finding the expression in a text of the Tanjur (the commentarial Tibetan canon). Those who have read the translation, *Mkhas grub rje's Fundamentals of the Buddhist Tantras*, will have gained some idea of the difference between the four classes of Buddhist Tantra. They will know that the Indian writer Ānandagarbha (in Tibetan, Kun-dgaḥ-sñing-po) was a celebrated commentator on the third class of Tantra called the Yoga-tantra, which itself is divided up into four sections. Of these sections, the one called "Purification of Evil Destiny" is especially interesting on the commentarial side, and Ānandagarbha has written a commentary on it, in which I happened to find the word, though here it was transcribed into Tibetan letters as *tsak-ka-li.*

Let me translate Ānandagarbha's key sentence: "Besides, there is a condition (*rkyen*) for generating those *mantras*; one both arranges them in the mind and arranges the *tsak-ka-li* of body." This shows that in order to effectuate the incantations, there is a simultaneous or parallel process in the mind and in the external world. In the mind the incantations are arranged, and in the external world the symbolic representations of the deity are arranged. It might be thought that those external representations, such as the miniature paintings, are serving as meditation props, helping the performer to visualize the particular deity or deities. This is certainly a valid function, but Ānandagarbha intends something more than that. To see the point, one should ascertain how this particular meditation fits into the general theory of Buddhist meditation.

Tsoṅ-kha-pa's *Lam rim chen mo*, section on *zhi gnas* "calming (of the mind)", shows that various scriptures as well as Kamalaśīla's *Bhāva-*

1. The *tsak-ka-li* word transcribes an original Sanskrit term *cakkali*, which is not found in the Sanskrit dictionary. However, the Monier-Williams *Sanskrit-English Dictionary* has the word *cakkala*, which presumably means the same, and is inappropriately defined in the dictionary as presumably "circular", being equivalent to the word *cakrala*. However, here the word means an iconographic device. The painted miniatures are usually square; miniature tankas are rectangular. There is no reason why the device cannot be circular or triangular.

nākrama II and *Bhāvanākrama* III allow that one may accomplish *samādhi* by taking the body of the Tathāgata (the Buddha) as a meditative object. This is thoroughly orthodox, because it is associated with "mindfulness of the Buddha", which is said to generate an infinity of merits. Besides, there are the merits of not losing mindfulness of the Buddha at the time of death. When the body of the Buddha, as meditated upon, becomes vivid and firm, this is the "calming" of keen faculty. The meditator can then continue, as is indicated in the Mahāyāna scriptures, by bowing, making offerings and fervent aspirations before that contemplated body—all of which is included in merit accumulation; and then go on to confess sins and take vows before that contemplated body—all of which is included in purification from obscurations. The latter seems to pertain to "discerning (the truth)" (*lhag mthong*). Thus there are numerous benefits from holding thought on the body of the Buddha. Also, there is a well-defined procedure for such a contemplation. Tsoṅ-kha-pa quotes the *Bhāvanākrama* III:

> In regard to that, first the yogin fastens his mind on the formal body of the Tathāgata as it is seen and as it is heard, and then is to accomplish calming. He orients his mind continuously on the form of the Tathāgata's body, yellow like the color of purified gold, adorned with the (32) characteristics and the (80) minor marks, dwelling within its retinue, and acting for the aim of the sentient beings by diverse means. Generating a desire for the merits of that (body), he subdues fading, excitement, and the other faults, and should practice meditation until such time as that (body) dwells in front and is seen clearly.

In the same place, Tsoṅ-kha-pa makes a distinction between the initial reflected image in the mind of the external replica, such as a painting or metal casting; and the advanced vivid recollection of that body as naturally present in the mind. The latter attainment involves what is called the "basis of the meditative object". He states: "Some place an icon in front, and viewing it with the eye, make a quick contemplation. This has been elegantly refuted by the teacher Ye-śes-sde: *samādhi* is not accomplished by what the senses are aware of; rather it is accomplished by what the mind is aware of." Tsoṅ-kha-pa means that the measure of success in this kind of meditation is in the degree to which the meditative object is completely transferred to the mind, so that both the subtle and rough parts of the body appear vividly in the mind as though alive there. Such a "basis of meditative object" is divorced from the physical characteristics of the particular medium of the replica, such as the painting ingredients and the particular features brought in by reason of a metal casting.

Nevertheless, in the initial stage one does well to use a good replica as a "meditative prop".

Let us return to that sentence of Ānandagarbha's. He seems to indicate the more advanced stage which Tsoṅ-kha-pa refers to as the "basis of meditative object" in the mind. This is not the phase in which one is looking at the *tsak-ka-li* (because *samādhi* is not accomplished by what the senses are aware of). Rather, the *tsak-ka-li* is covered or unviewed. In such a case, at an appropriate point in the service the *tsak-ka-li* can be uncovered to constitute a revelation.

Mkhas-grub-rje writes: "Now if someone were made only to enter the *maṇḍala* and not to be conferred Initiation, what would be the advantage? If one takes the refuge vow and beholds the *maṇḍala* with faith, there is the advantage that he becomes purified from sins accumulated for many aeons and plants in his stream of consciousness (*saṃtāna*) the disposition (*vāsana*) of becoming in future times a receptacle fit for entering the profound *mantra* path (i.e. the Vajra-yāna)." In this connection, recall the passage from the Lcang skya Hutukhtu: "Then, in order to reveal the *maṇḍala* . . ." Those explanations by Mkhas-grub-rje and the Lcang skya Hutukhtu show that there is no revelation of the *maṇḍala* just by exhibiting it, or by the disciple's mere seeing it. Likewise a *maṇḍala* is not revealed when it is published in some modern book and even if thousands of persons buy the book and look at it. But one can take Mkhas-grub-rje's remarks as meaningful by presuming that the mental ritual is directly correlated with the hidden external representation, which thus becomes a seat of power.

Ānandagarbha's mention of arranging *mantras* in the mind has to do with what is called in Tibetan books the *nges don* ("final meaning") of the *mantra*, when it is pronounced in the mind during meditation rather than in outward spoken form, in which case it would be called *drang don* ("provisional meaning"). There is now a good treatment of the "meditation of dwelling in the flame and in the sound" in the English version of Mkhas-grub-rje's book. In alternate words, the *mantra* has two main levels—that of its ordinary muttered expression, when it has the meaning of the waking state; and that of its extraordinary meditational expression, when it has the meaning of the dream state. One may notice as analogous the two stages in contemplation of the meditation object, mentioned above, as the initial reflected image in the mind and the advanced vivid recollection of the object abiding naturally in the mind.

The Meaning of Initiation

Mkhas grub rje's contains a wealth of information on the subject of initiation; and it is safe to say that not before its publication was such a survey of the topic available in depth. However, there is also the fine treatment of initiation according to the *Kālacakra Tantra* in Mario E. Carelli's introduction to his Sanskrit edition of Nāropā's *Sekoddeśaṭīkā* (Baroda, 1941). The present essay is not intended to substitute for those expositions —to which the readers' attention is invited—or to substitute for the specialized treatment in my forthcoming *Yoga of the Guhyasamājatantra; the Arcane Lore of Forty Verses.*

The word "initiation" is the translation of the Sanskrit word *abhiṣeka*, which is rendered into Tibetan as "conferral of power" (*dbaṅ bskur*). Among the germane issues are: (1) whether one must be initiated in order to meditate upon a certain deity; (2) whether the disciple is really "initiated" by going through the formal motions of initiation; (3) whether the procedures of initiation by the gurus are the same as what one could read in a text or manual on the topic (or whether the book could be so understood).

(1) The preceding essay on preparation of disciples for evocation of deities shows that it is not necessary to be initiated in order to evoke a deity. The simplest example of this is of course meditation on the Buddha or on one of the transcendent Bodhisattvas such Avalokiteśvara, as these meditations were practiced in countries with Mahāyāna Buddhism. In fact, such meditations as these do not even require "permission", but the theory of "permission" arose with Tantric deities. Naturally, such meditations on both non-tantric and tantric deities have gone on in countless cases without any formal initiation ceremony of the type developed in tantric Buddhism. And also for tantric deities, I cited in the foregoing part what Mkhas grub rje said: "Now if someone were made only to enter the maṇḍala and not to be conferred Initiation, what would be the advantage? . . ." By *maṇḍala* is meant both the residence and residents (the deities). The idea here is that one does not need to be initiated in order to meditate on a deity, but one must get the permission (*anujñā*) to so meditate, and with that permission comes the directions for the meditation. For example, a number of Westerners have studied with the Tibetan Lamas in northern India and Nepal and been given an individual deity to meditate upon, usually along with some verses directed toward that deity, e.g. Vajrasattva. This requires only a preparation of the disciple and a decision by the guru that such and such is the appropriate deity for that person to meditate upon. But, in addition, it is possible to get an initiation in connection with a certain deity, say Avalokiteśvara; and this initiation gives the person so initiated the right to be instructed in the entire cult of that deity, and therefore in the procedures of gaining various siddhis (occult powers) through that cult. Besides, the higher initiations through such deities as Guhyasamāja are intended to empower the candidate to attempt the supreme goal of Buddhahood in the present life.

(2) The next point is by no means inconsequential because a number of

Westerners have now gone through initiation ceremonies as conducted, for example, in North India by the Tibetan refugees; and the present writer and his wife so participated in the great *Kālacakra* initiation conducted by H.H. the Dalai Lama in 1970. Some Westerners have written on these topics in a manner to suggest to the reader that they know something about the Tantra in question by virtue of "getting initiated." This is far from the truth: in fact, initiation is meant to qualify the candidate to receive the teachings of the Tantra, because the seventh of the fourteen fundamental transgressions (cf. *Mkhas grub rje's*, p. 328) is "to tell the secrets to immature (i.e. uninitiated) persons."

I went into another aspect of this problem in my talk before the International Conference of Orientalists in Japan (1970), which was published in their *Transactions* (No. XV, 1970):

> Buddhism teaches three kinds of insight (Pāli, *paññā*; Sanskrit, *prajñā*), that consisting of hearing or learning (*śrutamayī prajñā*) that consisting of meditation or pondering (*cintāmayī prajñā*), and that consisting of putting into practice or cultivating in one's life (*bhāvanāmayī prajñā*). There is a revelatory example of the first one from my recent stay in Dharmsala, Himachal Pradesh of India. In March, 1970, H. H. the Dalai Lama conferred the Kālacakra Initiation via loudspeaker to over 10,000 Tibetans. Afterwards I asked a learned Lama how His Holiness could possibly initiate so many, when initiations were usually given to small groups of proven disciples. The Lama answered: filled with faith they came from far-off distances at considerable sacrifice; that showed their suitability. I could add: and they sat for hours, listening respectfully and patiently, often under a hot sun without drinking facilities. The idea here is that the one who has faith and endures hardship to hear the teaching has the first level of insight in the Buddhist sense, the insight consisting of hearing. Naturally, few of these persons ever go on to the second stage, the insight consisting of pondering, which in conventional Buddhist theory should involve the laid-down procedure of Buddhist meditation. Again, still fewer, having heard with faith and having pondered again and again, go to the third stage of being exemplars of putting that teaching into practice, the insight of cultivating in one's life.

Therefore, it is undeniable that a person participating in an initiation learns more about the procedure than he knew before. Moreover, there are various vows that are given during the initiation and which the candidates usually have to repeat three times; and of course the serious acceptance of vows and adherence to them in the future, is a matter that differs from person to person. We must conclude that the mere fact that a person underwent an initiation in the sense of being there and cooperating, does not prove that he is "initiated" (empowered), but neither can initiation be categorically denied in his case if he went through all the motions.

(3) The final point is whether anyone, just by reading a Tantra (say the *Guhyasamājatantra*) knows what the work is talking about, and how its procedures, say of initiation, are actually conducted. This is an important issue because most of the criticism of the Tantras as being a degenerate cult stems from persons reading a sentence or so of a Tantra and assuming that they know, by such brief indications, what in fact the procedures are when, as is necessary for actual performance, the procedures are enacted in extension. For example, at the above-mentioned Kālacakra initiation I observed and photographed the candidates for initiation with their eye-bands made of red cloth; but whereas the texts do speak of this eye-band, one would have supposed it to be upon the two eyes, but in fact it was wound about the forehead. Then I similarly observed that the candidates, now presumably initiated, replaced the eye-band with the petal of the Champa flower pasted in the middle of the forehead (in the position of the third eye), and this also appears as part of the oral instructions. Among the offerings presented to H. H. the Dalai Lama as the officiant and initiator, was not a girl, as one might expect from the books, but seven pots graced with peach blossoms (see illustration), representing the female consort, here the earth goddess. But the significance of the seven pots were not understood by me through attendance at that initiation—as it was similarly not understood by the thousands of attendees—but rather through consulting the manuscript notes (in my possession) of the late F. D. Lessing who witnessed the great Kālacakra festival in 1932 when it was put on in Peking by the old Panchen Lama; and I was able to combine my observations with his.

It is easy to give an answer to the present problem, although it may not satisfy the critic, whose judgment is usually obdurate: Of course, one does not understand the basic Tantra just by reading it. The reason is that understanding a Tantra is being able to do it, since the Tantra is a course of action, not a philosophical exposition; and the basic Tantra is not so sufficiently detailed that a person reading it could just go ahead and do it according to the indications of the text. Therefore, in Tibetan tantric practice, the *Guhyasamājatantra* (among Father Tantras) and the *Śrī-Cakrasamvaratantra* (among Mother Tantras), and a few other Tantras, became the main Tantras actually engaged in with the full complement of cult—because such Tantras as these have the richest literature of commentaries and associated *sādhanas* (evocation of deity) and lineages brought into Tibet from India. That is to say, the practitioners of these Tantras do not believe they can understand the basic Tantra of the cult just by reading

PLATE 5. Seven lamas with pots (one pot hidden from view). Kālacakra ceremony, March 20-23, 1970, Dharmsala, India. Describing the equivalent ceremony held in Peking, 21-27 October 1932, Ferdinand Lessing wrote in the *Deutsch-Chinesische Nachrichten*, Tientsin, 6 November 1932 (in German): "Seven lamas . . . proceed to the podium, each with a large water pot (*kalaśa*). They move it to and fro. It symbolizes the young lady (Tib. *rig ma*) of the initiation who plays such a great role in this cult."

it; even though they have a superior background for understanding it by reading it, if it were possible to achieve understanding this way. Again this is not to deny that a certain Tantra, by reason of varying lineages, was sometimes practiced differently by its proficients, in short, that the basic Tantra was sometimes understood differently in the authoritative lineages.

Now, I began this chapter by pointing out that Mantrayāna begins with initiation. "Mantrayāna" is a synonym of Vajrayāna (the Diamond Vehicle), and a natural question is: why call it "Mantrayāna", or what is the meaning of "mantra" in the title Mantrayāna? I have in my possession a Tibetan text which explains this matter as part of the preliminary explanations for the one to get the higher initiations of the Tantra; and these explanations follow the schools of Mitrajoki and Abhayākaragupta's *Vajrāvalī*.[2]

Mantrayāna. That Tibetan work, which I shall refer to in short as the "Initiation Preliminary," explains:

> It says in the *Vajraśekhara*: "The characteristic of *mantras* is the mind of all Buddhas, accomplishes the dharma-heart, possesses the Dharmadhātu—that is said to be the characteristic of *mantras*." For that reason, it is said that mantra is the non-dual wisdom (jñāna) of bliss-void belonging to the mind of all the Buddhas; and it is said that mantra is the deities; and it is said that mantra is the calling after the characteristic of deities; and it is said that mantra is to be kept secret from unworthy vessels (*snod ma yin pa*). Besides, there are three kinds: *gsaṅ sṅags* (mantra), *rig sṅags* (vidyā), and *gzuṅ sṅags* (dhāraṇī).
>
> (1) *Gsaṅ sṅags*. The *gsaṅ* ("secret") is as stated in the *Śrī-Saṃpuṭa* (Chap. One): "It is secret because outside the scope of Viṣṇu, Maheśvara, Brahmā; śrāvakas and pratyekabuddhas." As to *sṅags* (mantra), since it incorporates the meanings of the previous explanations, it is *mantra* by protecting the mind from signs (from sense objects) and discursive thought (vikalpa), as explained in the Continuation of the *Śrī-Guhyasamājatantra* (i.e. Chap. XVIII). It is as stated in the work *Dbaṅ yon tan rim pa*: "The meaning of the expression 'mantra' is explained as the non-duality of void and compassion. I have explained *man-* as the Great Insight (mahāprajñā) not separate from the character of the void, the breath of Vajrasattva. *Tra* has the meaning of protecting. The breath of the Tathāgatas is the method of non-duality of void and compassion." The expression *sṅags* stands for *mantra*. In explanation, *man-* is

2. Mi-ṭa (Mitra) daṅ rdo rje 'phreṅ ba'i dbaṅ chen skabs kyi sṅon 'gro'i chos bśad.

mind, and *tra* is protecting, so it means protecting the performer's mind from signs and discursive thought. As to how it protects, the purpose of mantra is the recitation of the mantra through non-dual engagement of means and insight (upāya-prajñā). That method of cultivation generates the non-dual wisdom of voidness and compassion in the practitioner's stream of consciousness; and because of that method, it is called "mantra".

(2) *Rig sṅags.* The *Vajraśekhara* states: "Countering *avidyā* (nescience) by overcoming the darkness of passion and by overcoming of defilements, it is called *vidyā*." Hence, it is the preeminent return to destroying faults; and that is the purpose of *vidyā* (occult science).

(3) *Gzuṅs sṅags.* The same work states: "The character of *dhāraṇī-s* is to hold the Buddha-dharmas; its holding is called 'holding of dharmas' and 'virtue'." Hence, it is the preeminent return to holding of merits; and that is *dhāraṇī*.

Besides, Buddhaguhya explains in the *Dhyānottarapaṭalaṭīkā* (Toh. 2670, Derge Tanjur, Rgyud, Thu, 4a-3): "Here a *vidyā* is a deity with the form and shape of a female, as well as the sound, gesture (*mudrā*), etc. which manifests that (deity). The reverse of that (i.e. a male deity, etc.) is the characteristic of *mantra*." And the same author says (7b-3): "The passage means that if even Rishis cannot make a *mantra* successful when they are not in Meditation (*dhyāna*), how much less could other performers (*sādhaka*)!"

That is the mysterious world into which the initiate enters. And the *Guhyasamājatantra* (Chap. XVIII, Bhattacharyya ed., p. 156.16-17) states:

> The pledge (*samaya*) and vow (*saṃvara*) said to be liberated from worldly conduct, when protected by all the "diamonds" (*vajra*), is pronounced "practice of *mantra*."

This passage indicates that the tantric devotee enters upon a new and perhaps secretive life that starts with the vows and pledges of his initiations. The word "vow" (Tibetan *sdom pa*) is a statement taken ritually and ordinarily uttered three times; it is in a form easily understood and must hold together, adhere in the disciple's stream of consciousness. The vows are usually of a general nature, holding for the entire Tantra in which the candidate is initiated and for the entire time after his initiation. On the other hand, the "pledge" (Tibetan *dam tshig*) is less comprehensible and may require commentarial or oral expansion to get the meaning. The pledges are not general, but may apply to a particular element of the

Tantra and to a special phase of the practice. Frequently they are in a negative form, pointing to what the disciple should avoid or not engage in.

The vows that are taken by the disciples during initiation are sometimes shared between different initiations and sometimes peculiar to a certain initiation in which case they are termed "unshared". Examples are one petition and two vows which Geshe Rabten of Dharmsala asked me to translate from Tibetan on behalf of the Europeans who were attending the Kālacakra initiation held 21-23 March, 1970. Each one of these is to be repeated three times by direction of the guru (who in this case was H.H. the Dalai Lama):

A. (Petition): Thou my teacher with great joy art the sole savior from the ocean of phenomenal life attended with such dangers as the great water monster of birth, old age, and death. I bow to thee the great lord who is steadfast in the way of the great enlightenment. Grant me that same pledge! Grant me the thought of enlightenment! Grant me the three refuges of Buddha, Dharma, and Sangha! O lord, pray introduce me into the exalted city (=the *maṇḍala*) of great liberation!

B. (Common vow between the Bodhisattva and the Tantra path): I take refuge in the three jewels, confess all my sins, hold mentally the sympathetic joy with the virtues of (other) living beings, as well as with the Buddha's enlightenment.

C. (Unshared vow, peculiar to the Kālacakra Tantra): Having conferred upon me the sublime initiation of the irreversible wheel, O lord, pray explain the reality of the gods of the wheel, the wondrous action of the hierophant, the pledge of all the Buddhas, and the highest secret of the vow. So as to serve the aim of all sentient beings may I forever be a hierophant!

The fact that these three utterances are given here in sequence is no indication of their actual location in the long and elaborate Kālacakra initiation ritual. The time of petition for initiation is when the disciples made the gesture (*mudrā*) of the universe (the four continents and Mt. Meru).

The pledges are special to the different families of Tathāgatas and to different phases of the path. For example, there is the pledge to refrain from the fourteen fundamental transgressions of the Anuttarayoga Tantra. The fourteen are given in *Mkhas grub rje's* (p. 328 note) as follows:

1. To disparage one's master.
2. To transgress the directives of the Buddha.
3. To express anger toward "diamond brothers".
4. To abandon love of the sentient beings.

5. To abandon the Mind of Enlightenment.
6. To disparage the Doctrine of one's own or of another's tenets.
7. To tell the secrets to immature persons.
8. To abuse the five *skandhas* for their nature belongs to the five Buddhas.
9. To have reservations concerning the natures intrinsically pure.
10. To have love for the wicked.
11. To apply discursive thought to the wordless natures.
12. To have belittling thoughts toward the believers.
13. To not adhere to the pledges in the way they were taken.
14. To disparage women, who are the nature of insight.

After Tsoṅ-kha-pa's individual commentary on those fourteen in his *Dṅos grub kyi sñe ma* (PTT. Vol. 160, p. 70-1,2) he groups them in this way (my summary including material from his individual commentary):

A. *Concerning Dharma.*
- (1) Teacher of the Dharma. No. 1 "to disparage one's master" (*ācārya*).
- (2) Associates in accomplishing the Dharma.
  - (a) Good associates. No. 3 "To express anger toward diamond brothers" who are fellow initiates of the same master. No. 12 "To have belittling thoughts toward the believers" who are fit vessels for the path.
  - (b) Bad associates. No. 10 "To have love (*maitrī*) for the wicked", especially those who damage and destroy the Doctrine, but one should have compassion (*karuṇā*) for them.
- (3) Dharma to take to heart. No. 2 "To transgress the directives of the Buddha" which are the three vows (of the Vinaya, the Bodhisattva, and the Mantrayāna). No. 6 "To disparage the Doctrine of one's own (mantrayāna) or of another's (prajñāpāramitāyāna) tenets. No. 7 "To tell the secrets to immature (uninitiated) persons"; but Tsoṅ-kha-pa rejects a certain learned opinion that it is a transgression to show esoteric substances such as icons, the *ḍamaru* drum and so on, because the Tantras state the fault in what is revealed to the ear, not in what is revealed to the eye.

B. *Concerning Path*
- (1) Basis of Path. At the time one has generated the Mind of Enlightenment: No. 4 "To abandon love of the sentient beings" by acting waywardly toward the sentient beings. No. 5 "To abandon the Mind of Enlightenment" by abandoning the true nature of the mind.
- (2) Nature of Path.
  - (a) The Stage of Generation (*utpatti-krama*). No. 8 "To

abuse the five *skandhas* for their nature belongs to the five Buddhas", such abuse including all injury, mortification, and suppression. (My forthcoming *Yoga of the Guhyasamājatantra* will clearly show why this transgression applies to the Stage of Generation, because in this Stage there is the meditation of associating the *skandhas* with the respective Buddhas).

(b) The Stage of Completion (*saṃpanna-krama*). No. 9 "To have reservations concerning the natures (*dharma*) intrinsically pure". No. 11 "To apply discursive thought to the wordless natures".

(3) Ancillaries of the Path. No. 13 "To not adhere to the pledges in the way they were taken" because pledges are the substance of the path, whether of the Anuttarayoga or of the Yoga Tantra. No. 14 "To disparage women, who are the nature of insight" because women are a hindrance to the path. "Women" are both the mundane kind and the supramundane kind of Vajravārāhī (the Diamond Sow), etc. "Insight" is the knowledge of great bliss (*mahāsukha*). One disparages women either by way of lusting for them or (in overt conduct) by reason of lusting for them.

Initiation of the Mirror

Again, while I do not intend to compete with *Mkhas grub rje's* authoritative material on initiations—those of the flask and the higher initiations of Anuttarayoga Tantra; nor can a written account take the place of actual participation in these tantric initiation rituals, it is still useful to present one here as found in written form. The "initiation of the mirror" is one of the six in the Guhyasamāja Akṣobhya ritual that corresponds to the role of the five flask initiations as portrayed in *Mkhas grub rje's*. Besides the intrinsic interest of this initiation, it is especially picked for its brevity, because initiation rituals are frequently of considerable length and detail whereby their presentation would require too much space for present purposes. This is translated from Tsoṅ-kha-pa's work, "*Dbaṅ gi don gyi de ñid rab tu gsal ba*" (Clarifying the realities belonging to the meaning of initiation) (PTT, Vol. 160, p. 111-3,4). Previously (p. 109-4-6) he had listed the six initiations as (1) initiation of water, (2) initiation of the diadem, (3) initiation of the *vajra*, (4) initiation of the bell, (5) initiation of the mirror, and (6) initiation of the name. Now for the "initiation of the mirror."

* * *

The placement of the mirror initiation in this phase which is the fifth stage, is as done by Klu byaṅ (*Nāgabodhi). In that (i.e. his method) there are two parts, starting with the "eye opening" (rite).

I. The method of "eye opening" proceeds by reciting and applying (of ointment). (The *guru*) places in a gold or silver vessel the golden eye ointment consisting of butter and honey. While the disciple imagines on his eyes the syllable PRAṂ, (the *guru*) applies (the eye ointment) with a probe (*śalākā*), reciting OṂ VAJRANETRA APAHARA PAṬALAṂ HRĪḤ ("Oṃ. Remove the film that is on the diamond eye! Hrīḥ."). He repeats the verse (of the *Vairocanābhisaṃbodhi-tantra*): "Just as the King of Healing (*bhaiṣajya-rāja*) with his probe removed the worldly film, so may the Buddhas dispel your film of ignorance, my son!" While he is so reciting, they imagine that the knowledge eye is opened upon removal of the nescience film.

II. Having had his eye opened in that manner, (the disciple) should look upon all *dharmas* as reflected images. So (the disciple) may accomplish that, he (the *guru*) shows a mirror incanted with an ĀḤ, and recites:

> All *dharmas* are like reflected images,
> clear and pure, without turbulence;
> ungraspable, inexpressible, truly arisen
> from cause and action (*hetu* and *karma*).
>
> Just like Vajrasattva in a mirror that is
> clear, pure, without turbulence; so also
> the Buddhas, universal lords, themselves
> abide in the heart of thee, my son.
>
> Now that you have so understood the *dharmas*
> as without intrinsic nature and without
> location, may you perform incomparably the
> aim of sentient beings, so they may be born
> as sons of the Protectors!

Those verses enjoin (the disciple) to understand in general that all *dharmas* are like a reflected image, and in particular that the Vajrasattva dwelling in one's heart is like a reflected image in a mirror.

* * *

When the third of those three verses speaks of the *dharmas* "as without intrinsic nature" and "without location" it refers respectively to the first and second verses. This is because when the second verse proclaims that "the Buddhas . . . themselves abide in the heart of thee", this is possible with the Mahāyāna position of the "Nirvāṇa of no fixed abode" (*apratiṣṭhita-nirvāṇa*), so the Buddha natures (*Buddha-dharma*) can be understood to abide in the disciple's heart while abiding elsewhere. Therefore the second verse is expressed from the standpoint of supreme truth (*paramārtha-satya*), while the first verse, stressing that the *dharmas* are "like reflected images" is expressed with conventional truth (*saṃvṛti-satya*). Since these are crucial points for grasping Mahāyāna Buddhist thought, it is well to expand a little.

The mirror is incanted with an ĀH, which suggests breath come to a stop on the mirror and thereby creating insubstantial shapes. The *guru* recites the first verse, "All *dharmas* are like reflected images . . ." to show that all mundane *dharmas* are without intrinsic nature, yet truly arisen from cause and action, i.e. in Dependent Origination (*pratītya-samutpāda*). This is the scope of conventional truth, or *saṃsāra*.

Then the *guru* recites the second verse to show that when the mind is smooth and clear like a mirror, i.e. when it is plunged in *samādhi*, it can reflect the form of Vajrasattva, treasured in the disciple's heart. But also in this case the Buddhas dwell in the heart, meaning that there is no limitation to their dwelling—whether in this person's or that person's heart, or elsewhere—and so this refers to the supramundane *dharmas* that are without location. This is the scope of supreme truth, or "Nirvāṇa of no fixed abode," not limited to either *saṃsāra* or *nirvāṇa*, but both.

The third verse then alludes to the meaning of this initiation. First the disciple's knowledge eye is opened and then he is brought to a new understanding—about mundane and supramundane *dharmas*—so he can now perform the aim of sentient beings. This shows the meaning of initiation as "maturation" of the candidate, in this case, maturation through the "initiation of the mirror".

8

OFFERING MATERIALS AND THEIR MEANINGS

Among the profusion of ritual implements and other substances of the tantric cults, the offering materials are paramount because they are the most wide-spread in all the cults and of course stem from practices far more ancient than Buddhism itself. The usual Sanskrit word for "offering" is *pūjā*; the word for "food offering" is *bali*; and for "burnt offering", *homa*. Besides, the notion of an "offering" is generalized, as will be seen below by their classifications.

Classification of Offerings

In tantric commentaries one frequently notices the terminology of "outer" and "inner" offerings. Sometimes the category "secret" is added. Usually the commentators take for granted that the reader knows what is meant. However, some sources do give explanations, and two such will now be presented.

Kukuri-pā, in his *Mahāmāyāsādhanamaṇḍalavidhi* (Toh. 1630, Derge Tanjur, Rgyud, Ya, 238b-4), states:

> Then he makes offering with outer offerings, from "water for the feet" down to "music." The "inner offering" is the offering to the host (*tshogs*) (of deities) after one has enjoyed the ambrosia. The "secret offering" is the pleasure of the two organs. The "ultimate (*anuttara*) offering" is the contemplation of non-duality.

The second passage is found in the manuscript remains of the late Professor F. D. Lessing. Some lama, perhaps a lama-teacher of his during the China years, wrote out in Tibetan script a classification of offerings but without indication of a textual source. Here is my translation:

Outer offerings (*phyi'i mchod pa*). The diversity of offerings as feasible, such as *maṇḍala*, incense, flower, water for the feet, perfumed water, feet-cooling water, food, lamp, music.

Inner offerings (*naṅ gi mchod pa*). Having meditatively created offerings by way of deities, after they have clearly arisen in one's mind in the manner of largesse, one offers them individually to the magnanimous host of deities.

Secret offering (*gsaṅ ba'i mchod pa*). Having enjoyed great ecstasy (*mahāsukha*) as the deities dissolve in oneself, one should make offering in the sense of inseparability of means and insight.

Goal offering (*don gyi mchod pa*). As the true-nature of all offerings dissolves in true nature and spontaneously appears, one offers them in the sense of no hindrance to one's liberation.

Symbolic offerings (*rtags kyi mchod pa*). As one sees delightful things, such as flowers, clean water, grains, he makes offering of them to the *guru* who is the jewel and the great compassionate one.

Illustrative offerings (*mtshon pa'i mchod pa*). (Showing that one is) free from clinging and attachment to offering of personal substances, to wit, the body and personality aggregates (*skandha*) one offers them.

It is apparent that Kukuri-pā's four kinds match four of the six in the second list given by Dr. Lessing's lama teacher. The three of the same title (outer, inner, and secret) easily agree; and Kukuri-pā's category of "ultimate offering" seems to be the "goal offering" of the other list. Among the two extra ones, the symbolic offerings made to the guru are obviously a Tibetan addition because Tibetan Buddhism added a refuge in the *guru* to the traditional three refuges in Buddha, Dharma, and Sangha. (Notice that the same Tibetan word, *rtags*, is used for the substances, herbs, etc., inserted in the flasks; and that the usage, while seemingly different, may well be intimately related). The illustrative offerings are a special feature of the "perfection of giving" (*dāna-pāramitā*) of the Bodhisattva path.

Of those various categories, the outer offerings and symbolic offerings are discussed in the present essay; the inner offerings are featured by the "five ambrosias" in the Tantric Ritual essay; the secret offering is the main theme of the material on Twilight Language; the ultimate offering is alluded to in various places of this work, particularly by the description "contemplation of non-duality."

That leaves only the category of illustrative offerings to be further discussed here. In an article of the *Indo-Iranian Journal* (III, 1959, pp. 121-22) I cited Buddhaguhya's commentary on the *Mahāvairocana*, about the "inner burnt offering" (T. *naṅ gi sbyin sreg*) (and even though he uses the word for "inner" the material fits the "illustrative" category). Here I repeat my translation of the passage about this kind of offering:

> Moreover, one destroys the five *ātmaka-skandha* in Voidness (*śūnyatā*), and also destroys the forms of sense objects (*viṣaya*), such as the external "hearth" (*agnikuṇḍa*), in Voidness. In the same way one individually destroys the issuances of six-doored perception (*vijñāna*); and when they do not issue and are stopped, in the same way the "thought of enlightenment" (*bodhicitta*) which destroys and stops those is itself stopped by the non-issuing Insight (*prajñā*); and that abiding in the non-discursive (*avikalpa*) *samādhi* is the Inner Burnt Offering. Hence, one stops the "fire of wind" (*vāyv-agni*) by the non-issuing Insight, and "One makes the burnt offering to fire with the mind (*manas*)." "Stops the fire of wind" means "restrains the *prāṇa* and *āyāma*." "One makes the burnt offering to fire with the mind" means "one burns thought immobile (*añinjya* or *āniñjya*)."

Here *prāṇa* has the special meaning of winds (*vāyu*), and *āyāma* refers to the mental component; together they make up the term *prāṇāyāma*; since perceptive consciousness rides on these winds, the stopping up of these winds (cf. my section on The Nine Orifices) is tantamount to the burnt offering of mind.

Finally, while it is convenient to have this classification into six for discussion purposes, the fact that the texts generally mention only the first three (outer, inner, and secret), or even just the first two, suggests that the set of six can be reduced to the three, or in any case there is considerable overlap.

The Four Offerings

Buddhaguhya, who has been cited above, is among the greatest commentators in the field of the three lower Tantras (Kriyā, Caryā, and Yoga), and among his most remarkable works is the commentary on the Tantra *Sarvadurgatipariśodhana*, his *Artha-vyañjana-vṛtti* (later I shall cite at length his explanation of the *maṇḍala*). In this work (PTT. Vol. 76, p. 35-2) he presents a personification of four offerings into goddesses of various colors, by the following scheme:

Offering	*Color*	*Buddhist Meaning*
perfumed incense	white	morality (*śīla*)
flower	yellow	deep concentration (*samādhi*)
lamp	red	insight (*prajñā*)
perfume	green	mind of enlightenment (*bodhicitta*)

The first three Buddhist terms constitute a well-known set, called from early Buddhist times "the three instructions;" and the famous compendium of the (Hīnayāna) Buddhist path by Buddhaghosa, the *Visuddhimagga*, is divided into three parts by these very headings. The "mind of enlightenment" is the foundation of the Bodhisattva path of Mahāyāna Buddhism.

Perfumed incense is used to purify (fumigate) the room, and so it represents morality as a purifying activity of the personality, hence also the color white. In the case of the celebrated Mahāyāna Buddhist scripture that is translated under the title *The Lotus of the True Law*, the original word for "lotus" here is *puṇḍarīka*, which is really the white lotus; and this lotus for centuries symbolized in China purity, especially moral purity.

For the flower with the meaning of *samādhi*, we may refer to the writings of D. T. Suzuki:[1]

> The legendary story of the origin of Zen in India runs as follows: Sakyamuni was once engaged at the Mount of the Holy Vulture in preaching to a congregation of his disciples. He did not resort to any lengthy verbal discourse to explain his point, but simply lifted a bouquet of flowers before the assemblage, which was presented to him by one of his lay-disciples. Not a word came out of his mouth. Nobody understood the meaning of this except the old venerable Mahakasyapa, who quietly smiled at the Master, as if he fully comprehended the purport of this silent but eloquent teaching on the part of the Enlightened One. The latter perceiving this opened his golden-tongued mouth and proclaimed solemnly, "I have the most precious treasure, spiritual and transcendental, which this moment I hand over to you, O venerable Mahakasyapa!"

The same writer mentions the special lines that sum up the message of Bodhidharma, who introduced Zen into China with his arrival in A.D. 520.[2]

1. *Zen Buddhism; Selected Writings of D. T. Suzuki*, ed. by William Barrett, (New York, 1956), p. 59.
2. *Ibid.*, p. 61.

"A special transmission outside the scriptures;
No dependence upon words and letters;
Direct pointing at the soul of man;
Seeing into one's nature and the attainment of Buddhahood."

Hence, yellow—and notice the reference to "golden-tongued mouth"—apparently refers to the official color of Buddhism and its emphasis on training the mind.

For the representation of insight by the lamp, *Mkhas grub rje's* (p. 183) has the verse (addressed to the deity):

Pray enjoy these lamps,
Auspicious and triumphant over harmful elements,
Virtuous and dispelling of darkness,
Which I offer with devotion.

The color red is of course that of fire, and shows that the illumination is from a flame. Insight (*prajñā*) in this role of a fire is explained in the *Kāśyapaparipṛcchā*, as cited and expanded near the end of Tsoṅ-kha-pa's *Lam rim chen mo*:

> Kāśyapa, thus, for example, when two trees are rubbed together by the wind, and fire arises (from the friction), (that fire) having arisen, burns the two trees. In the same way, Kāśyapa, (when natures are analysed) by the most pure discrimination (*pratya-vekṣaṇā*), the faculty of noble Insight (*ārya-prajñā*) arises; and (that Fire) having arisen, it burns up that most pure discrimination itself.

In order to get the sense of perfume colored green that stands for the mind of enlightenment, one can refer to *Mkhas grub rje's* (pp. 31-32), for the third Abhisaṃbodhi when Gautama "saw directly that Samantabhadra of the former thought of enlightenment under the shape of an upright five-pronged white thunderbolt in his own heart," for which reason (*infra*), perfumes are offered to the heart. See the note to those pages of *Mkhas grub rje's*: Samantabhadra is the knowledge of the pledge. This agrees with D. T. Suzuki, *Studies in the Laṅkāvatāra Sūtra* (pp. 230-36), on the *Avataṃsaka-sūtra*'s ten vows of the Bodhisattva Samantabhadra. In Tibet the green Samantabhadra is the Bodhisattva aspect of the "primordial Buddha" (*ādibuddha*) (for which see Tucci, *Tibetan Painted Scrolls*, I, p. 236), and protector of the Tibetan Rñiṅ-ma-pa sect. Here "primordial Buddha" means knowledge of the vow of enlightenment, or seed *bodhicitta*. The applicability of perfume is suggested by *Mkhas grub rje's* (p. 181) verse to the deity: "These auspicious perfumes . . .", because the word translated "auspicious" is *bzaṅ po*, part of the Tibetan name Kun-tu-bzaṅ-po (Samantabhadra), "entirely auspicious," so the perfume conveys the auspiciousness of the "mind of enlightenment". This seems also to be the meaning of the Green Tārā, because of the legend that in one of her former lives she was a queen who vowed that in her future lives she would always be a woman and would eventually in the incarnation of a woman become a Buddha, which she did become.

Oblations to the Deities

Concerning the offerings to the deities to be residents and the offering of seats, with the oblations and others such as the "feet-cooling water", cf. *Mkhas grub rje's*, pp. 178-83. *Sṅags rim* (237b to 238a) states the places where they are offered: The feet-cooling water, because it washes the feet, is imagined as offered to the feet (of the deity). The bath, to the entire body (i.e. to the reflected image of the body). The oblations, in front or to the head. The flower, to the head. Perfumed incense and lamp, in front. Food for the gods, in front, to the hands, or to the face. And one imagines the perfume offered to the heart. Those (locations) are common to all rites.

Mkhas grub rje's (p. 177) has a fine summary statement of the oblations used for the invitation:

> The invitation must be done with an oblation (*arghya*), which therefore must be prepared beforehand. The vessel for that is of gold, silver, and so forth; and a copper vessel is auspicious for all (invitations) in common. For appeasing rites (*śāntika*) and their superior *siddhi*, barley and milk are required. For rites to increase prosperity (*pauṣṭika*) and their middling *siddhi*, sesamum and sour milk are needed. For dreadful rites (*abhicāruka*) and their inferior *siddhi*, ordinary urine together with millet, or blood, is offered up. Parched rice, fragrant odors, white flowers, *kuśa* grass, and sesamum mixed in pure water, which are auspicious for all rites in common, are prepared and incensed with the odors of incense. One blesses the oblation by reciting seven times an appropriate one among the general *dhāraṇīs* of the Vidyārāja and of the three Families, among the *dhāraṇīs* of all the rites of the individual Families, or among the *dhāraṇīs* of Invitation.

That passage, however, does not give the complete list of oblations in the several cases. *Sṅags rim* (236b to 237a) sets forth two lists of seven oblations each. For appeasing rites, there are 1. barley, 2. milk, 3. white flowers, 4. kuśa grass, 5. sesamum, 6. parched rice, and 7. ambrosia.

For prosperity rites, there are 1. sesamum, 2. sour milk, 3. yellow flowers, 4. kuśa grass, 5. perfume, 6. yellow water, 7. ambrosia. A similar list was not presented for dreadful rites.[3]

Perhaps the most important of all special rites in the category of "appeasing" is the cult of Bhaiṣajya-guru (the Healing Buddha). The elaborate layered structure for the offerings in this case is indeed impressive.

Among the "prosperity" rites, the most eagerly pursued is the cult of the "three divinities of long life"—in the iconography, the Buddha Amitāyus, with Uṣṇīṣavijayā and the White Tārā in the foreground.

In the coercing service, included among the "terrible rites," there is, for example, the offering made to the Lord of the Dead, Yama, and his retinue. A Tibetan text in my possession, the *Drug bcu pa*, mentions the food offering (*bali*) to be the "three sweets and three whites" (dkar gsum mṅar gsum), which the Sarat Chandra Das *Tibetan-English Dictionary* explains to be molasses, honey, and sugar; and milk, curds, and butter. In the ritual, these offerings in large precious vessels are imagined to become a vast ocean of ambrosia. (This is perhaps also the meaning of the item "ambrosia" in the above two lists of seven oblations each). In this service, there is a large triangular construction called "*zor*"—in my text "gtor zor gñen po" (adversary *zor* for the offering)—for combating the evil spirits. On the pinnacle of the triangle is a skull with headdress—the whole giving a scare-crow appearance. The offerings are shown in more imaginative form in the Yama-offering tankas of Tibet, of which a sample is reproduced. The kinds of materials included in these coercing representations are listed by Lessing,[4] for example, the animals to gratify the sight of the fierce deity, the eight offerings in bowls in the foreground, and so on. In Lessing's manuscript remains, I notice the description of what is called in Tibetan the *dkar rgyan*, ornament of the three white things: the round offering; with flame-shaped ornament ending in sun, moon, and "fiery tongue" (the *dkar rgyan*); this is surmounted by the "black arrow" and a piece of black cloth.

Among the miscellaneous special offerings, there is the elaborate Tibetan rite of what Schubert[5] calls the "rice maṇḍala" and Lessing[6] a "thanksgiving offering". Lessing explains that it was first offered, according to legend, by Indra himself to the newly-born Śākyamuni Buddha; and that it

3. This is the threefold grouping of rites requiring a burnt offering (*homa*) and is very ancient, going back to the Vedic period. See F. D. Lessing, *Yung-Ho-Kung*, pp. 139-61, for the *homa* rites classified as four; in the latter case, the third group of "terrible rites" is divided up into "controlling" and "destroying".

4. Lessing, *Yung-Ho-Kung* (Stockholm, 1942), p. 104.

5. Johannes Schubert, "Das Reis-Maṇḍala," *Asiatica, Festschrift Friedrich Weller* (Leipzig, 1954), pp. 584-609.

6. F. D. Lessing, "Miscellaneous Lamaist Notes, I; Notes on the Thanksgiving Offering," *Central Asiatic Journal*, II:1 (1956), 58-71.

PLATE 6. Zor for Yama and Yama Offerings.

is coupled with a rite, on which he himself did much study,[7] called the "bath of the Buddha." In the course of the rites associated with Avalokiteśvara (the 11-headed variety, with an "eye-wound" in each of his thousand hands), this deity is invoked to slake the thirst of the starving ghosts (preta) in the verse:[8]

> May the starving spirits be satiated,
> bathed, and always cooled by the streams
> of milk flowing from the hands of
> Ārya-Avalokiteśvara.

The officiant, acting the role of Avalokiteśvara, pours some water to his left or right, or into a small bowl placed to the right of the food vessel, while making the incantation, OṂ ĀḤ HRĪḤ HŪṂ OṂ MAṆI PADME HŪṂ. OṂ JALAM IDAṂ SARVA-PRETEBHYAḤ SVĀHĀ. "Oṃ Āḥ Hrīḥ Hūṃ. Oṃ Maṇi Padme Hūṃ. Oṃ, this water to all the starving spirits, Svāhā." Observe that milk is one of the "three whites".

Materials Inserted in the Flasks

The Buddhist Tantras and their commentaries frequently mention certain ritual materials in sets as the five herbs, five perfumes, five essences, five grains, and five jewels; and sometimes the five ambrosias. The different works do not always itemize the members of each set the same. Tsoṅ-kha-pa's *Sṅags rim chen mo*, folio 193a, has a number of these lists for the items to be placed within the ritual flask. Of course, these materials do not necessarily all go into the same flask, and the *Sṅags rim*, 193b to 194a gives various theories. According to *Mkhas grub rje's* "Preparation of the flask" (pp. 287, ff.) there are two main kinds of flask, the victorious flask (*vijaya-kalaśa*) for the time of initiation and the action flask (*karma-kalaśa*) for general sprinkling purposes. The gods are generated in the victorious flask.

I found a number of itemizations of the fivefold sets in the commentaries on the *Vajra-vidāraṇa-dhāraṇī*. The commentary by Smṛti relates these to the body, speech, mind, marvellous action (*karma*), and merits (*guṇa*) of the deity, as shown in the following table, along with more or less standard listings in each set.

7. F. D. Lessing, "Structure and Meaning of the Rite Called the Bath of the Buddha According to Tibetan and Chinese Sources," *Studia Serica Bernhard Karlgren Dedicata*, pp. 159-171.

8. My own translation of the Tibetan verse which I find reproduced by Lessing in his manuscript study of the "Hundred-fold Offerings". I do not possess the Tibetan work he utilized, but only the very abbreviated form of the rite in a little treatise entitled, *Gtor ma brgya rtsa śin tu bsdus pa*.

PLATE 7. Maṇḍala Offerings for the Kālacakra (Peking 1932).

TABLE 7

MATERIALS IN THE FLASKS

SUPERINTENDENCE		SYMBOLIC SUBSTANCES (RTAGS)
Body	Herbs (5):	bṛhatī, kaṇḍakāri, white aparājita, white and red daṇḍa flower
Speech	Perfumes (5):	sandal, musk, saffron, aloe, incense
Mind	Essences (5):	sesamum, salt, butter, molasses, honey
Marvellous Action	Grains (5):	mustard seed, barley, fodder barley, sesame, peas
Merits	Jewels (5):	sapphire or another precious gem, coral, gold, pearl, crystal

The commentary (Toh. 2687) by Jñānavajra says of the five essences, (1) the essence from earth is sesamum; (2) from water is salt; (3) from cream is butter; (4) from a tree, molasses, (5) from flowers, honey. The commentary (Toh. 2681) by Vimalamitra substitutes for (1) and (2) the fire-crystal and the moon-crystal (presumably as the essence of the sun and the moon).

The greatest variety seems to be in the list of herbs. The list in the table is from the *Sṅags rim chen mo*. Jñānavajra gives instead: vyakri, seṅkri, jirikarṇikā, hasa, hasadeva.

Also, the *Sṅags rim*, folio 195b-3, states that the herbs, grains, and jewels are explained in the *Hevajra-tantra* tradition as tokens (*rtags*) respectively of the mind of enlightenment, heart, and bodily color, of the maṇḍala-deities. On the same folio, Tsoṅ-kha-pa quotes Kukurāja's *Samayogamaṇḍalavidhi* (Toh. 1671), "The five herbs are the mind of enlightenment of the compassionate one; the grains are the self-existence of the gods; the five kinds of jewels are the light of their bodies; the essences are the heart-realm of knowledge; the perfumes are the victorious merits of virtue." Of course, these correspondences in commentaries on the Anuttarayoga Tantra differ from those which Smṛti gives in a Kriyā Tantra commentary, and this suggests that the commentaries on the different Tantra divisions, Kriyā, Caryā, Yoga, and Anuttarayoga, may have their own way of working out the correspondences to the fivefold sets.

9

SYMBOLISM OF THE MAṆḌALA-PALACE*

I. Varieties of maṇḍala symbolism

The Tibetan diagrams called *maṇḍala*, usually in the form of square paintings, have aroused much interest in the West. These *maṇḍalas* are especially depicted with an ornamented circular border which encloses a two-dimensional form of a four-sided palace. The present study is not meant to convey a thorough account of the rich symbolism involved, but to show what light can be cast on the subject by selected passages from authoritative works. For this purpose, the abbreviation PTT with volume number will be used for citations from the Japanese photographic edition of the Peking Tibetan canon. The abbreviation *Sṅags rim* refers to Tsoṅ-kha-pa's *Sṅags rim chen mo* in a separate Peking blockprint. The works of Ratnākaraśānti (known to the Tibetans as Śānti-pā) have been especially helpful.

Introducing the palace

The palace demands a proper setting. For example, in Ratnākaraśānti's *Mahāmāyāsādhana* (*Sādhanamālā*, No. 239), we read: "One should contemplate as below, a spot of earth made of diamond; across, a diamond enclosure; above, a tent; in the middle, a dreadful burning ground" (adho vajramayīṃ bhūmiṃ tiryag vajraprākāram upari vajrapañjaraṃ

* Under the title "Contributions on the Symbolism of the Maṇḍala-Palace," the first part of the present study was published in *Études tibétaines dédiées à la mémoire de Marcelle Lalou*. (Adrien Maisonneuve, Paris, 1971), which may be consulted for the Tibetan and Sanskrit passages here omitted.

madhye ghoraśmaśānaṃ vibhāvya). The text continues: "In the midst of that, one sees a palace with a single courtyard and made entirely of jewels—with four corners, four gates, decorated with four arches, having four altars, and radiant with nets and so on, and with nymphs" (tanmadhye kūṭāgārām ekapuṭaṃ sarvaratnamayaṃ paśyet—caturaśraṃ caturdvāraṃ catustoraṇabhūṣitam / hārādyair apsarobhiś ca bhāsvad vedīcatuṣṭayam //).[1]

Besides, the palace can be understood as the transformation of the body, in the context of which *Sṅags rim* (234a-6) cites the Explanatory Tantra of the Guhyasamāja, the *Vajramālā*: "The body becomes a palace, the hallowed basis of all the Buddhas" (/ lus ni gźal yas khaṅ du gyur / /saṅs rgyas kun gyi yaṅ dag rten/). When the body of the yogin has this transformation he is called the Diamond Being (Vajrasattva), as in this passage of the *Śrī Paramādya-tantra* (PTT, Vol. 5, p. 172-2):

> . . . Surrounded by a diamond line, beautified with eight posts, decorated with four gates, arches, altars, banners and half-banners, and so on. How is Vajrasattva understood as the principal meaning there? Because he has marks born of the sky, is supreme without beginning or end, the great self-existence (*svabhāva*) of Vajrasattva is said to be the Glorious Supreme Primordial (*śrī paramādya*).[2]

Explanation of the parts of the palace

Undoubtedly, the Tanjur (commentarial portion of the Tibetan canon) contains many commentaries on the basic palace terminology. Invariably, such elements as the four gates are identified with categories of the Buddhist path, thus indicating that Vajrasattva is the synthetic paragon of all Buddhist accomplishments. The first solution comes from the *Sarvarahasyanāma-tantrarāja* (PTT, Vol. 5, p. 58-5), verses 117-123 in my counting:

> 117. Where the *maṇḍala* is explained is the sublime mental *maṇḍala*. The palace is knowledge (*jñāna*), erection of an edifice of consciousness.
>
> 118. The four outer corners establish equality of measure. The mind of maitrī, etc. is explained as the four lines.
>
> 119. The recollection praxis of *dharma* is explained as the

1. The Tibetan translation (Tohoku No. 1643, Derge Tanjur, Rgyud ḥgrel, Ya, 270a-7, f.) enables us to establish Sanskrit-Tibetan equivalences for some important terms: S. vajramayīm bhūmim, T. rdo rjeḥi sa gźi. S. vajraprākāra, T. rdo rjeḥi ra ba. S. kūṭāgāra, T. gźal yas khaṅ. S. puṭa, T. khyams. S. aśra, T. gru. S. dvāra, T. sgo. S. toraṇa, T. rta babs. S. hāra, T. dra ba. S. vedī, T. stegs bu.

2. This passage introduces some more terms of which the equivalences are not in doubt: S. sūtra, T. thig. S. stambha, T. ka ba. S. vedī, T. kha khyer. S. ardhahāra, T. dra phyed.

diamond line. The liberation from all views is explained as the knowledge line.

120. The holy collection of morality is referred to as "ornament" (*alaṃkāra*). The thoughts of independence, and so on, have realized the five hopes.

121. The four liberations (*vimokṣa*) are the gates. The four right elimination-exertions (*samyak-prahāṇa*) are the arches and involve posts.

122. The four stations of mindfulness (*smṛtyupasthāna*) are understood as the four courtyards. The four bases of magical power (*ṛddhi-pāda*) are the four gate projections (*niryūha*).[3]

123. The seven ancillaries of enlightenment (*bodhyaṅga*) are the adornment with garlands and flower bundles. The eightfold Noble Path is explained as the eight posts.

Following are extracts from the commentary on the foregoing by Ratnākaraśānti, his *Śrī-sarvarahasya-nibandha-rahasya-pradīpa-nāma* (PTT, Vol. 76, p. 12-1,2,3):

> "Sublime" (*dam pa*) because it is comprised by the Saṃbhoga-kāya. "Knowledge" means insight (*prajñā*) . . . The equality of the four sides in terms of external measurement, is the "four lines"; in reality, it is friendliness (*maitrī*), etc., that is, friendliness, compassion, sympathetic joy, and impartiality. Because they take the sentient beings as object, the four boundless states (*apramāṇa*) of friendliness, etc. are called "boundless". When they take as object the sentient beings involved with the realm of desire, they are called the "pure abodes" (*brahma-vihāra*) . . . (In the first case, see verse 119) the line is the reality (*tattva*); (in the second case,) it is the knowledge (*jñāna*) . . . The five hopes are the faculties of faith, etc.

Turning to the Guhyasamāja-tantra cycle, there are two main commentarial traditions, that headed by Buddhajñānapāda and that headed by the tantric Nāgārjuna. Here one finds an interesting, but overly brief, explanation in Buddhajñānapāda's *Caturaṅga-sādhanopāyika-samantabhadra-nāma*, PTT Vol. 65, p. 19, which has been overly expanded in Samantabhadra's *Caturaṅga-sādhana-ṭīkā-sāramañjarī-nāma*, PTT Vol. 65, p. 116, f. The following summary will present the principal details of this position:

The officiant recites the formula *Oṃ śūnyatājñānavajrasvabhāva ātmako 'ham*. He then imagines in the triangular *dharmodaya* (T. *chos ḥbyuṅ*)

3. Here is the equivalence, S. niryūha, T. sgo khyud.

a lotus adorned with a viśvavajra. (These words point to the maṇḍala-palace). From the wheel of BHRŪṂ syllables ârise Vairocana together with his consort. (These words point to the divine residents of the maṇḍala). The four corners show that there is no inequality of Buddhahood and Complete Buddhahood in comparison with Buddhahood and Incomplete Buddhahood. The four gates mean excellence by way of mindfulness (*smṛti*) and faculty (*indriya*). The mindfulness is said to imply the four stations of mindfulness, the four right elimination-exertions, and the four bases of magical power; faculty means the set beginning with faith. Besides, the stations of mindfulness have three levels by way of the three insights, that consisting of learning, of pondering, and of cultivation. Preliminary to all the rest is faith (*śraddhā*), so that is the Eastern Gate. The four right elimination-exertions or four strivings (*vīrya*) are the Southern Gate. To the Western Gate are assigned the mindfulness generated by analysis of the doctrine (*dharma-pravicaya*) as well as the four bases of magical power. The Northern Gate has one-pointed *samādhi* which implies the five faculties (*indriya*) and five powers (*bala*). The four arches are the four Dhyānas; and these are encircled by the four-part perimeter (*nemi*) of *samādhis*, the four called Śūraṃgama, Gagaṇagañja, Vimala, and Siṃha-vijṛmbhitạ. This part is well-ornamented with objects of worship. Because the nine divisions of scripture are intended to please and attract the sentient beings, they are represented by the fluttering banners of eight different colors and tinkling bells, called the ninefold miscellany (*prakīrṇa*). "Knowledge-mirror" is expanded as net (*hāra*), half-net (*ardha-hāra*), mirror, flower-garland, and so on—representing the seven ancillaries of enlightenment. The eight decorated posts stand for the purity of the eight liberations. The diamond line stands for turning the wheel of the doctrine by the diamond method, which is the method of incantation (*mantra*). The five·offerings (flowers, powdered incense, lamp, perfume, and food for the gods) represent the Dharmadhātu. Besides, the palace is to be studded with as many jewels as possible.[4]

In the case of Nagarjuna, there is his *Piṇḍīkṛta-sādhana*, which fortunately has been edited by Louis de La Vallée Poussin in his edition of the *Pañca-krama* (Gand, 1896). Verse 23 has the setting of the palace: "When one draws together the four *maṇḍalas*, there is the *maṇḍala* in a spot of diamond earth (*vajrabhūbhāga*). There one should contemplate a palace arisen from the syllable BHRŪṂ:—"

> 24-26. With four corners, four gates, decorated with four arches, associated with four lines, adorned with eight posts, beautified with nets and half-nets, and with *maṇi-vajras* and half-moons. Studded

4. Here we have S. nemi, T. mu khyud.

(*khacita*) with *vajraratnas* [in all the joints of corners and] in the joints of the gates and gate projections. [Has a line struck for the outer circle]. With flasks, posts, and the Mahāvajra; also birds on the series of heads. Adorned with bell-banners; also with *cāmaras*, and so on".[5]

On this, Ratnākaraśānti has well commented in his *Piṇḍīkṛta-sādhanopāyikā-vṛtti-ratnāvalī-nāma* (PTT, Vol. 62, p. 74). He has employed the classifying terminology of "hinted meaning" (*neyārtha*) and "evident meaning" (*nītārtha*), which turns out to be here the distinction between the conceptualized and then externally-represented *maṇḍala* on the one hand, and the body *maṇḍala* on the other.

A. *Hinted Meaning*. The spread of the rampart perimeter about the four corners amounts to four *aṅguli*, because it is the purity of "sameness knowledge" (*samatā-jñāna*). "Four gates" means accompanied with gates in each direction, because they are the purity of the four gates to liberation and the four stations of mindfulness. "Four arches" means the special structures over the four gates as a lovely decoration; because they are the purity of the four Dhyānas. Likewise, "associated with four lines" means with the two Brahmā lines or with the (four) basic lines,[6] because they are the purity of the four pure abodes. "Adorned with eight posts" means with their positions in the directions of the eastern square (*koṣṭhaka*) of the *cakravartin*, etc. since they possess various jewels and are marked with vajras, mirrors, etc., because they are the purity of the (eight) liberations of meditation. Likewise, "beautified" means that the net, which has a lord, and the half-net, which is without a lord, are beautified with *maṇi-vajras* and half-moons, because they are the purity of the seven ancillaries of enlightenment. "All the joints of the corners" means joints of the four directions; likewise, the "gate projections" are the outer parts and the "joints" are the inner parts. They are "studded with vajraratnas," i.e. with *vajras* marked with *ratnas* that slightly stand out and emanate light, because they are the intrinsic nature of the five knowledges. Likewise, flasks are placed on both sides of each gate, that is, eight golden flasks; among them,

5. La Vallée Poussin's reading *krayaśīrṣas tu yakṣinī* has been corrected to *kramaśīrṣaṃ tu paksinī*. In the *Sṅags rim*, 188a-4,5,6, this *kramaśīrṣa* is identified with the "elephant trunks" (S. *sūcikā*, T. *śar bu rnams*).

6. The two Brahmā lines (North-South and East-West) cross each other and so can be counted as four segments. The basic lines are the directional lines constituting the sides of the square. See the diagram in Ferdinand D. Lessing, "The Eighteen Worthies Crossing the Sea," in the *Sino-Swedish Expedition* Publication 38 (Stockholm 1954), p. 126.

the Jaya and Maṅgala are in the East; the Pratihārya and Siddhi in the South; Vijaya and Śānti in the West; Siddha and Nirmita in the North—because they are the nature of the eight *siddhis* of *źi ba*,[7] etc. The posts are eight, since there are two each at each gate; their adornment is as before. "Mahāvajra" stands for the eleven *vajras*, because they are the purity of the Stages.[8] "Birds on the series of heads" means that on the summits of the arches, there are two peacocks (*māyūra*) in the East, two swans (*haṃsa*) in the South, two *cakravākas* in the West, two *jīvaṃjīvakas* in the North, because they are the purification of passion (*rāga*). Likewise, "bell-banners" are banners along with bells which give out peals from the tops of the banners, and are possessed of nets of banners and bells. Again, "with *cāmaras* and so on" means *cāmaras* (i.e. whisks made of yak tail), flower garlands. "Adorned" means adorned with those (bell-banners, etc.), which are the purity of the nine divisions of the sacred scripture. (The foregoing:) Hinted Meaning (*neyārtha*).

B. *Evident Meaning*. Among those, "Meru" is the body. "Eight peaks" are the eight orifices.[9] "Viśva-vajra" and "viśva-padma" are the two organs by division into male and female. The "palace" is the body itself. "Four corners" are the front, back, right, and left sides. "Four gates" are the mouth, the secret place (*here:* the heart), navel, and Brahmarandhra. The four arches are the two eyes and the two ears. The four lines are Rus sbal ma (*Kūrmī), Zla ba ma (*Candrikā), Lha sbyin ma (Devadattā), and Nor rgya ma.[10] The eight posts are the two shoulders, both the arms and the legs and the two thighs. The "net" is the basic veins; the "half-net" is the subsidiary fibres, totalling 72,000. The half-moon is the

7. The term *źi ba* may be a slip. It is equivalent to the rite of appeasing (*śāntika*); this is the first of the three or four rites aimed at *siddhis* (occult powers or success) of various kinds. For the list of eight siddhis, cf. Mkhas grub rje's *Fundamentals of the Buddhist Tantras*, tr. by F. D. Lessing and A. Wayman (The Hague, 1968), pp. 220-1.

8. The Stages are of course the ten Bodhisattva Stages and the Buddha Stage, making a total of eleven.

9. The eight orifices are presumably the usual nine minus the Brahmarandhra; cf. Tsoṅ-kha-pa's commentary on the Six Laws of Nāro-pā, the "*Yid ches gsum ldan*". (PTT Vol. 161, p. 10), where it is taught that in order to have a transit through the Brahmarandhra (here called the "Golden Gate"), it is necessary to inhibit the transits (Ratnākaraśānti would call them the "oozing") of *vijñāna* through the other eight orifices.

10. Earlier in this same work by Ratnākaraśānti, PTT Vol. 62, p. 69-3, he had also mentioned this tortoise lady (*kūrmī*) as a vein (*nāḍī*) and in like fashion the moon lady (*candrikā*). Presumably the four ladies are equivalent to the four goddesses of the heart, Traivṛttā, Kāminī, Gehā, and Caṇḍikā, who are placed in the four directions according to the discussion in *Sṅags rim*, 435a-6, where a fifth goddess Māradārikā is added in the middle. In this theory of the heart having the initial structure which spreads to the other *cakras* of the body, the four goddesses of the heart, representing the four sensory objects, seem to well correspond to the first four lines of the *maṇḍala*.

> *bodhicitta*, which is the part of means (*upāya*) incorporating the part of insight (*prajñā*). The *vajra* is the *vajra* of the secret place. *Ratna* is its peak. "Corner part" is the left nostril; "joint of the gate projection" is the right nostril. Their "*vajra*" is perception (*vijñāna*). Jewel is the substance oozing therefrom, and which possesses it. Flask is the belly. Post is the back. Mahāvajra is the six elements. Birds are the ten winds, because they move about. Bell is the tongue, because it makes sounds. Banner is the central channel. Cāmara is the hair of head. The flower garlands included in "and so on" are the intestines. "Deer" are the eight perceptions. (The foregoing:) Evident Meaning (*nītārtha*).

Then there is a passage in Vajravarman's commentary, the "Sundarālaṃkara", on the tantra *Sarvadurgati-pariśodhana*, PTT Vol. 76, p. 133, which is worthwhile presenting to show a somewhat unorthodox way of interpreting the same parts of the palace, and in particular to introduce the obscure Tibetan term pha-khu (=pha-gu): "The four boundless states of friendliness, etc., are the four gates. The four samādhis are the four arches. The eight liberations are the eight posts. The four noble Truths are the four sides (*logs*). The four Dhyānas are the jewelled *pha-khu*.[11] Finally, the nine *samāpattis* are the nets and half-nets".

Those commentaries on the parts of the palace, attributing to them the categories of Buddhist ascension, agree rather consistently on the basic parts to be so treated symbolically. In addition, the books go into further technicalities of construction, which are elaborately developed in the *Sṅags rim*, chapter on Preparatory Rite (*sta gon gi cho ga*), subsection "Explaining the meaning of the lines which are 'struck'" (*btab paḥi thig rnams kyi don bśad paḥo*). Besides, this subsection has valuable information for our present discussion. In particular, *maṇḍala* paintings show two circular strips, the outer ring and the inner enclosure of the lotus. Already we have noticed in the setting of the palace that there is a diamond enclosure. *Sṅags rim* (178b-3) cites Kluḥi Blo (*Nāgabuddhi), "The arch (*toraṇa*) has a pinnacle of diamond; beyond that is the outer wall which has the good light of a diamond garland". With reference to the inner enclosure, *Sṅags rim* (175a-2) cites the same author, "Outside the inner circle, one should draw the four lines completely equal". The following passage of *Sṅags rim* (178a-2, ff.) insists that the expression "diamond enclosure" (*vajraprākāra*) means both the outer wall of the world and the Dharmodaya (fecund source of all the natures of the world). They are, so to say, the outer and inner boundaries of the world. Accordingly, the

11. The *Sṅags rim* (187a-1) defines the *pha-gu* as follows: "The "*pha- gu*" goes upon the structure up to the summit of the gate side, as the structure runs" (/ pha gu ni rtsig paḥi steṅ nas sgo logs kyi rtse moḥi bar du rtsig pa ji ltar soṅ ba bzin yod do /).

four equal lines according to the *Sṅags rim* are really boundless, just as was set forth above from the *Sarvarahasya-nāma-tantrarāja*:

> The equal measure of the "fire mountain" (S. agniparvata, T. me ri) in all directions has the meaning of equal measure of emitting rays, but it is not the case that the four small parts (segments) do not continue further. Hence, (he) says that one does not prepare the painting of powdered colors as its ceiling: it continues on without measure. In all the directional angles, the fire heap keeps on; within that, the diamond enclosure has the nature of the outer wall of the world (*mahācakravāla*) which is thick and compact. Furthermore, this *ācārya* [presumably Kluḥi Blo] maintains that the meaning of its contemplation goes from the wind-maṇḍala below to the Akaniṣṭha above, so it is necessary to understand likewise the "strips" (*snam bu*) of the diamond spot. The sort of *vajra* may be either five-pronged, three-pronged, or a *viśva-vajra* (crossed thunderbolt); and if painted, is to be made accordingly. Our school holds that the circular line which encloses the *vajra* and the *padma* symbolizes the Dharmodaya; and if there is contemplation of the Dharmodaya, it is (done) that way.

According to that position of Tsoṅ-kha-pa, although the texts frequently describe the *dharmodaya* as a triangle, one should contemplate it as an inner circle in the case of conceiving the *maṇḍala*.

The Triangular Dharmodaya

The Dharmodaya as a triangle is apparently shown in a *maṇḍala* in my possession only in photographic form (original presumably in Stockholm, the Hedin collection). Unfortunately, it is not sufficiently clear for further reproduction.

Here, what I take to be the Dharmodaya triangle is within the inner circle which is surrounded by four petals, suggesting the *maṇḍala* of the heart, described later in my essay on the Inner Zodiac. Previously it was noted that in the *Caturaṅga-sādhana* the officiant imagines a lotus adorned with a *viśvavajra* (a crossed thunderbolt) in the triangular Dharmodaya (=*dharmadhātu* as source of natures). Presumably that is also what Śrīdhara refers to in his *Kṛṣṇayamāri-sādhana-nāma* (PTT. Vol. 85, p. 298-5), verse 18:

> (From which) rightly arises the auspicious member—
> a white triangular Dharmodaya,
> located above like the sky,
> with a viśva-padma-vajra in the middle.

Maṇḍala of the Triangular Dharmodaya

In the present case the "diamond thread" which surrounds the inner circle is strung with skulls; and within the triangle, instead of the *viśvavajra*—which is a stiff structure—there is what seems to be a free representation of the *svastika* in its meaning (as Buddhaguhya will be cited below) of the union of means and insight, or of the male and female, symbolized by the *vajra* and the *padma*. This becomes clear when the small, diffuse, triangular area of the photograph is viewed under a microscope. The figure within the triangle seems to consist of two scarves crossing each at their mid-points where they are tied together, which the artist has embellished in wave fashion. On the facing page is a drawing of the central area only of this particular *maṇḍala*.

* * *

The figure within the drawing is such that it can be turned in any direction. In any case, the triangle, while drawn pointing downwards, need not be so construed because it is part of a two-dimensional representation of the three-dimensional palace. In the *Guhyasamājatantra* tradition, as in Tsoṅ-kha-pa's annotation commentary on the *Pradīpoddyotana* (PTT. Vol. 158, p. 13-3), there is a triangle called the "E-triangle" (after the shape of the letter "*e*" in an Indian alphabet) meaning the lotus of the *vidyā*, and also meaning the three liberations (the voidness, wishless, and signless).

II. Symbolism of maṇḍala ritual

Mkhas grub rje's *Fundamentals of the Buddhist Tantras*[12] contains a fund of basic data, but scattered here and there for our present purposes. Let us recall the line cited from the *Sarvarahasya-nāma-tantrarāja*, "Where the *maṇḍala* is explained is the sublime mental *maṇḍala*," on which Ratnākaraśānti comments: "'sublime' because it is comprised by the Saṃbhoga-kāya". This indicates that the *maṇḍala* can be understood to represent the palace of the Akaniṣṭha heaven, where according to Mahāyāna tradition (say, the *Laṅkāvatāra-sūtra*), Gautama was initiated as a Complete Buddha with the body called Saṃbhoga-kāya. This Akaniṣṭha heaven is considered to be at the top of the world at the limit of the "pure abodes" of the "Realm of Form" (*rūpa-dhātu*). Mkhas grub rje's work contains the tradition that this Saṃbhoga-kāya teaches only Bodhisattvas of the Tenth Stage. The implication is that the *maṇḍala* constitutes the re-establishment of the heavenly arrangement. It amounts to saying that mythologically the advanced Bodhisattvas ascend to the Akaniṣṭha heaven to receive the instruction of the Saṃbhoga-kāya, and that in practice they construct a

12. *Op. cit.*, note 7, above.

maṇḍala. Mkhas grub rje's work clarifies that the *maṇḍala* must be more than constructed: it must be realized. The *maṇḍala* is constructed in the order of steps generally employed in the Tibetan hieratic paintings. First, there is a sketch according to the rules. In the Tantra, this is called the *karma*-line, which is white. Then, areas are given appropriate colors. In the Tantra, this is called the *jñāna*-line, with lines of five colors representing the five Buddhas; and Mkhas grub rje explains that five sets of threads of five colors, making a total of twenty five, are twisted together, to constitute the *jñāna*-line. Lastly, the details are put in. In the Tantra, this is the last stage of *maṇḍala*-construction, the erection of an edifice.

Besides, that author Vajravarman (*op. cit.*, p. 133, fol. 5) says, "There are two fruitional *maṇḍalas*, with the method of the Dharmakāya and with the method of the Saṃbhogakāya". He goes on to illustrate the "method of the Dharmakāya" as the five knowledges which are the nature of the five Buddhas, starting with the Dharmadhātujñāna which is the basis of all supramundane knowledge and which has the nature of Vairocana. If one follows the terminology in the tradition of the *Mahāvairocana-tantra* which leads up to the two *maṇḍalas* of the Japanese Shingon school, the method of the Dharmakāya might be a *maṇḍala* representing the Diamond Realm (*vajradhātu*) and the method of the Saṃbhogakāya might be a *maṇḍala* representing the Nature Realm (*dharmadhātu*). The *maṇḍala* of the Diamond Realm is inexpressible, and that of the Nature Realm is expressible.[13]

The reflected-image maṇḍala

The following materials are based on six verses in a Tantra of the Yoga class referred to briefly as the *Sarvadurgati-pariśodhana* (Purification of all evil destiny).[14] While there are several extensive commentaries on this Tantra preserved in Tibetan translation, I shall translate here only the one by Buddhaguhya in his work of reconstructed title, *Durgati-pariśodhanārtha-vyañjana-vṛtti*. First the six verses (*śloka*) of the Tantra (PTT. Vol. 5, p. 84-4,5) translated from the Tibetan:

1. One should start by blessing the place with a rite of whatever be the sort, i.e. vihāra, upavana, stūpa, devakula, ārāma, etc.

2.-3. One should draw the outer maṇḍala in that place which has been blessed, to wit, possessed of four corners, four gates, four arches; adorned with four staircases and garland, lions, bulls; adorned with silk, tassels, pendant necklaces, garland, bells, yak tails.

13. *Ibid.*, pp. 204-5.

14. The full title of the Tantra as entered in the catalogs of the Tibetan canon is: Sarvadurgati-pariśodhana-tejorājasya tathāgatasya arhate samyaksambuddhasya kalpa nāma.

4. One should adorn it with the seals (mudrā) of diamond, jewel, lotus, svastika. It should possess eight lines, and be adorned with outer gate projections.
5A. One should dress it in nine parts and render the gates and gate projections into three parts.
5B. The casting of thread with diamond line is the casting of thread of the center maṇḍala.
6. Like the wheel of the law, it has sixteen spokes along with a nave. It is possessed of a triple series, and the spokes are to be doubled.

Next I translate Buddhaguhya's commentary on these verses in the section which he calls "the concise meaning of the *maṇḍala*" (PTT, Vol. 76, p. 22-1 to 23-1). Because of certain illegible spots in the photographic edition I also consulted the Narthang Tanjur edition. I shall use superscript letters, starting with "a" to indicate the paragraphs of my annotation which follows the translation.

* * *

Now I shall teach about the reflected image of the conceptual basic *maṇḍala*. Why so? Because this is said to be the external *maṇḍala*. As to its being external, the method of constructing the reflected image *maṇḍala* of powdered colors appears in the sensory domain of the five sense organs. The "*maṇḍa*" is the inner palace; and the "*la*" is the wheel possessed of spokes, and possessed of strips, gates, and corners.[a] The meaning expressed below has the pure tones from the mouth (of my guru).

1. *The vihāra and the upavana*. It is said that the *vihāra* (temple) kind is made within the confines of a monastery. The *upavana* (grove) kind occurs variously on a spot of ground that is smooth.

The stūpa, devakula, ārāma. The *stūpa* kind occurs where there are relics of the body. The *devakula* (chapel) is a residence for mundane gods. The *ārāma* (garden) is drawn in a place where many persons congregate.

With a rite of whatever be the sort. "Of whatever be the sort" indicates of whatever sort of place, of whatever sort of implements, and of whatever sort of incantation expert, incantation assistant, and patron. The "rite" involves the place, rite of investigating, (permission) of a visible king, or of an invisible deity, and so forth. In this case there is the sequence: (1) the spot where it will be done; and the search for a good spot; (2) begging permission to do the stipulated activities according to the rules; (3) using incantation (*mantra*), gesture (*mudrā*), and deep concentration (*samādhi*) to bless it into the mind of enlightenment which is the nature of the five knowledges; (4) examining the self-existence and characteristic of earth; (5) contemplating according to the rite; (6) beseeching to know according to the rite, doing the ritual methodically, and not wavering in *samādhi*.[b] Why so?

One should bless the place. There are four kinds of blessing: (1) blessing the place into the true nature of knowledge; (2) blessing the place of the *dharma-maṇḍala* arisen from the *samādhi*-mind; (3) blessing the place of conceptual names into the *dharmadhātu*; (4) blessing the *maṇḍala* of powdered colors as a place of material marks, into a dwelling place for the Buddha.

2.-3. *In that place which has been blessed*. In the manner that a thousand ounces of silver are changed into gold by using gold paint, it is said that one blesses the defilement into purity by using the paint of *samādhi*-knowledge.

One should draw the outer maṇḍala. Cognition manifests. One must visualize the *samādhi-maṇḍala*. The outer *maṇḍala* is a reflected image of that, and since that is the required basis, one speaks of an "outer *maṇḍala*"; and in order to symbolize that, there is the expression "outer *maṇḍala*".

Possessed of four corners and four gates. It exhibits the four corners as symbols of having the four knowledges; and exhibits the four gates as symbols of having the four kinds of marvellous action (*phrin las*).[c]

Possessed of four arches; adorned with four staircases and garland. The "arches," the terrace steps of the *maṇḍala*-stand, are made of terrace steps in the gateways. The "staircases" are made of small stairs from the arches. The "garland" consists of the staircases and arches, and is beautified by eight intervals (or segments) which appear along with the garland. Besides, it is ornamented by possession of the "arches" consisting of the four boundless states, with the "staircases" consisting of the four means of conversion, and with the "garland" consisting of infinite compassion; and it also exhibits the eight liberations.[d]

Adorned with lions and bulls. There are "lions" since the one with great compassion of means is not frightened of *saṃsāra*. There are "bulls" in the sense of infinite marks of right powers.

Adorned with silk, tassels, pendant necklaces, garland, bells, and yak tails. They are on the left and right of the gates. "Silk," or *pañcarāga* (five-colored), has the meaning of five kinds of knowledge. "Tassels," or *trirāga* (three-colored), are the pure nature of body, speech, and mind. "Pendant necklace" is a hanging necklace of pearls, standing for the Bodhisattva's joy. "Garland" is a pearl garland surrounding the circular necklace; this means the set of requirements for samādhi. "Bells" are combined with the necklaces; because they are the purity of speech, they cause the teaching of Dharma to the living beings; and made of pearl, they circle the border of the *maṇḍala*. "Yak tails," Himalayan, extend out; free from fault, they stand for no shifting in the mind of enlightenment.[e]

4. *One should adorn it with the seals* (*mudrā*) *of diamond, jewel, lotus,*

and svastika. The "diamond" means a round fence of diamond, i.e. an unconstructed fence like diamond consisting of wisdom-knowledge (*vidyā-jñāna*). With a garland of "jewels" there is the inner circle of the palace; it arises through all sorts of other merits. "Lotus" is the special thing with the various seats for goddesses; it means the aim of living beings with the great compassion of skill in the means while being unattached. The "*svastika*" is an angular cross of *vajras*, like the moon. It is a symbol of the union of means (*upāya*) and insight (*prajñā*). "Adorn it" means ornamentation to beautify the reflected image, and ornamentation to clarify the apperception of inner symbols.

It should possess eight lines and be adorned with outer gate projections. The "lines," i.e. threads, mean contemplation in the manner of the mind of enlightenment. Having "eight" means it is decorated with four directional threads and four inner threads, making eight. Possessing the eight kinds means that the person with the eight good-luck symbols on his body, has the symbols of completion. "Outer gate projections" are the gate-bends (*sgo khug pa*), standing for the means of entering by *samādhi* comprehension. "Adorned" with those kinds, means three levels (*sum rim*) in the gates, exhibited by twelve gates. This means that in order to turn the sentient beings of the three realms away from the twelve members of dependent origination, there is the Buddha in the method of the twelve acts. Adorning the strips (*snam bu*) with a quadruple series (*bżi rim*) is a symbol of purifying the four kinds of birthplace by means of the four knowledges. That is the meaning of adorning it.[f]

5A. *One should dress it in nine parts and render the gates and gate projections in three parts.* This means that because one purifies with compassion the three realms and the nine stages, one explains the single face of the *maṇḍala* as having nine (parts). "One should render the gates and gate projections" means that one should render the gates and gate projections by the union of calming (the mind) and discerning (the truth); and because that perfects body, speech, and mind, one explains that there are three parts.[g]

That finishes the teaching of Indra differentiation.[h] Now to teach the meaning of the inner. Why so?

5B. *The casting of thread with diamond line is the casting of thread of the center maṇḍala.* "Diamond" is taken as the family (*rigs*), because it is blessed into mind of enlightenment. The "line" is taken as the thread which is the means of showing this and that. The "center" is taken as a round palace which is the symbol standing for the *dharmadhātu*. The "thread" is the diamond thread of wisdom (*vidyā*) and is to be taken as the great bliss (*mahāsukha*) of the mind of enlightenment. From that "thread" with the magical performance (*prātihārya*) of blessing, emanate the rays of knowledge (*jñāna*) which exhort the illustrious hearts of the noble ones and bless by performing the aim of sentient beings. Casting the "son thread", i.e. the thread that is blessed and is emanating the light of knowledge, means casting the sky thread (*gnam thig*) and the earth thread (*sa thig*). By so casting the pure brahmā thread, it is blessed into purity or brahmā.[i]

6. *Like the wheel of the law*. Here "wheel" means that when it has a nave and spokes there is capability as a wheel. Like that example, when one has a Teacher, retinue, place, etc., because he teaches the law, there is the wheel (set into motion). The one with a wheel is like an offering. Because right knowledge cuts off the defilement kind of suffering, it is said to be the wheel of the law; it is the understanding that perceives the meaning after cutting down the nets of intellect. "Net" is a term that takes as one the sixteen constructed with having spokes, and is a symbol showing that. The *dharmadhātu* is primordially pure (*ye nas rnam par dag pa*); the nave is a symbol showing that. The spokes are a symbol of the perfection of compassion with skill in the means; and *dharma* is the realm exhibited at the nave. The wheel is exhibited as marvellous action (*phrin las*), and the spokes are exhibited as the nature of compassion. The "net" as a symbol of showing, is taken as the reflected image which shows the world. In order to take it that way, the garland of jewels which shows knowledge surrounds the circle; and through the arising of desire there is the Saṃbhogakāya. One posits the example of the horse-*maṇḍala*.[j] What is the reason for that?

It has sixteen spokes along with a nave. The "nave", which is the circular palace of the center, is the Dharmakāya. "Along with" means that the garland of jewels surrounds the circle and through the arising of desire there is the Saṃbhogakāya. The "spokes", i.e. the wheel, exhibit the nature of the sixteen *sattvas* who are the perfection of compassion, and are the Nirmāṇakāya.[k] Why so?

It is possessed of a triple series. The "series" is exhibited as three entrances within from without, and three exits from within. The exits from within are exhibited as the nave, the garland of jewels, and the spokes. Among them, the nave represents the symbol of All-kenning (*kun rig*) Vairocana, the Dharmakāya, "Series" is a term for arising of the special (*āvenika*). The garland of jewels represents the Buddhas of the four families as well as the Mother of the family, i.e. the Saṃbhogakāya in great bliss. The spokes of the triple series are the Nirmāṇakāya, i.e. they represent the Nirmāṇakāya as the nature of the supramundane retinue of sixteen *sattvas*, etc. After the diamond fence, the created circle (*nirmita-cakra*) should be understood as mundane and supramundane. The triple series of entrances from without represent the three levels (*sum rim*) in the gate. There is the term "entrance from without" because one arouses the mind in the Great Vehicle in the series of performing the aim of living beings by way of the body and speech of the Tathāgata; and by installing the living beings that way among the Bodhisattvas.[1] Now to teach the aim of the wheel:

The spokes are to be doubled. This means that the spokes are doubled at the nave of the wheel, but the pairing does not include the garland of jewels of the center. Moreover, it is because the garland of jewels and the aforementioned doubling take rise from the nave, that the spokes are to be doubled. It is said that there is doubling for the sake of performing the aim of living beings by way of the means and insight.

The concise meaning of the *maṇḍala* is finished.

* * *

Subsequently (p. 27-1) Buddhaguhya has an explanation of *maṇḍala* ornaments: "(The text) mentions "canopy" because this is the *guru* of the three realms; "banner" because victorious over the Māras; "adornment" (*vibhūṣaṇa*)—marvellous action of compassion; "umbrella"—mind of enlightenment; "yak-tail (whisk)"—marvellous action; "tassels"—compassion; "food"—benefit and morality of body; sixteen golden flasks which show the seal (*mudrā*) of the *dharmadhātu*; five flasks that are filled with the water of the five families—the knowledges of the five families; "lamp"—insight; "strewn food offering" (*bali*)—compassion; "food and drink"—food for the gods, diverse foods having the hundred flavors, offering water having the eight aspects, and so on."

* * *

Here are my comments on the above:

a. Buddhaguhya here defines the word *maṇḍala* in terms of the contained, *maṇḍa*, and the container or holder, *la*. For more information, see *Mkhas grub rje's*, especially pp. 270-71. Guiseppe Tucci, *The Theory and Practice of the Mandala* is recommended for a general treatment and mainly for the theory of "residents" of the *maṇḍala* (in contrast to the *maṇḍala* of "residence"). Two French scholars have studied the *maṇḍala* as portrayed in the *Mañjuśrīmūlakalpa*; first Marcelle Lalou, *Iconographie des étoffes peintes* (1930), and more recently, Ariane Macdonald, *Le Maṇḍala du Mañjuśrīmūlakalpa* (1962). For individual *maṇḍalas*, the most remarkable contribution is now *A New Tibeto-Mongol Pantheon*, Parts 12-15, published by Prof. Dr. Raghu Vira† and Prof. Dr. Lokesh Chandra (International Academy of Indian Culture, 1967), the individual parts containing an enormous number of *maṇḍala* representations with deity lists.

b. The different parts of the rite are written up more extensively in *Mkhas grub rje's*, pp. 279, ff.

c. When the knowledges are given as four, there is the correspondence system of the Yoga Tantra (cf. *Mkhas grub rje's*, pp. 232-33); and so the knowledges are the Mirror-like, Equality, Discriminative, and Procedure of Duty, with respective Bodhisattva activity of Mind of Enlightenment, Perfection of Giving, Perfection of Insight, and Perfection of Striving.

d. The four boundless states were already set forth in the section on parts of the palace. The four means of conversion are (1) Giving, equal to the Perfection of Giving, (2) Fine, pleasant speech, (3) Acts in accordance, (4) Oneself serving as an example. The "eight liberations" were stated earlier to represent the eight posts; for the ancient Buddhist theory of the eight, see, for example, Paravahera Vajirañāṇa Mahāthera, *Buddhist Meditation in Theory and Practice*, pp. 484-86; and the annotated version in Étienne Lamotte, *Le traité de la grande vertue de sagesse*, Tome III (1970), pp. 1291-99.

e. When five knowledges are mentioned, then the Dharmadhātu-knowledge is added to the other four. The set of requirements (T. *tshogs*) is variously stated in the books, but they more or less amount to the set stated by Asaṅga (cf. A. Wayman, *Analysis of the Śrāvakabhūmi*, p. 60): personal success, success of others, virtuous craving for the doctrine, going forth (to the religious life), restraint of morality, restraint of senses, knowing the amount in food, practice of staying awake in the former and latter parts of night, conduct with awareness, seclusion, elimination of hindrances, and right dwelling in *samādhi*.

f. For the eight good-luck symbols, see the next section of this chapter. The twelve members of dependent origination are in English translation: (1) nescience, (2) motivations, (3) perception, (4) name-and-form, (5) six sense bases, (6) sense contact, (7) feelings, (8) craving, (9) indulgence, (10) gestation, (11) birth, (12) old age and death. The twelve acts of the Buddha are (*Mkhas grub rje's*, p. 25): (1) the descent from Tuṣita, (2) entrance into the womb, (3) rebirth, (4) skill in worldly arts, (5) enjoyment of the harem women, (6) departure from home, (7) arduous discipline, (8) passage to the terrace of enlightenment, (9) defeat of the Māra host, (10) complete enlightenment, (11) (turning) the wheel of the law, (12) departure into Nirvāṇa. The strips (*paṭa*) are shown surrounding the inner palace square in the drawing of the Dharmodaya. For the four kinds of birthplace, see my essay, "Buddhist Genesis and the Tantric Tradition" (note 1); but how the four knowledges can purify them certainly needs further explanation.

g. The term "nine stages" is somewhat obscure (the same expression occurs in the Narthang edition of this text). However, as it is coupled with the "three realms" the meaning should be the nine *samāpatti*-s (equilibrium attainments), for which see *Buddhist Meditation in Theory and Practice*, pp. 454-68. The nine *samāpatti*-s are the four *dhyāna* stages of the realm of form (*rūpa-dhātu*), the four stages of the formless (*arūpya*-s), and the stage called "cessation of ideas and feelings" (in Pāli: *saññā-vedita-nirodha*). Union of calming and discerning is in Sanskrit, *śamatha-vipaśyanā-yuganaddha*.

h. The use of the word "Indra" here requires explanation. Vajravarman's commentary on the same *Sarvadurgatipariśodhana* (PTT. Vol. 76, p. 121-3), mentions that there are two kinds of Indra, the one of the hundred offerings (*śatakratu*) and the one of a thousand eyes. Here the one of the hundred offerings is in point, because Buddhaguhya in his commentary (p. 33-3) says that Indra is the "*yon bdag*" (Sanskrit, *yajamāna*), i.e. patron of the sacrifice. However, the term Māhendra (belonging to Great Indra) is used in the Buddhist Tantras to mean "earth".[15] So far there has been a differentiation of the sanctified spot of earth, so this must be the main use here of the word "Indra".

i. Blessing (*adhiṣṭhāna*) is one of the four kinds of *prātihārya* according to *Mkhas grub rje's*, p. 26 (note), the other three being Initiation, Marvellous Action, and Deep Concentration. For the knowledge thread and *brahmā*-lines, see *Mkhas grub rje's*, pp. 284-87. While Mkhas-grub-rje does not use the terminology "sky thread" and "earth thread", his explanation is immediately applicable. The meaning of course is that the knowledge thread is really in the sky; and so the thread on earth must be imaginatively lifted to the sky and imbued with the knowledge which is there, then brought down to earth as the "knowledge line", which accordingly is a "son thread," blessed with knowledge.

j. Concerning the wheel of the law, in non-tantric Buddhism one may take Vasubandhu's *Ārya-Akṣayamatinirdeśa-ṭīkā* (Derge Tanjur, Toh. 3994, 6a-4, ff.): "'In the manner of a wheel' means there is a wheel by reason of a nave, spokes, and rim; so also from among the Tathāgata's Eightfold Noble Path, right speech, right bodily action, and right livelihood are understood as the aggregate of morality, like the nave. The four, right understanding, right conception, right mindfulness, and right effort are understood as the aggregate of insight, like the spokes. Right *samādhi* (i.e. the aggregate of *samādhi*) is the pacification of all *prapañca* (expansion of sense attachment), hence like the rim." Notice that Buddhaguhya's number sixteen in a multiple of four, and can be taken as

15. This is clear enough in the *Pañcakrama* (ed. by de La Vallée Poussin), Vajrajāpakrama, verses 19-22, which set forth the Buddha elements streaming forth from one or other nostril from their bases in various element *cakras*, here called "*maṇḍala*" (vortex). Verse 19 speaks of the *hutabhuṅ-maṇḍala*, i.e. the vortex of fire (*hutabhuj*) which is red and departs from the right nostril. Verse 20 uses the expression *vāyu-maṇḍala* for the vortex of wind which is greenish yellow and departs from the left nostril. Verse 21 has the term *māhendra-maṇḍala* for the earth vortex which goes forth in a golden ray from both nostrils. Finally, verse 22 has the term *vāruṇa* ("related to Varuṇa") for the water vortex which is the white ray also leaving through both nostrils. Here *māhendra* (related to, belonging to, fit for Great Indra) is a name of the earth.

one in the sense of a net. But when Buddhaguhya explains the spokes as the nature of compassion, it does not agree with Vasubandhu's understanding of them as the aggregate of insight. A further divergence is when Buddhaguhya takes the nave to stand for the *dharma* realm, while Vasubandhu puts here the aggregate of morality, and evidently counts the entire wheel as representing the *dharma*. And when Buddhaguhya takes the circle (hence the rim) as the knowledge garland, the disagreement is complete. That still does not clarify the "horse-*maṇḍala*" (same reading in the Narthang Tanjur). But the previous use of the word "Indra" suggests that "horse" refers metaphorically to the "horse sacrifice" (*aśva-medha*), since in this sacrifice as portrayed at the opening of the *Bṛhadāraṇyaka Upaniṣad*, the horse parts sum up the world, and the *maṇḍala* is also the world.

k. The sixteen *sattvas* are certainly the set of sixteen Bodhisattvas which Buddhaguhya lists in his commentary, p. 24-2,3 and where he calls them the "Bodhisattvas of the Bhadrakalpa (fortunate eon)". His list is not quite the same as in any of the *maṇḍalas* of the *Niṣpannayogāvalī*, but the closest lists are in the *Mañjuvajramaṇḍala* and *Durgatipariśodhana-maṇḍala*, wherein the Sanskrit names are established. Here is Buddhaguhya's listing together with directional meaning:

East (who do not swerve from the true nature of mind):
    Maitreya, Mañjuśrī, Gandhahasti, Jñānaketu.
South (who have purity of view and practice):
    Bhadrapāla, Amoghadarśi, Ākāśagarbha, Akṣayamati.
West (who have a host of merits):
    Pratibhānakūṭa, Mahāsthāmaprāpta, Sarvāpāyañjaha, Sarvaśokatamonirghātamati.
North (who have eliminated the two obscurations—of defilement and knowable):
    Jālinīprabha, Candraprabha, Amṛtaprabha, Samantabhadra.

The most notable omission is that of Avalokiteśvara, but he might be present with the name "Amoghadarśi" (whose vision does not fail), especially since the *Dharmadhātu-Vāgīśvara-maṇḍala* of the *Niṣpanna-yogāvalī* in its list of sixteen Bodhisattvas includes Avalokiteśvara and omits the name Amoghadarśi. Some years ago, when I was reading the list in the *Dharmadhātu-maṇḍala*, the Mongolian lama Dilowa Gegen Hutukhtu told me that those sixteen belong to the Tenth Stage (and so according to *Mkhas grub rje's* are in the retinue of the Saṃbhogakāya). This then is what Buddhaguhya means in his next paragraph by "supra-mundane retinue".

l. The three exits from within are: (1) the nave—Vairocana as Dharmakāya; (2) the garland of jewels, which is the rim—the Buddhas in Sambhogakāya form; (3) the sixteen spokes—the *sattvas* as Nirmāṇakāya. The word "*āvenika*" may refer to the special group of eighteen attributes peculiar to a Buddha, called the unshared natures (*āvenika-dharma*); the most elaborate exposition of the eighteen is now in Lamotte (*op. cit.*), Chap. XLI (pp. 1625-1703). The three entrances from without are the special kind of body, speech, and mind. The "diamond fence" was previously stated to be the round, unconstructed fence consisting of wisdom-knowledge. Earlier in Tsoṅ-kha-pa's passage it is called the "fire mountain" and the outer wall of the world. In fact, it is the hallowed circle, blessed into diamond, and the demonic elements are all outside: they cannot cross the "fire mountain".

The Mt. Meru Maṇḍala

Previously Ratnākaraśānti's exposition of the body-*maṇḍala* mentioned that Meru represents the body. Then Buddhaguhya's description of the *maṇḍala*-rite spoke of a person having the eight good-luck symbols on his body. The meaning of these remarks relates to the temple banner of Mt. Meru, but we must start with the *maṇḍala* of Mt. Meru, here reproduced.[16] Meru is in the center of the four continent system of the realm of desire (*kāmadhātu*).

In a small Tibetan text[17] I noticed a description which goes with this *maṇḍala* and therefore also helps explain the temple banner (below). In my translation of the passage I shall restore in part the well-attested Sanskrit names[18] along with numbers that agree with those on the Mt. Meru Maṇḍala.

(The Maṇḍala:) OṂ VAJRABHUMI ĀḤ HŪṂ ("Oṃ. The diamond spot of earth. Āḥ Hūṃ"). (There appears) the golden spot of earth which belongs to Great Indra (*māhendra*). OṂ VAJRAREKHE ĀḤ HŪṂ ("Oṃ. The diamond sketch. Āḥ Hūṃ"). (There appear):—

16. The Meru maṇḍala with names in Tibetan and Chinese was produced by the Peking Buddhist Institute among the years when the late Professor F. D. Lessing was there, and probably in the late 1930's when he participated in the Hedin expedition. Professor Lessing prepared a Sumeru diagram accordingly (see *Yung-Ho-Kung*, pp. 105-106) and his further remarks are helpful (especially p. 103).

17. The *Byaṅ chub lam gyi rim pa'i dmar khrid myur lam gyi sṅon 'gro'i ṅag 'don gyi rim pa khyer bde bklag chog bskal bzaṅ mgrin rgyan żes bya ba*, which was published in a book of minor Tibetan works with Western format. My copy, which has no entry of date or place of publication, was purchased at the Tibetan press in Dharmsala, H.P. (India) in Spring 1970.

18. These names are given by Professor Lessing (note 16, above) and probably stem from the *Mahāvyutpatti*, chapter on the four continents, especially Nos. 3047-3059 in the Sakaki edition, which I have utilized.

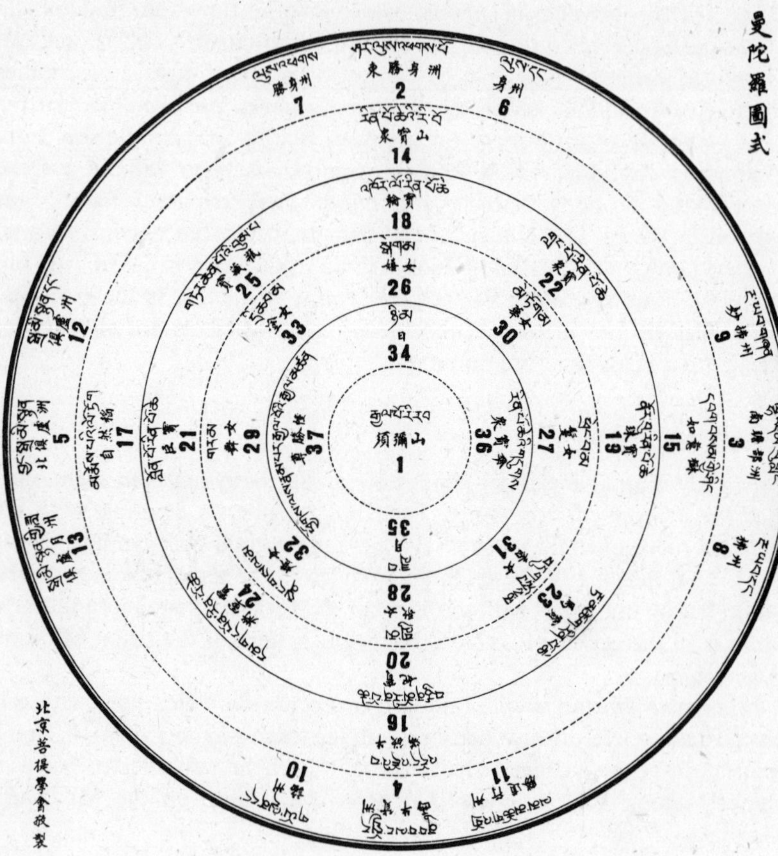

PLATE 8. The Mt. Meru Maṇḍala (Tibetan-Chinese).

1. Su-Meru, the King of Mountains, in the center, surrounded on the outside by the Cakravāla of iron mountains;
2. Pūrvavideha (Videha of the East),
3. Jambudvīpa in the South,
4. Aparagodānīya (Godānīya of the West),
5. Uttarakuru (Kuru of the North),
6. Deha,
7. Videha,
8. Cāmara
9. Aparacāmara (the Other Cāmara),
10. Śāthā,
11. Uttaramantriṇa,
12. Kurava
13. Kaurava,

Names of continents and lesser continents

14. the Mountain of Gems,
15. the Wish-granting Tree,
16. the Cow of Plenty,
17. the Harvest Without Ploughing,
18. the jewel of the wheel,
19. the jewel of the gem,
20. the jewel of the woman,
21. the jewel of the minister,
22. the jewel of the elephant,
23. the jewel of the excellent horse,
24. the jewel of the general,
25. the flask of great treasure,
26. the play lady,
27. the garland lady,
28. the song lady,
29. the dance lady,
30. the flower lady,
31. the incense lady,
32. the lamp lady,
33. the perfume lady,
34. Sun,
35. Moon,
36. the Precious Umbrella,
37. the Banner Victorious over the Quarters.

In that list the eight ladies (Nos. 26 through 33) are goddesses frequently depicted in Tibetan banners as holding the individual offering indicated by their names (play, garland, song, dance, flower, incense, lamp, perfume).[19]

19. See Lessing, *Yung-Ho-Kung*, p. 135.

PLATE 9. Mt. Meru Temple Banner.

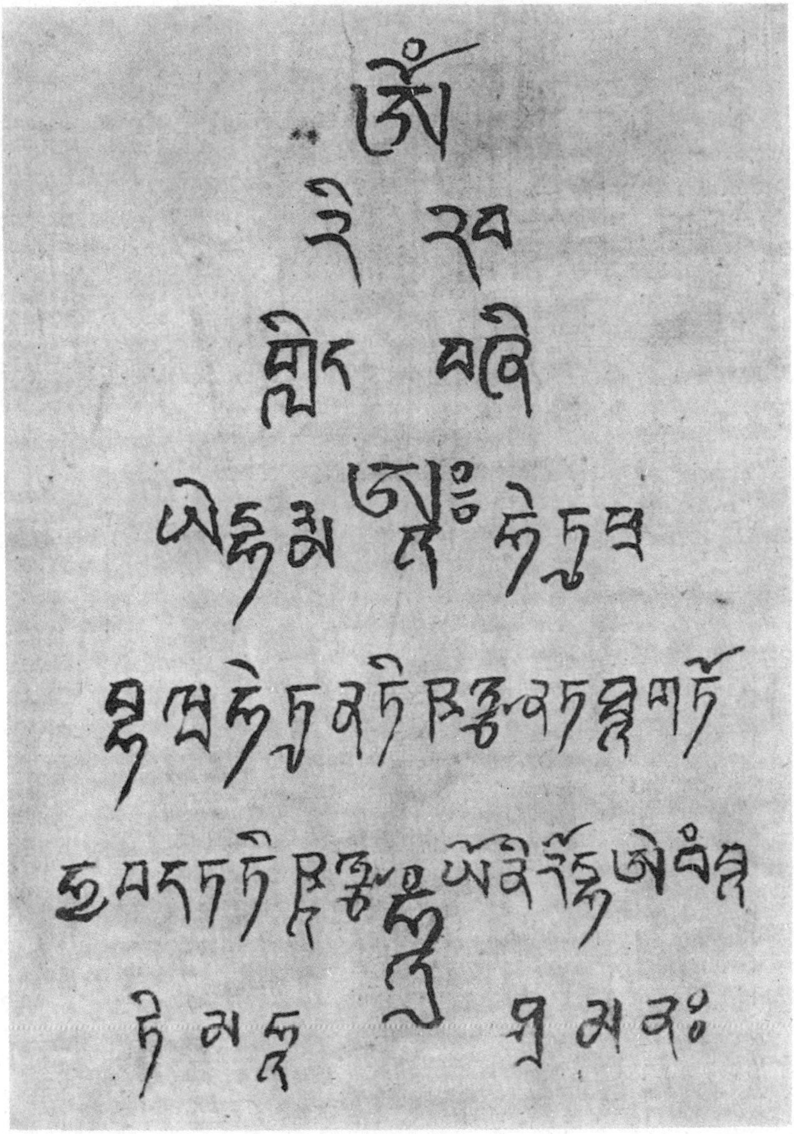

OṂ
Sumero
Four Continents
ĀḤ
Whatever natures have arisen through causes, their cause the tathāgata has declared and whatever is their cessation—speaking thus is the great ascetic (Mahāśramaṇa)
HŪṂ

PLATE 10. Reverse side of the Temple Banner

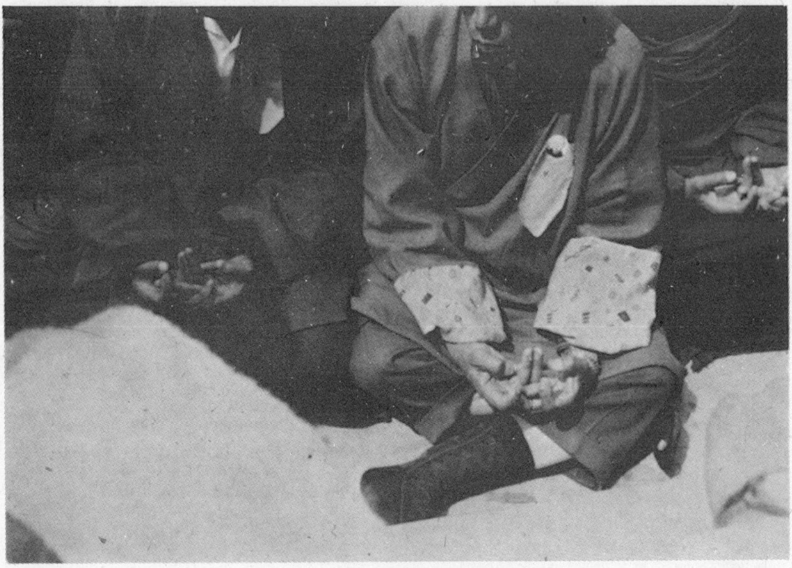

PLATE 11. Mudrā of the four continents and Mt. Meru. Enacted by the candidates during petition for the Kālacakra initiation.

The Mt. Meru Temple Banner

All that data is immediately applicable to the Tibetan temple banner reproduced here and combines with *Mkhas grub rje's* (p. 175). The first two evocation stages are not visible in the temple banner: (first) "he must imagine an earth surface made of many jewels and strewn with gold sand;" and second he has the diamond sketch or plan. The next (or third) evocation stage is visible in the banner at the bottom (*Mkhas grub rje's*): "Upon it he imagines an ocean of milk. . . . In the middle of this, he imagines a four-sided Sumeru mountain, adorned on all four sides with rows of stairs made of gold, silver, sapphire, and amber, all over which spring up wish-granting trees decorated with a thousand fluttering victory banners." In the case of the body as Meru, Ratnākaraśānti refers to the sides as "front, back, right, and left", which are respectively East, West, South, and North.[20] On the temple banner in the manner of a retinue, the three white crescent shapes are the Eastern continent Pūrvavideha (middle), with two minor continents Deha and Videha. The Southern continent is represented by a blue square—the one for Jambudvīpa not visible, presumably because the meditation is taking place in this continent (=India); the two visible squares are the lesser Cāmara and Aparacāmara.

20. See the correspondence table, *Yung-Ho-Kung*, p. 102.

The three red circles are the Western continent Aparagodānīya along with the lesser continents Śāṭhā and Uttaramantriṇa. The three yellow truncated triangles are the Northern continent Uttarakuru and its two minor companions Kurava and Kaurava.

The temple banner shows wish-granting trees but not the Mountain of Gems, the Cow of Plenty, or the Harvest Without Plowing. Then there is the list of the seven jewels of the World Emperor (*cakravārtin*), and it is said (*Sūtrālaṃkāra*, Bodhipakṣa chapter) that the Bodhisattva has seven jewels comparable to the imperial seven. The Bodhisattva jewels are the seven limbs of enlightenment (Nos. 19-25 of the thirty-seven natures accessory to enlightenment, listed in my first chapter): mindfulness is comparable to the jewel of wheel, joy to the jewel of gem, the cathartic to the jewel of woman, *samādhi* to the jewel of the minister (or treasurer), analysis of the doctrine to the jewel of the elephant, striving to the jewel of the excellent horse, equanimity to the jewel of the general. All seven world-emperor's jewels are depicted on the temple banner on the observer's right. From top down, there are the wheel and the imperial gem (=wish-granting gem, *cintāmaṇi*), the woman and the treasurer, the elephant, the general, and the horse. In the case of the body-*maṇḍala*, the yogin naturally has the seven limbs of enlightenment.

In the middle along with the Sun and Moon, there are the external offerings, starting with the five offerings to the senses, on observer's left: mirror (the plain one), *ḍamaru* drum, and auspicious (incense) flask (*bhadrakalaśa*); on the right: food and conch shell (the one which is held). Beneath these five are a total of twelve offerings. Among these there stand out, on the left: lamp (candles) and flower (lotus); on the right: incense (incense burner) and perfume (shell with scented water). These are the four basic offerings discussed in my Offering Materials chapter, and are shared between the list in the Mt. Meru Maṇḍala, above, and *Mkhas grub rje's* (pp. 179-183). However, the remaining four goddess offerings in the Mt. Meru Maṇḍala, namely, play, garland, song, and dance, are not represented in the temple banner; but the remaining four in *Mkhas grub rje's* list of eight are apparently represented: oblation, feet-cooling water, mirror (the other one with rays) for washing the divine body, food for the gods. The remaining four offerings (of the twelve) appear to be various kinds of herbs. All those offerings go with Sun, Moon, and stars in the intermediate space. In the Divinity chapter, Padmavajra mentions one meaning of the Dharmakāya as the set of planets, asterisms, etc. It is difficult to know if this meaning applies here. But in the section "Explanation of parts of the palace" it was observed that the set of five offerings represents the Dharmadhātu.

The star groups depicted on the banner are each rough approximations to two famous constellations. The one associated with the sun is obviously meant to be the circumpolar constellation Ursa Major, called the Great Bear, the Plough, Great Dipper, and by other names. It amounts to seven stars called in Indian mythology the Seven Rishis, who are the 'mind-born sons' of Brahmā. The one associated with the moon is even more deformed, but its six stars can hardly constitute any constellation other than the Pleiades, because among the group of twenty-seven or twenty-eight asterisms (*nakṣatra*), the ancient Indian works always had the moon starting out in the Pleiades, called in the Indian language Kṛttikā. The Indian Śaivitic war-god Kārttikeya owes his name and his six heads to the legend that he was fostered by the six wet-nurse stars of this constellation.

In the sky (the part of the temple banner above the Sun and Moon) (*Mkhas grub rje's*, p. 175): "Above it, he is to imagine a canopy (appearing) in an instant. On top of that, he generates the complete characteristics of an eaved palace and generates within it various seats; and he may also generate within the palace *stupas* of the varieties 'victorious' and 'radiant'." At this upper level there are the eight good-luck symbols or emblems that are on the yogin's body-*maṇḍala*. Buddhaguhya's commentary on the *Sarvadurgatipariśodhana* (PTT. Vol. 76, p. 26-4) just prior to setting forth the eight, defines "yoga" of "yogin" by way of its Tibetan translation (*rnal 'byor*, "sticking to tranquillity"): "tranquillity" (*rnal*) is true nature (*dharmatā*) and "sticking to" (*'byor*) is knowing. Then Buddhaguhya says: "Yoga displays (itself) as the eight emblems (*rtags*) on the true nature of body. The eight emblems of good luck (*aṣṭa-mangala*) are: the endless knot (*śrīvatsa*) which is lotus-like; the wheel (*cakra*) which is frightening; the banner (*dvaja*) which is victorious; the umbrella (*chattra*) which is dignified; the lotus (*padma*) which is luminous; the flask (*kalaśa*) of acute mind; the conch (*śaṅkha*) of purity; the golden fish (*matsya*) of auspicious mind." The Mt. Meru Maṇḍala has two entries, the Precious Umbrella (No. 36) and the Banner Victorious over the Quarters (No. 37), which appear to be the same as two of the above eight emblems, namely the umbrella and the banner. Besides, the Maṇḍala entry "flask of great treasure" (No. 25) may very well be the emblem "flask". As to those emblems being on the yogin's body, in an early article[21] I translated from a commentary of the Yoga Tantra a certain list of the thirty-two characteristics that included for the Buddha's hands (although usually the feet are credited with these characteristics: the "lion's seat" (*siṃhāsana*), "fish" (*mīna*), "banner of victory" (*dvaja*), "thunderbolt" (*vajra*), the "hook" (*aṅkuśa*), the "flask" (*kalaśa*), the Nandyāvartta, the Śrīvatsa, the "conch shell" (*śaṅkha*), the "lotus" (*padma*), and the Svastika.

Let us now treat the three-storied palace which rests on the cloud atop Mt. Meru.

21. "Contributions Regarding the Thirty-Two Characteristics of the Great Person," *Sino-Indian Studies; Liebenthal Festschrift* (Visvabharati, Santiniketan, 1957), pp. 243, ff.

Speaking about the eaved palace on the summit of Mt. Meru, Lessing[22] states that it is Indra's palace called Sudarśana. This continues the association with the name "Indra" since the golden spot of earth from which the evocation began is called "belonging to Great Indra". The tiny structure on the top of the palace roof is more difficult. It may very well be a stylized part of a stūpa. It will be recalled that *Mkhas grub rje's* mentions two kinds of stūpas that can be generated in the palace. Like the standard stūpa, this structure—as the photograph is seen with a microscope—also has on its very top the crescent moon surmounted by the sun, in turn surmounted by a hook-like curve that should represent fire. While the usual representation of a stūpa does not show lotuses in the superstructure, in fact two lotuses are mentioned in that position in the stupa description recently published in a Tibetan educational manual.[23] These lotuses, although tiny, are visible in the tiny roof structure atop the three storied palace, which considered as a reliquary house might contain the three kinds of relics.[24] The two lotuses shown in the roof structure should be (lowest) the "lotus which is the throne for the flask" (*bum gdan padma*) and the other one (higher) the "lotus which supports the parasol" (*gdugs 'degs padma*).

Finally, the top of the temple banner is described from Buddhaguhya's *maṇḍala* exposition previously translated. The pendant necklace is a hanging necklace of pearls, standing for the Bodhisattva's joy. The silk (scarves)—five-colored—have the meaning of five kinds of knowledge.

22. *Yung-Ho-Kung*, p. 104.

23. The / *'briṅ rim slob deb kyi kha skoṅ las / rig gnas don bsdu* /, Tibetan Cultural Printing Press, Kashmir House, Distt. Kangra, Dharmsala (H.). India, 1970.

24. *Mkhas grub rje's*, pp. 106-107, shows that the corporeal relics of the Buddha are of the Nirmāṇakāya, that the *dhāraṇīs* are relics of the Dharmakāya, and so, inferentially, the icons are relics of the Saṃbhogakāya. The *dhāraṇīs* do not have to be in the form of incantations. In fact, the most frequent one is the sentence of the law which is repeated on the reverse side of the Temple Banner—the sentence, "Whatever natures have arisen through causes . . ." This famous passage is among the most ancient sayings of Buddhism, being known from the celebrated account of the conversion of the disciples Śāriputra and Maudgalyāyana.

10

TANTRIC RITUAL AND SYMBOLISM OF ITS ATTAINMENTS

Ritual in the Buddhist Tantras somehow always revolves about the "three mysteries of the Buddha"—his Body, Speech, and Mind, and how the tantric performer correlates his own body, speech, and mind with those "mysteries" or secrets. That will be my first concern. Then I shall turn to various topics of the Anuttarayoga Tantra, a note on mundane occult attainments (*siddhi*), the "five ambrosias" of the Stage of Generation, finally the three ritual observances (*vrata*) and other matters of the Stage of Completion. The "three mysteries of the Buddha" are the life of all these discussions.

Orientation toward the "Three Mysteries"

It was already pointed out that the officiant correlates his body to the Body Mystery by means of gesture (*mudrā*), his speech to the Speech Mystery by means of incantation (*mantra*), and his mind to the Mind Mystery by means of intense concentration (*samādhi*). I now go into these in reverse order, because *samādhi* is the part which is shared with non-tantric Buddhism and in fact is a feature of Buddhism from its outset.

According to *Mkhas grub rje's* (pp. 198-201), which should be consulted on these points, calming (the mind) (*śamatha*) and discerning (the truth) (*vipaśyanā*) are the backbone of both the "Pāramitā-yāna" and the "Mantra-yāna". Mkhas grub rje points out that the specific techniques of developing these two essential ingredients of *samādhi*—as one can read about them extensively in ordinary Buddhist texts—are not mentioned in

3 gates – Σ-triangle

the Tantras for the simple reason that the contemplation, according to the rules, of the *yoga* of the deity brings the complete characteristics of calming. Likewise, for discerning reality, one must have the voidness contemplation, which is an essential element in the Buddhist Tantras even though they do not treat voidness in the manner of a Mādhyamika treatise, with its refutations of the opponent and the like. This voidness contemplation in tantric practice is illustrated in the meditation on sound (see those same pages of *Mkhas grub rje's*) where the sound contemplation is carried out to the extreme limit of silence, whereupon one reaches the voidness. This is called "freedom at the limit of the sound," a freedom abiding in the Dharmakāya. This is explained for the lower Tantras in Śrī-Dīpaṃkarabhadra's *Vāg-āśrita-dhyāna-nāma* (PTT, Vol. 79, p. 251 to p. 252), where the sound of the *dhāraṇī*-garland (*mālā*) is associated with what he calls the "stage of generation," and the sound of the void with the "stage of completion." This author, Dīpaṃkarabhadra, has written a work well-known in the *Guhyasamāja* tradition (the *Guhyasamājamaṇḍala-vidhi*). He states: "There are two kinds of sound which cut off all *karma* of living beings—the sound of the void and the sound of the garland." He then says that there are six kinds of sound of the void. These are his six, with brief citation of his further explanation:

(1) That based on body and speech. This relies on the magical practice born of the body through the profound unborn true nature (*dharmatā*), which is void.

(2) That based on sense objects (*viṣaya*). This arises in the five gates of the profound true nature, while the yogin is devoid of intellectual activity (*buddhi*).

(3) That based on mind (*citta*). This is based on memory.

(4) That based on the natural disposition of a knowable entity. Here the yogin is entirely devoid of views, and true nature appears as an illusion (*māyā*).

(5) That based on time. There are three cases: (a) the time of cognition, when cognition is cut off while sound dissolves within (one). (b) the time of comprehension, when there is realization of non-self (*anātman*). (c) the time of the "year's recitation," when there is the harvest of true-nature.

(6) That based on personal transformation. This is voidness of basis (*hetu*). In the case based on (a spot of) body, there is gradual decrease (of phenomenal manifestation); and in the case based on mind, there is transcending of *saṃsāra*.

Besides, the Tantras usually have different meditative objects from the non-tantric Buddhist ones. Tsoṅ-kha-pa's *Lam rim chen mo* (*śamatha* section) cites the author Bodhibhadra (his *Samādhi-sambhāra-parivarta-nāma*) for a classification of meditative objects that emphasizes tantric examples. Following is a tabulation of this author's material.

TABLE 8

MEDITATIVE OBJECTS FOR CALMING (THE MIND)

I. By looking inward		*II. By dwelling on what is seen outside*	
A. DWELLING ON THE BODY	B. DWELLING ON WHAT IS BASED ON THE BODY	A. OUTSTANDING	B. ORDINARY
1. As the aspect of a god	1. On the breath	1. Dwelling on the body	(not listed)
2. As the unpleasant thing of skeleton, etc.	2. On the subtle signs (*sūkṣma-nimitta*) 3. On the drop (*bindu*)	2. Dwelling on speech	
3. With outstanding signs like *khaṭvāṅga*	4. On the member rays 5. On rapture (*prīti*) and pleasure (*sukha*)		

Passing to the second topic, it is of course the officiant's use of *mantra*, or a string of these in the form of *dhāraṇi*, to correlate his speech to the Speech Mystery. *Mkhas grub rje's* section on "The four members of muttering" (pp. 186, ff.) already has so much authoritative material on this subject that I can do little more than refer the reader to his treatment. However, the little that I can add is to continue Dīpaṃkarabhadra's exposition. He states that there are five kinds of sound-garland, which I here give with abbreviated notice of his individual explanations.

(1) Meditation of dwelling in the sound held in accordance with the "stage of generation." Here the aim is, after much recitation, to have the sound-garland eventually sound itself, whereupon the sound is issuing in voidness, and is a reflected image of the Buddha's realm.

(2) Meditation on dwelling in the sound of the garland of letters. The officiant imagines a garland of vowel letters at the root of his nostrils between the eyes; eventually it should become "bright" and be associated with ecstasy.

(3) Meditation of dwelling in the garland sound of the body-speech-circle causing a state of consciousness. The word "body" means the bodies of deities who are the "circle" and "speech" is their speech. Whirling this garland, one becomes liberated from the garland of egoistic views, and consciousness dwells in the realm of profound true nature.

(4) Meditation of dwelling in the garland-sound of intrinsically pure natures (*dharma*). This is a method of liberation from false appearances, cutting off of discursive thought, transcending the conventions of singleness and multiplicity, so that one arrives at the realm of the Buddha.

(5) Meditation of dwelling in the sound which produces the path which

is the true-nature of the stage of completion. This is for the disciple of faith who has already become a "solitary hero" of the stage of generation and having donned the armor of the gods is now a beginner of the stage of completion. He has gained a superior capacity to pursue the aims of others. Seated on a pleasant seat, he imagines on his tongue a HŪṂ from which issue a myriad rays of blue diamond, the ends of which are encircled by a *dhāraṇī*-garland of his tutelary deity which is revolving to the right. Outside of that is another garland composed of vowels, revolving to the left; and outside of the latter is another garland, composed of consonants, revolving to the right. The mind dwells on the set of three garlands; so dwelling the yogin destroys the faults of body, speech, and mind. When those three kinds of faults are destroyed, then dwelling on the first garland, he reaches the Nirmāṇakāya of Vajravidāraṇa; by the second one, he reaches the Saṃbhogakāya; and by the third, the Dharmakāya. By dwelling on the rays of the HŪṂ he reaches the body of Vajravidāraṇa inseparable from the three bodies. As to how he dwells on them—he dwells on the first garland in the manner of a dream; dwells on the second one imagining it to be like water; dwells on the third one as though it were sky. Finally, he dwells on the rays of HŪṂ as the profound realm of the Buddha.

Dīpaṃkarabhadra's exposition is a sample of the rich material on this subject in the Buddhist Tantra, here part of the theory of becoming a Buddha through the Kriyā Tantra deity Vajravidāraṇa, who is Vajrapāṇi.

The third correlation is of course by way of *mudrā*, which means a "seal". I refer to the author Buddhaguhya, commentary on *Durgatipariśodhana* (pp. 32-5), where he states that there are three kinds of *mudrā*: (1) the *mudrā* which is not transcended. It is not transcended by reflection on true nature (*dharmatā*). (2) the illustration *mudrā*. The illustration with *mudrā* is, e.g. of five colors. (3) the hand-gesture *mudrā*. It is a gesture of empowering with the fingers of the hand. Furthermore, a *mudrā* is said to be "illustrious" because it pleases and because it is non-dual. That is Buddhaguhya's brief but masterful explanation. There is learned information belonging to the Tibetan tradition in *Mkhas grub rje's* (especially pp. 228-49). One can find much material on *mudrā* following the Japanese tradition in E. Dale Saunders, *Mudrā*; in this case, it is practically all on the third kind of *mudrā*, the hand gesture. Concerning the second kind of *mudrā* mentioned by Buddhaguhya, this appears to be exemplified later in this essay as the "six *mudrās*" which in fact are the six ornaments of the Buddhist tantric deities; that is to say, these ornaments illustrate or stand for the six perfections. His first kind of *mudrā* appears to be, for example, those also mentioned in this essay as the three Inner Seals and three Outer Seals, because these seals do not illustrate something else, but are themselves the true-nature experiences aimed at, hence are not transcended; likewise the final topic of four *mudrās* falls in this category. In any case, the correlation of *mudrā* is with the Body Mystery.

Four Kinds of Yoga

Tsoṅ-kha-pa frequently cites Abhayākaragupta's great commentary called the *Āmnāya-mañjari* (*Man sñe*) and in the *Sṅags rim chen mo* (402a-b) he refers to this work for describing three kinds of *yoga*, namely the yoga of eating, yoga of washing, yoga of lying down; and then adds a fourth one called yoga of getting up. I now translate all four descriptions:

> *Yoga of eating.* At the time of taking food, including drink and the like, one should be mindful of oneself as the deity; and having empowered the food to be like ambrosia (*amṛta*), should enjoy it by thinking that it is a divine offering.
>
> *Yoga of washing.* It is to be done as in the phase of initiation.
>
> *Yoga of lying down.* Having convinced oneself that the nature of voidness which consists of the true form of co-natal bliss is the nature of the Clear Light, he should lie down with what consists of Insight and the Means.
>
> *Yoga of getting up.* He should get up upon being exhorted by the sound of the *ḍamaru* drum, or by the song of the goddess.

The "Yoga of eating" is of course involved with the section on "five ambrosias" as also with the "inner offering" in the classification of offerings in the previous chapter on Offering Materials. The "Yoga of washing" is evidently the sprinkling rite of initiation. The "Yoga of lying down" shows that the union of Insight (*prajñā*) and Means (*upāya*) takes place within the yogin. The "Yoga of getting up" agrees with our later discussion to the effect that the yogin, or the "Means" within him, is roused, made to rise by the sound of Insight.

External materials and mundane siddhis

The Stage of Generation in the Anuttarayoga Tantra has in this Tantra class the most in common with the lower Tantras, especially the Yoga Tantra. One thing in common is the feature of what are called "mundane *siddhis*", although the Stage of Generation is frequently credited with the "eight great siddhis" (still mundane). The second stage in the Anuttarayoga Tantra, called Stage of Completion, is credited with the possibility of supramundane *siddhi*, or Buddhahood. Therefore, at this point we may call attention to *Mkhas grub rje's* (p. 211): "In this Tantra it is set forth that by taking recourse to external materials such as the sword (*khaḍga*), one accomplishes the (*siddhi*) *khaḍga-vidyādhara*, and so forth." This is simply a repetition of the remark in *Sṅags rim chen mo*, folio 92b-4, at which place there is no further information. Buddhaguhya slightly expands the list in his commentary on the *Durgatipariśodhana* (PTT, Vol. 76, p. 40-3), calling them "tokens of siddhi" (*dṅos grub kyi rtags*), and mentioning the sword (ral gri), trident (rtse gsum), wheel (cakra), and adding "etc." (la sogs pa). With this slightly longer list to indicate typical members of the series, one can get further with the passage in the *Āryasiddhaikavīrasādhanaṁ* (*Sādhanamālā*, No. 71, Vol. I, p. 143-44): "Then at the time of the moon or of the sun, he takes in his hand a sword (*khaḍga*) made of natural iron; and gazing at the moon he recites (the mantra) until such time as he is liberated and becomes a *vidyādhara* of the sword. In like fashion, having applied the domineering substances of eye ointment, foot ointment, mid-forehead ointment—the thunderbolt (vajra), wheel (cakra), trident (triśūla), arrow (śara), mallet (mudgara), noose (pāśa), hook (aṅkuśa), etc. are accomplished." Furthermore, *Mkhas grub rje's* (p. 216, note) states: "Contemplating the deity and performing rosary muttering, while taking recourse to such substances as malachite (lig-bu-mig) and lamp-black (or antimony) (srod-añjana), one attains whatever he desires."

Merit is also counted as a success (*siddhi*) according to what we read in Jñānavajra's *Puṇyavardhanī-śrījñānamālā-nāma* (PTT. Vol. 79, p. 251-4):

> . . . Having personally invited the gods of the *maṇḍala*, one confesses to them any sinful, unvirtuous deeds. Then, he implores them for the desired object. If it is accomplished, he should make a huge banquet for others. Then, on a day of thunder he should convey to a large river the materials of the burnt offering and so on. On the East side of the town he should make various roarings of the conch-shell, set up parasols and victory banners. On the South side he should sound various drums and set up streamers. On the West side he should ride on a horse or elephant, sounding the ḍamaru drum along with the sounds of musical instruments and the gong. On the North side, he should sound the bells and cymbals and hang various silks. Then he should confess whatever accumulation (of goods) he has amassed. Having done that ritual three or seven times, that yogin will undoubtedly attain to all facets of merit like the burning of a dry tree.

The Five Ambrosias

One of the most striking identifications of the five Buddhas is with the five kinds of ambrosia (*amṛta*) in a context where they are explained as blood, semen, human flesh, urine, and excrement. This context is the conclusion of *yoga* in the Stage of Generation (*utpatti-krama*) in the Anuttara-yoga-tantra, preliminary to the Stage of Completion (*saṃpanna-krama*). Tsoṅ-kha-pa (A.D. 1357-1419), founder of the Gelugpa sect in Tibet, sets forth this topic in his reform of the Tantras, called *Sṅags rim chen mo*, with the views of numerous authorities.[1] Now, I wish to signal some of the essential ideas.

Because the preceding main part of the *yoga* has wearied body and mind, there is this rite of enjoying the ambrosia, envigorating the body. The *yogin* imagines at the top of his head a lunar disk marked with an *Oṃ*. From this *Oṃ* ambrosia trickles down moistening the finest particles all the way to his feet. But that is the end result of an evocation process, which is variously described, and presumably connected with the celebrated Hindu account of the churning of the ocean to extract the *amṛta*, over which the gods (*deva*) and demigods (*asura*) fought.

In these texts cited by Tsoṅ-kha-pa one starts with three vessels of authorized kind, skull bowl, and so on,—one in front containing liquid offering materials (Skt. = *bali*), such as milk, and two more on the right and left sides containing solid offering materials, such as meat and fish. However, Tsoṅ-kha-pa says that, if these materials are not available, one can use just water. Presumably the *yogin* is sitting with crossed legs. He "generates" the offering materials in three steps or evocations, stacking up a wind, on that a fire, and on the latter a skull bowl, the latter itself resting on a trivet of skull bowls. In that skull bowl, level with his own head (or is it his own head?), he generates from ten germ syllables, starting with *Hūṃ*, the five ambrosias and the five kinds of flesh. Here there is the flesh of cow in the east, of dog in the south, of elephant in the west, of horse in the north, and of man in the middle. In the intermediate directions and center there are the five ambrosias, and Tsoṅ-kha-pa quotes from the *Mahāmudrātilaka*:

> Ratnasambhava is blood, Amitābha is semen;
> Amoghasiddhi is human flesh, Akṣobhya is urine;
> Vairocana is excrement. These are the five best ambrosias.[2]

The *yogin* stacks the three germ syllables, *Oṃ*, *Āḥ*, *Hūṃ*, in that order, apparently at the level of the crown of the head, level of the eyebrows, and level of the little tongue, uvula. These syllables irradiate, and attract the ambrosia of the Buddhas and Bodhisattvas of the ten directions, as well as the ambrosia in the oceans.

The upward evocation can be interpreted in terms of "centers" of the

1. The section herein treated occupies almost four folios of the *Sṅags rim chen mo*, beginning 394*b*-4.
2. *Sṅags rim chen mo*, 395*b*-5.

body by reference to the Table of the preceding section. There the wind disk is in the navel and the fire disk in the throat. The third evocation, that of the skull bowl, would thus correspond to one's own head. This upward "generation" naturally reminds one of Viṣṇu's Three Steps. In fact, in the Hindu legend of the churning of the ocean of milk, Viṣṇu himself is seated on the mountain Mandāra, which constitutes the churning stick. This scene is beautifully depicted in Plate 5, M. S. Randhawa's *Basohli Painting* (Government of India, 1959). Among the objects which arose from the churning process were the divine cow Surabhi, the seven-headed steed, and the white elephant Airāvata. These three may account for three kinds of flesh generated in the skull bowl. Flesh of man in the middle may derive from Viṣṇu's central position. Alone flesh of dog is not accounted for in the Hindu legend. Hence this remarkable yogic evocation described in the Buddhist Tantras seems intimately related to certain legends about Viṣṇu.

In evaluating this curious description of the five ambrosias, which in this literature are said to purify the offering materials, it is well to observe that Tsoṅ-kha-pa in the Bodhisattva section of his Steps of the Path to Enlightenment, the *Lam rim chen mo*, speaks of the impropriety of certain gifts. For example, the Bodhisattva must not give food and drink polluted with excrement and urine, spittle, vomit, pus and blood; or give forbidden flesh.[3] It is my opinion that Tsoṅ-kha-pa bothers to mention this in the light of the Tantric doctrine of the five ambrosias.

The Three Ritual Observances (vrata)

The word *vrata* for a ritual observance is of ancient usage in India. The standard Tibetan equivalent is *brtul źugs*, and the present materials happen to be mainly based on the Tibetan passages using this term. As the attainments are discussed in the Mother Tantra of the Anuttarayoga Tantra, they usually come in the order of first the ornaments of the deities and next the symbolization of the ecstatic song and dance by the magic wand (*khaṭvāṅga*), the drum (*ḍamaru*), and the skull bowl (*kapāla*).

During Tsoṅ-kha-pa's explanation of the three higher initiations (the Secret one, the Insight-knowledge, and the Fourth) in the *Sṅags rim chen mo*, he brings in (fol. 310b to 311a) the terminology of the three kinds of *vrata* (ritual observance).

For the first one, called "*vidyā-vrata*" (ritual observance of the *vidyā*), he says:

> Because the prajñā herself is the concrete means for perfection of

3. This prohibition is part of a lengthy statement about the impropriety of giving, occurring in the Tashilunpo edition of the *Lam rim chen mo* on folio 230*a*, where Tsoṅ-kha-pa mentions Asaṅga's *Bodhisattvabhūmi* as the source of this particular material.

> the illustrious non-oozing bliss, the "ritual observance of the goddess consort (*vidyā*)" is the understanding by the beginners and so on, "I must not omit the condensed reflection (*bsdus rtogs pa*) in any period."

The phrase "in any period" can be understood by materials in my forthcoming *Yoga of the Guhyasamājatantra* that the *vidyā-vrata* is the contact with the goddesses at the junctures, i.e. morning, noon, sunset, and midnight. The "condensed reflection" is presumably the co-natal knowledge (*sahaja-jñāna*) which Tsoṅ-kha-pa in that context says is explained in the phase of the third Initiation, i.e. the *prajñā-jñāna* (Insight-Knowledge). This agrees with *Mkhas grub rje's* (pp. 318-19, note), that this initiation takes place in the "wombs" (*bhaga*), i.e. in the four *cakras* of the body belonging to the goddesses Locanā, etc.

Then he explains the one called "*vajra-vrata*" (ritual observance of the diamond). This "diamond" turns out to be the inner diamond which is the one mind of enlightenment as the intrinsic nature of the five knowledges. One has ritual observance of this diamond when he practices all the rites while free from discursive thought.

The third one is called "*caryā-vrata*" (ritual observance of the engagement). There are three forms: (1) The first engagement is to apply oneself to accomplishing the three inner "seals" (*mudrā*), which are (a) one's own body as a divine body; (b) the indestructible sound of the "heat"; (c) the *saṃvṛti* mind of enlightenment which is the basis for enjoying the great bliss (the three symbolized by the *khaṭvāṅga*, etc.). One can also understand the three as external "seals" by taking the first one as the Father (yab), the second as the Prajñā, and the third as the *mantra* being recited. (2) The second engagement is the ritual observance of engagement together with the yoginī who wears the five ornaments; by having this observance, one applies himself to generating the five kinds of knowledge, which are the pure Dharmadhātu knowledge, and so forth. (3) The third engagement is the application to arousing the mind of enlightenment which has the indivisibility of void and compassion, that is to say, if one has achieved the capacity of the four divine stances, the supernormal faculties, etc.—applying them to accomplish the aim of sentient beings; and if yogins and yoginīs go outside (the fold) through worldly occupations —applying the power of all one's own inner ornaments for their aim.

Ornaments of the Deities

There are six ornaments called *mudrās* (seals) worn by the deities and said to represent the six perfections (*pāramitā*) of the Bodhisattva, according to the final verse in Durjayacandra's *Saptākṣarasādhana* (No. 250 in the *Sādhanamālā*).

The Green Tārā, showing the six ornaments.

Besides, five of the six are made to represent the five Buddhas according to *Hevajratantra* (I, vi, 11) and, consistently, according to the Explanatory Tantra, the *Saṃpuṭa* (PTT. Vol. 2, p. 260-3). Nāro-pāda's explanation of the ornaments in his *Vajrapada-sāra-saṃgraha-pañjikā* (PTT. Vol. 54, p. 36-1,2,3,4) accordingly concerns itself with the set of five. Hence a sixth ornament (the sacred thread) is left over; and besides there are some variants in stating certain ornaments, for example, as found in Tsoṅ-kha-pa's *Sbas don* commentary on the *Śrī-Cakrasaṃvara* (PTT. Vol. 157, p. 90-2). I only found the actual itemization of the ornaments with correspondences to both the perfections and the Buddhas, in Kloṅ-rdol bla-ma's collected works, Vol. Ga (p. 74-5 in Dalama's edition, Vol. I), for which a sixth Buddha (Mahāvajradhara) has to be allotted. Nevertheless, the fact that the various contexts in which I find the list of these ornaments do not correlate them explicitly and respectively with the six perfections; and, furthermore, that the indications already given connect them with the five kinds of knowledge, shows that it is more practical to set up the intended correspondences with this in mind (n.b., in the order of the *Hevajratantra* list):

TABLE 9

THE FIVE ORNAMENTS

ORNAMENT MANIFESTED	BY WHICH BUDDHA	FOR WHICH KNOWLEDGE
1. Head ornament (mukuṭa)=maṇi of head, or cakra of head	Akṣobhya	Mirror-like
2. Ear-ring (kuṇḍalam)	Amitābha	Discriminative
3. Necklace (kaṇṭhikā)	Ratnasambhava	Equality
4. Bracelet (arms and legs) (rucakam)	Vairocana	Dharmadhātu
5. Belt (mekhalā or kāyabandhanam) or sacred ash (mahābhasman)	Amoghasiddhi	Procedure-of-duty

According to *Sṅags rim*, 302a-1, ff., when one has already entered into the *vidyā-vrata*, which is the regular contact with the divinity at the *sandhis* (dawn, etc.), he then is to enter into the *caryā-vrata*. Tsoṅ-kha-pa makes a distinction as to whether it is a woman or a man that enters the *caryā-vrata*. A woman generates herself into the form of Vajravārāhī (the Diamond Sow), Nairātmyā (She who is Selfless), or the goddess of the family indicated by the thrown flower (in the flower initiation; cf. *Mkhas grub rje's*, p. 315). A man generates himself into Hevajra, etc. In either case, the person must then attract, by means of the rays from the seed in his heart, the knowledge being and then make it enter, whereupon he should convince himself that from the transformation of Akṣobhya, etc. the respective ornaments appear on his person. That is why the ornaments are called "*mudrās*" (seals). For each ornament a respective mantra is set forth to be cited thrice. Tsoṅ-kha-pa states that those mantras are taken from the *Vajrapañjarā*, Chap. Nine. In short, the yogin and the yoginī try to gain the five ornaments, "avoiding the 'sacred thread'" (precept of the *Śrī-Cakrasaṃvaratantra*, Chap. 27), at least in this phase.

Now to Nāro-pāda's explanations of the five ornaments: He goes through the explanations twice, first for the 'hinted meaning' (*neyārtha*) and next for the "evident meaning" (*nītārtha*):

neyārtha: One wears the *cakra* so as to bow to the guru, ācārya, kāmadeva.
One wears the ear-rings on the ears so as to not hear any harsh words directed toward the guru, holder of the *vajra*.
The necklace for reciting with mantra; the bracelets for avoiding any killing of living beings; the belt for recourse to *mudrā*.

nitārtha: One wears the *cakra* so as to honor and have a transit of the "drop" (*bindu*) of the *bodhicitta* (mind of enlightenment) which is called "guru, ācārya, kāmadeva". One wears the ear-rings on the ears so as to destroy the harsh words and to preserve the words of agreement. One ties on the necklace for the purpose of cessation through reciting the mantra, since it "protects the mind" (man-tra). The bracelets to avoid any killing of living beings, where "living being" means the mind, and one should not kill it. The belt so as to take recourse to a *mudrā*, i.e. the *karma-mudrā*.

Those explanations of the ornaments turn out rather close to the correspondences of "perfections" as given by Kloṅ-rdol bla-ma, because the assignment of *prajñā-pāramitā* is consistent with the explanation of *mudrā*, especially *karma-mudrā* (the visible consort) since the word *prajñā* is often used for the consort in this tantric material. In the standard order of the perfections, these run: 1. Giving—necklace; 2. Morality—bracelets; 3. Forbearance—Ear-ring; 4. Striving—head ornament; 5. Meditation—Sacred thread; 6. Insight (*prajñā*)—belt (or sacred ash)—which happens to be the order of the six ornaments in the *Śrī-Cakrasaṃvaratantra*, Chap. 27. Notice that this introduces the extra ornament, the "sacred thread" (*brahmasūtra*, or *yajñopavītam*), which is identified with the

Buddha Mahāvajradhara who, in the Gelugpa sect founded by Tsoṅ-kha-pa, is the Ādibuddha.

The lord and the Buddhist tantric deities represented iconographically have all six ornaments. Reference to B. Bhattacharyya's *The Indian Buddhist Iconography* shows that the sacred thread can be formed of a number of materials. Sometimes it consists of a snake, sometimes of bone ornaments, and frequently the material is not specified. It is of course always indicated when the iconographical description specifies six mudrās (*ṣaṇmudrā*), because this means the five as have been discussed above plus a further one which is the "sacred thread". It is noteworthy that this one is associated with the perfection "meditation"; this is perhaps a recognition that all the principal deities of the Buddhist tantric pantheon are contacted through meditation. But this does not justify the misnomer "Dhyani Buddhas" (the texts speak only of Buddhas, Tathāgatas, or Jinas).

The khaṭvāṅga, ḍamaru, and kapāla

Pictures of the legendary Padmasambhava (8th century magician in Tibet) have frequently appeared in the West in books on Tibet; and many persons have noticed the peculiar wand held with his left arm that is called the *khaṭvāṅga*. Former travellers in Tibet have spoken about the mysterious rite called Chöd, and the drum called *ḍamaru* (large sized variety) used in that mysterious cult. (Note that the spelling *ḍamaru* is standard, but when transcribed into Tibetan the word is generally written *ḍāmaru*). Tibetan iconography frequently depicts the skull-bowl (*kapāla*), full of blood, held by some fierce figure. Those three are the attributes or hand symbols of the *ḍākinīs*, typified by Buddhaḍākinī (saṅs rgyas mkha' 'gro) as depicted in the *Rin 'byuṅ* collection (Lokesh Chandra, *A New Tibeto-Mongol Pantheon*, Part 9, *Rin 'byuṅ* 141). On the facing page the three attributes are made more salient:

All three are also taken together in a passage which Tsoṅ-kha-pa cites in the *Sṅags rim chen mo* (311a-4), running as follows: "It is said in the *Kun spyod* (evidently the *Yoginīsaṃcārya*), 'The *khaṭvāṅga* is the body of a god; the *ḍamaru* is insight (*prajñā*);' and 'Mantra is the drinking skull (*kapāla*).'" In the foregoing treatment of the three ritual observances, this place in the *Sṅags rim chen mo* was alluded to in exposition of the *caryā-vrata*. In summary:

Symbol	*Inner Seal*	*Outer Seal*
khaṭvāṅga	one's own body as a divine body	Father (yab)
ḍamaru	indestructible sound of the "heat"	Prajñā (the Insight consort)
kapāla	basis for enjoying bliss	Mantra being recited

Buddhaḍākinī, showing the *khaṭvāṅga*, *ḍamaru*, and *kapāla*.

Because the Father (yab) and Prajñā as the Mother (yum) can be combined as Father-Mother (yab-yum), the *khaṭvāṅga* and the *ḍamaru* are frequently mentioned together, for example, *Sbas don* (p. 57-2): ". . . along with the *khaṭvāṅga* with skulls marked with a *vajra*, and the beating of the *ḍamaru* with the sound of HŪṂ . . ." The particular correspondence system which Tsoṅ-kha-pa uses in the above part of the *Sṅags rim chen mo* is consistent with his citation in the same work (426a-5) of a passage from the celebrated master of the Mother Tantra named Lui-pa, including: "The *khaṭvāṅga* is the divine body; Prajñā is the sound of the *ḍamaru*. The lord who has the *vajra* is day; the yoginī is night." A passage in the *Hevajra-tantra* seems to contradict the above, if we are to accept Snellgrove's translation (Part I: I, vi, 11): Wisdom (is symbolized) by the *khaṭvāṅga* and means by the drum. But note his own edited Sanskrit (confirmed by the Tibetan):

> . . . prajñā khaṭvāṅgarūpiṇī
> ḍamarūpāyarūpeṇa . . .

It seems possible to translate this in a manner consistent with Lui-pa:

> Prajñā is embodied for (or has the body belonging to) the *khaṭvāṅga* i.e. is the *ḍamaru*, by embodiment for the means.

My interpretation appears supported by the somewhat obscure line of the *Śrī-Cakrasaṃvaratantra* (Chap. 35): "For cheating untimely death, a body is applied to the *khaṭvāṅga*."

Tsoṅ-kha-pa was undoubtedly aware of the seeming discrepancy between the tradition he is following and the *Hevajratantra* (in common with the *Saṃpuṭa*), and in his *Sbas don* commentary on the *Śrī-Cakrasaṃvara-tantra*, p. 90-2, he treats the topic along with analysis of the expression "*khaṭvāṅga*". Notice that *khaṭvā* means a "cot" or "couch"; so *khaṭvāṅga* (with *aṅga* in the meaning of "body"): "the body on the cot". Tsoṅ-kha-pa writes:

> The reality of the "*prajñā* body" (śes rab yan lag) is explained as the *khaṭvāṅga* or the embrace by the body of the *prajñā* lady. Nag-po-pa states in his *Maṇḍala-vidhi*: "The *prajñā* body is on the cot;" this means that the *prajñā* lady is to be taken as the cot.

That is to say, if "*prajñā* body" is the *khaṭvā* body, then *prajñā* is the *khaṭvā* or cot. Hence, that *Hevajratantra* line (I, vi, 11), "Prajñā has the body belonging to the *khaṭvāṅga*," or "Prajñā has the form of the *khaṭvāṅga*," again possibly to be construed as meaning that Prajñā is the *khaṭvā*, the cot. While "embraced by *prajñā*" refers to the divine body on the *prajñā* cot. In the *Lam rim chen mo* (Bodhisattva section), in the course of explaining the "perfection of insight" (*prajñā-pāramitā*), Tsoṅ-kha-pa cites a work by Nāgārjuna: "Insight is the root of all this visible and invisible merit; hence, to accomplish both, one must hold on to Insight. It is the great science—the source of (present) nature, (future) purpose, and liberation; hence, with devotion from the outset, one must hold on to Insight, the Great Mother." This requirement to hold on to *prajñā* is of course the rationale for the tantric iconography that shows the Buddha in the tantric form of Mahāvajradhara embraced by Prajñā or by a goddess representing *prajñā*, while he holds on to her. This role of *prajñā*—and she is called "Mother of Buddhas and Bodhisattvas" in the Mahāyāna scriptures—will be clearer as we proceed.

Those observations are further certified by the *Hevajratantra* itself (I, vi, 17), and here Snellgrove wrongly adopted a reading *prajñākhaṭvāṅgo* against the evidence of "All MSS. khaṭvāṅga." The manuscript readings require a syntactical reevaluation; and thus correcting the passage, it can be retranslated: "The sound of the *ḍamaru* is the recitation; *prajñā* is the contemplation of the *khaṭvāṅga*. This is to be recited and to be contemplated by the engagement of the diamond-skull." Previously we observed that Prajñā is associated with the sound of the *ḍamaru*, and is the *khaṭvā*. How is this possible? Compare with K. Kunjunni Raja, *Indian Theories of Meaning*, chapter on Metaphor, giving from Gautama's *Nyāyasūtra-s* a list of possible metaphorical transfer of meaning, including (p. 234), "Location", "e.g. *mañcāḥ krośanti* (The cots cry). Here the term *mañca* (cot) is used to refer to 'the children on the cot'." Then giving from Patañjali's *Mahābhāṣya* the famous grammarian's relations involving transference of meaning, and as the first category, "Location", "e.g. *mañcā hasanti* (The cots laugh), *girir dahyate* (The hill is burning). Here the term 'cots' stands for 'the children in the cots' and the term 'hill' stands for 'the trees on the hill.'" In the present case, we can understand the word "cot" (*khaṭvā*) to have a metaphorical transfer. The *khaṭvā*—the stretched out canvas of a cot—is the *ḍamaru*'s recitation; and—as a student at Columbia University Mr. Lex Hixon, suggested to me—perhaps because a drum is stretched material analogous to a cot. As to the kind of suggestion involved, see Raja (*op. cit.*, pp. 302-03) where we find that poetical suggestion (*dhvani*) is of two sorts: *avivakṣita-vācya* (an implicit expression that is not intended to be told) based on the metaphorical transfer (*lakṣaṇā*); and *vivakṣita-vācya* (an implicit expression that is intended to be told) based on the literal meaning (*abhidhā*). In the present case, we obviously have an example of metaphorical usage whose message was not intended to be told, because part of the secrecy code of the Tantra. Still I am here telling it, through the fortunate confluence of explanations from diverse sources, and also because, if it is proper for Westerners to tell many wrong things about the Buddhist Tantras, it is surely proper for someone to tell some right things that have come to his notice.

But we are far from exhausting the subject! What does the *Hevajratantra* mean by the "engagement of the diamond-skull"? We have already noticed that "diamond" in this context is the mind of enlightenment (*bodhicitta*). Hence, "diamond-skull" means skull containing the conventional mind of enlightenment. But the skull is explained as the mantra being recited. So drinking from the skull is the yogin's recitation of the mantra; and he is no longer reciting it: the recitation is done by *prajñā*—the cot conveying him through those three severed heads on the *khaṭvāṅga* pole.

As to the skull bowl, the *Śrī-Cakrasaṃvaratantra* (Chap. 31) says: "Who would revile the skull of the embodiment of the Dharmakāya, arisen from the three sources—conch-shell (*śaṅkha*), mother-of-pearl (*śukti*), or pearl (*muktā*)!" Tsoṅ-kha-pa's commentary (*Sbas don*, p. 63-2,3,4) holds that the skull here refers to the skull of man. The reason the body of man is the best, is that it is the distinguished basis for accomplishing the Dharmakāya liberation and the knowledge of great bliss (*mahāsukhajñāna*). Those three, conch-shell, etc. are used to construct the skull in five sections (representing the five goddesses), as attached to the head-dress.

Shedding further light on the *ḍamaru*, Indrabhūti, in his commentary on the *Śrī-Cakrasaṃvaratantra*, the "*Sambarasamuccaya-nāma-vṛtti*" (Toh. 1413, Derge Tanjur, Rgyud, Tsa, f. 75b-2) writes:

> The words, "Now through himself emerging," mean that the yogin emerges from the realm of the heart, through exhortation of the sound of the *ḍamaru* drum, in the manner of deep sleep as the Dharmakāya of the Clear Light, dream like the Saṃbhogakāya, and waking state as the Nirmāṇakāya.

Therefore, when, as in Lui-pa's precepts, we take *prajñā* as the sound of the *ḍamaru*, it turns out that she, contemplating the yogin—the divine body on the couch—exhorts him to rise.

The Four Mudrā-s

There is a great deal of information about this topic in *Mkhas grub rje's*, and the extensive definitions by Padmavajra cited in the notes to that work, pp. 228-29, show the situation prevalent in the three lower Tantras. Here I wish to present some further material from the Anuttarayoga Tantra that happens to be consistent with the present chapter. The *Śrī-Cakrasaṃvara-tantra* concerns itself with this topic in Chap. 36; and Tsoṅ-kha-pa's

Sbas don commentary (p. 71-1) presents the explanation of the four *mudrā-s* in accordance with Abhayākaragupta's *Āmnāyamañjari*. Here the four *mudrā-s* are twice explained, that is, for the phase of the path in the Stage of Generation and in the Stage of Completion, and finally their fruit is established in terms of the four Buddha bodies.

TABLE 10

THE FOUR MUDRĀ-S

MUDRĀ	STAGE OF GENERATION	STAGE OF COMPLETION	FRUIT
Karmamudrā	Contemplation of an external prajñā only in the form of Kāmadevī (goddess of love).	The external prajñā, because she confers pleasure through the acts of embracing, etc.	Nirmāṇakāya
Dharmamudrā	The HŪṂ and other syllables contemplated in the body.	The inner prajñā, the *avadhūtī* (central channel).	Dharmakāya
Samayamudrā	Emanating and recollecting the *maṇḍala* circle (of deities) accomplished from the seed syllables, etc.	The materialization of diverse forms of the gods	Mahāsukhakāya
Mahāmudrā	Contemplating oneself as the body of the principal deity.	The *bodhicitta* with great bliss, which is the fruit of those *mudrās*.	Sambhogakāya

In that explanation, the Mahāsukhakāya is expanded as the *bodhicitta* of bliss-void.

11

TWILIGHT LANGUAGE AND A TANTRIC SONG

In my paper published in the Louis Renou memorial volume* I began, "Certainly the Vajrayāna is not now as obscure as when Prabodh Chandra Bagchi wrote his still valuable *Studies in the Tantras* (University of Calcutta, 1939). Nevertheless, both the form, the meaning, and illustrations of the expression *saṃdhā-bhāṣa* deserve a fresh approach based on primary sources." In the first section of the paper I concluded "that the correct forms are *saṃdhā-bhāṣā*, *saṃdhi-bhāṣā*, or *saṃdhyā bhāṣā*, and that they all intend '*bhāṣā* in the manner of *saṃdhi* (=*saṃdhā*)'." To continue:—

The Meaning of the Expression

Bagchi, in the same place (p. 27) writes, "Prof. Vidhuśekhar Śāstrī in the *Indian Historical Quarterly* (1928, pp. 287 ff.) has tried to determine the exact meaning of the expression *Sandhābhāṣā*. He has collected a large number of facts which justifies us in rejecting the old interpretation suggested by Mahāmahopādhyāya H. P. Śāstrī as 'the twilight language' (*āloāndhārī bhāsā*). . . . The large number of texts quoted by Prof. Vidhuśekhar Śāstrī has enabled him to interpret it as *ābhiprāyika vacana* or *neyārtha vacana*, i.e. 'intentional speech' . . . (V. S. Śāstrī) 'intended to imply or suggest something different from what is expressed by the

* "Concerning *saṃdhā-bhāṣā* / *saṃdhi-bhāṣā* / *saṃdhyā bhāṣā*," *Mélanges d'indianisme a la mémoire de Louis Renou* (Éditions E. de Boccard, Paris, 1968), 789–796. This original article may be consulted for the full first section indicated in my summary as well as for the Tibetan and Sanskrit passages omitted here.

words.'" This interpretation is general among modern discussions of the Buddhist Tantras; but Edgerton (*Buddhist Hybrid Sanskrit Dictionary*), takes *saṃdhā* as "esoteric meaning" whence *saṃdhā-bhāṣita* "expressed with esoteric meaning".

Candrakīrti's definition of *sandhyā bhāṣa* is extant in the Bihar manuscript of the *Pradīpoddyotana* (Plate I, 2d folio) and I transcribe the passage exactly as it occurs: / *viśiṣṭaruci-sattvānāṃ dharmatattvaprakāśanaṃ* / *viruddhālāpayogena yat tat sandhyāyabhāṣitaṃ* / "Whichever one reveals a truth of nature for sentient beings having superior zeal, and by the method of ambiguous discourse (*viruddhālāpa*)—that one is expressed in the manner of *saṃdhi*". (Here I assume a scribal corruption in the form *sandhyāyabhāṣitaṃ*; it should read *sandhyābhāṣitaṃ* but theoretically could be *sandhāyabhāṣitaṃ*). Unfortunately definition of the negative alternative, *na sandhyābhāṣitaṃ* is missing from the manuscript. It is easily translated from Tibetan: "Whichever one teaches with certainty a truth for the comprehension of sentient beings having dull senses and in a very clear way—that one is not expressed in the manner of *saṃdhi*."

There is an extended discussion of the "six alternatives" in Tsoṅ-kha-pa's commentary on the *Jñāna-vajrasamuccaya*, which is an Explanatory Tantra of the *Guhyasamāja*, as is also the *Saṃdhivyākaraṇa* referred to above. This discussion in Japanese Photo. edition is in Vol. 160, p. 164, ff. A significant remark occurs p. 165-2: "The learned men of Tibet say that the *neya* and the *nīta* are based on alternatives (*koṭi*) of meaning (*artha*); the *saṃdhyā*, on alternatives of word (*śabda*); the *yathāruta* and *na yathāruta*, on alternatives of both word and meaning". According to this remark, Edgerton's "esoteric meaning" for *saṃdhā* is incorrect, since his rendition attributes a given meaning, which is the province of either *neya* and *nīta*. Tsoṅ-kha-pa explains, p. 165-4, that the *saṃdhyā bhāṣā* is intended for candidates with keen senses and zeal for the highest *siddhi* (success) but the words for that goal are stated in ambiguous discourse. Since the chief goal is the "Clear Light" (*prabhāsvara*) and "the pair united" (*yuganaddha*), and *saṃdhā* refers to that goal, mentioned by Candrakīrti as *dharmatattva*—there is no certainty in the goal. Tsoṅ-kha-pa quotes the commentary (Candrakīrti's?) on *Guhyasamāja*, Chap. 1: "If even the Tathāgatas do not know the goal of the *samāja*, how much less do the Bodhisattvas know it!" This indicates that the current rendition of *saṃdhā-bhāṣā* as "intentional language" is incorrect, as is also Snellgrove's translation in that *Hevajratantra* passage, "secret language".

Of course, the words *saṃdhi*, *saṃdhā*, and *saṃdhyā* can all be used for "twilight". While the word *saṃdhyā* is especially used in this meaning, it is invalid to reject it in "*saṃdhā-bhāṣā*" arguing that *saṃdhi* or *saṃdhā* are the forms rather than *saṃdhyā*. There is little doubt from Candrakīrti's and Tsoṅ-kha-pa's remarks that Mahāmahopadhyāya H. P. Śastrī was right in translating the term as "twilight language".—The expression *saṃdhyā bḥāṣā* is rendered literally "language in the manner of twilight".

The term *saṃdhā-bhāṣā* ("twilight language") aptly refers to the ambiguity, contradiction, or paradox of the moment between darkness and light. In ancient India, these were "climactics", as represented in my article "Climactic Times in Indian Mythology and Religion." *History of Religions* 4:2 (Winter, 1965). It is only in recent times that Hindus have ceased to respond to the dawn and dusk (morning and evening twilights). The ancient Hindu well appreciated the paradoxical nature of Ushas, goddess of Dawn, whose ever-youthful appearance heralded another day of life, bringing men that much closer to death. When evening descended a host of spirits emerged: it was the time that the Māra host appeared to the meditating Gautama under the *bodhi*-tree. The twilights symbolized the sensitive points in the temporal flow when spiritual victory was possible. A special vocabulary was created to refer to these critical points and called in the Buddhist Tantras "twilight language". This should have been obvious from the outset of Western research in the Tantras. But the scholars' understanding was blinded by their preference to regard the Tantras as a repulsive literature, depicting degraded cults. Hence they concluded that the *saṃdhā-bhāṣā* was a kind of literary "cover-up" for dissolute practices. Of course, if the terms are understood in the latter sense, they are indeed understandable and positively not ambiguous, so the obvious rendition "twilight language" had to be rejected by early Western investigators of the Tantras.

There was surely a time in India when every learned Buddhist monk could understand the terminology *saṃdhāya . . . bhāṣitaṃ* found in verses Śāriputra is made to say in the *Saddharmapuṇḍarīka*, Chap. III (Edgerton's *Buddhist Hybrid Sanskrit Reader*, p. 55):

> Days and nights I spent, O Lord,
> mostly thinking just that; now, I shall
> ask the Lord whether I have failed or not.
>
> And as I so reflected, O Jinendra,
> the days and nights continually passed on.
> And noticing many other *bodhisattvas* being praised
> by the Preceptor of the world,
>
> And having heard this *buddhadharma*, I thought "Indeed, this is expressed in the manner of twilight; at the tree of enlightenment the Jina reveals the knowledge that is inaccessible to logic, subtle, and immaculate."

Illustrations of Saṃdhyā bhāṣā

The *Saṃdhibhāṣā-ṭikā* is written by Nāgārjuna, presumably the same tantric who authored the *Pañcakrama* of the Guhyasamāja system. In the Japanese Photo. edition, it is in Vol. 56, pp. 67-69. He lists his explanations of the "twilight" expressions in seven groups or rounds. It should be of interest to compare his explanations with those in the *Hevajratantra*, accepting the work of Snellgrove in most cases.

Hevajratantra	*Saṃdhibhāṣā-ṭikā* (1st round)
madhya (wine) *is madana* (intoxication)	is the ambrosia (*amṛta*) of heaven, to be drunk continuously.
māṃsa (flesh) is *bala* (strength)	is wind, is food, to be controlled.
malayaja (sandlewood) is *milana* (meeting)	the coming together of external states, sense organs, and perceptions (based thereon)—which is so to be contemplated; also the consubstantial joy (*sahajānanda*).
kheṭa (phlegm) is *gati* (going)	the passage of the wind; also, when one has the four *yogas*, he contemplates without holding it, i.e. lets it go.
śava (corpse) is *śrāya* (resort)	is the *yantra* of body, having infinite light (*amitābha*), and one should resort to that group.
asthyābharaṇa (bone ornament) is *niraṃśuka* (naked)	One should be convinced, "these very bones of mine are my ornaments."
preṅkhana (wandering) is *āgati* (coming)	is inhalation; and one should stop it from its violent acts.
kṛpīta (wood) is *ḍamaruka* (drum)	the undefeated sound; also, by controlling the *prāṇa* and *āyāma*, one beats it (the drum) and makes it even.
dundura (emission) is *abhavya* (non-potential)	is *vikalpa* (mental emission) and should not be elsewhere.
Kāliñjara (N. of a mountain) is *bhavya* (potential)	has *avikalpa* nature; also, while the wind is being inhaled there is no recitation.

padmabhājana (lotus vessel) is *kapāla* (skull)	is the four wheels (*cakra* [of the body] [one of which] is either the wheel at the head or the wheel at the navel; or it is the *kakkola* of the *karmamudrā*. . . . the four wheels are the *padmabhājana* . . .
tṛptikara (satisfying) is *bhakṣya* (food)	is the meditation to be eaten by the yogins.
mālatīndhana (jasmine wood) is *vyañjana* (herbs)	that scrutiny scraping the element is to be eaten.
catuḥsama (a potion of four ingredients) is *gūtha* (dung)	is Vairocana, hence is present through anointment of the body.
kasturikā (musk) is *mūtra* (urine)	is Akṣobhya, ditto.
sihlaka (frankincense) is *svayaṃbhu* (blood)	is Ratnasambhava, ditto.
karpūra (camphor) is *śukra* (semen)	is Amitābha, hence is present through anointment.
sālija (rice product) is *mahāmāṃsa* (human-flesh)	is Amoghasiddhi, hence is present the same way.
kunduru (resin) is the union of the two	is the union of sense organ and perception.
vola (gum myrrh) is *vajra* (thunderbolt)	is *vijñāna* (perception), or the external *vajra*.
kakkola (perfume) is lotus	is the secret lotus, or else the external secret *prajña*; by means of these, one acts in *yoga*.

That ends the first round of seven in Nāgārjuna's commentary and accounts for each item in the *Hevajratantra* list except for "*ḍiṇḍima* (small drum) is *asparśa* (untouchable)," omitted in Nāgārjuna's list, or omitted in manuscript copying. In the subsequent rounds Nāgārjuna treats the very same expressions with different comments, and *ḍiṇḍima* does appear in the third round.

Nāgārjuna's commentary suggests that the *Hevajratantra* has given the basic list of "twilight language". These are expressions for ambiguous *yoga* states, while "non-twilight language" refers to states of *yoga* that are not ambiguous. Both these alternatives should be distinguished from the other sets, *neyārtha, nītārtha*; *yathāruta, na-yathāruta*; and while a similarly extended discussion of the latter terms would take us afield from our main topic, some brief explanations, following Candrakīrti's *Pradīpoddyotana*, are in order. In tantric usage, *neyārtha* and *nītārtha* are alternative explanations for a given term, usually referring to a momentous or precious element of the body. For example, in the case of the expression "great blood", the *neyārtha* is ordinary human blood, the *nītārtha* is menstrual blood. The set *yathāruta* and *na-yathāruta* refer to the terms employed for given objective entities. When the term employed is standard, it is *yathāruta*. When the term is coined, apparently to enable the insiders of the cult to preserve secrecy even if the text falls into unworthy hands, it is *na-yathāruta*. In contrast, "twilight expression" does not refer to a definite given entity, and it is not a meaning (*artha*).

The Diamond Song

Immediately after the section on "twilight language" in the *Hevajratantra*, there is a tantric song in the type of language called Apabhraṃśa (sometimes identified with old Bengali), which is generally used for the mystic songs called Dohā. The Siddhas (tantric masters), such as Saraha and Kāṇha, have left a remarkable group of these songs, the collections of which are variously called *Dohā-koṣa*, *Caryāgīti-koṣa*, and *Caryāpadas*.

Of course, the various commentators on the *Hevajratantra* have each had to explain to some extent this tantric song, and Snellgrove, who edited and translated the *Hevajratantra* naturally used some of these materials for his version. Fortunately, the great tantric master Nāropā has reproduced the text of the song along with his explanations in his commentary on particular expressions of the *Hevajratantra* in the *Vajrapada-sāra-saṃgraha-pañjikā*, extant in Tibetan (PTT, Vol. 54, pp. 1 to 41), where his commentary on this portion occurs, p. 32-2, ff. This is a song of the engagement (*caryā*), and our foregoing section on tantric ritual shows that there are three kinds of *caryā*, more fully "*caryā-vrata*" (ritual observance of the engagement), symbolized by the *khaṭvāṅga*, etc. There is a considerable amount of information on this topic, pertaining to the "Stage of Completion" (*sampanna-krama*), in my forthcoming *Yoga of the Guhyasamājatantra*. As to the song itself, Nāropā's commentary provides an understanding of it that is hardly possible from reading Snellgrove's translation and notes. This is not to deny the value of the *Hevajra* context and Snellgrove's labors; in fact, his information that the *bodhicitta* (mind of enlightenment) is here in the head—where inferentially is Kollagiri—is a helpful addition, as are his notes generally. But that is also the meaning of "diamond-skull', as explained in my section on "ritual observances". One should observe that the song takes for granted the basic list of "twilight language" expressions. Notice also that the song serves as an expansion of the celebrated *mantra* OṂ MAṆI PADME HŪṂ, Oṃ, the gem in the lotus, Hūṃ. Snellgrove's text is adopted with a few modifications.

* * *

KOLLAIRE ṬṬHIA VOLA MUMMUṆIRE KAKKOLA
Vola (the diamond mind of enlightenment) dwells at Kollagiri (seizing bliss); Kakkola (the lotus) at Mummuṇi (the navel disk).
GHAṆA KIPIṬṬA HO VĀJJAI KARUṆE KIAINA ROLĀ
The diamond exhortation is uninterrupted. The diamond of all thoughts of enlightenment holds the intrinsic nature of the three worlds in melted form. The two organs congregate with friction.
TIHAṂ BALU KHUJJAI GHAḌE MAANĀ PIJJAI
Having united the vola and the kakkola, one should eat meat (=the five personality aggregates which are the nature of the five Tathāgatas, and which thereby lose self-existence, melting into the self-existence of the mind of enlightenment possessing the five knowledges, mirror-like, etc.); and having united those two, one should drink wine (i.e. ambrosia).
HALE KĀLIÑJARA PAṆIAI DUNDURU TAHIṂ VARJJIAI
Hail! The fortunate mind of enlightenment (Kāliñjara) should enter the antlers of the lotus. The unfortunate sense bases of eye, etc. (dunduru) should be avoided.
CAUSAMA KACCHURI SIHLA KAPPURA LĀIAI
He (the Lord) takes the fourfold potion (Vairocana), musk (Akṣobhya), frankincense (Ratnasambhava), and camphor (Amitābha) (because he is inseparable from them).
MĀLAINDHANA ŚĀLIJA TAHIṂ BHARU KHĀIAI
One should especially eat vegetables (mālaindhana) (=five aggregates) along with rice (śālija) (=the knowledge of the Tathāgata).
PREṂKHAṆA KHEṬA KARANTE ŚUDDHA NA MUṆIAI
Coming and going, one cannot comprehend the pure and the impure.
NIRAMŚUA AṂGHA CAḌĀBIAI TAHIṂ JA ŚARĀBA PAṆI
He pays no attention to the bone ornaments on his naked body (=the diamond of the mind of enlightenment, the nature of the five knowledges). The corpse (śarāba), i.e. the mind of enlightenment which is selfless, is situated at the tip of the nostril of the lotus.
MALAYAJA KUNDURU BAṬṬAI ḌIṆḌIMA TIHAṂ NA VAJJAAI
At the meeting (malayaja) of the diamond mind of enlightenment with the prajñā, there is union of the two organs. One does not touch the small

drum (ḍiṇḍima) (in any event, because it is "untouchable"—*Hevajra*'s "Ḍombī"; and ultimately, because everything has become unified).

* * *

Concerning the "coming and going" of that song, the *Saṃdhibhāṣā-ṭīkā*, as previously cited, has the explanation that it is inhalation (and exhalation). Such remarks point to the yoga practice of the "pot" (*kumbhaka*), which is treated in my subsequent section on Nine Orifices.

III

SPECIAL STUDIES

Both the one who is ignorant of the yoga of wind
And the one who knowing it does not practice it,
Are *saṃsāra's* worm,
Afflicted by all sorts of suffering.

Saṃvarodaya-tantra

12

THE NINE ORIFICES OF THE BODY

It is a well-known feature of Buddhist canonical literature that one of the chief early disciples of the Buddha, Maudgalyāyana (Pāli: Moggallāna) was credited with special magical powers (*iddhi* in Pāli, *ṛddhi* in Sanskrit) with which he often visited various other realms of the world than ours, such as the hells and heavens. *The Mahāvastu* (Vol. I) soon takes up an account of this disciple's visits to the eight great hells and other realms. These stories do not explain how he managed to accomplish the feat. It is only much later—as far as I know—in the Buddhist Tantra literature, that one can find an explanation of how a yogin can contact the subdivisions of the three worlds, according to the traditional Buddhist classification, that is to say, the realm of desire, realm of form, and formless realm. The realm of desire is said to include the six passion deity families, as well as men, animals, hungry ghosts (*preta*), and hell beings. The realm of form is called, for meditative purposes, the four dhyānas, and has further divisions. The formless realm also has its divisions of the bases of infinite space, infinite perception, and so on. These divisions are known from early Buddhist literature and are discussed acutely in the branch of literature called Abhidharma. According to the tantric literature as will be cited below, the way a yogin like Maudgalyāyana can gain entrance to those worlds is analogous to how a person might go there after death by reason of destiny. In short, the yogin concentrates in a special way on various body orifices that are deemed to be correlated with the beings of various realms, while the person who dies with his stream of consciousness passing through one orifice or another, goes to the appropriate realm of the intermediate state (*antarābhava*). The orifices themselves are made salient in ancient Indian literature. The rest may well have been strictly oral for centuries; but there are suggestions of the rather curious theory herein unfolded in the wide-spread injunction to think of a deity in the hour of death so as to go to the realm of that deity. Such a teaching is found in the Hindu classic, the *Bhagavadgītā*, and the famous American Sanskritist Franklin Edgerton once collected many materials on this subject for an article in *Annals of the Bhandarkar Institute* (1927).

The nine orifices are referred to in the *Śvetāśvatara Upaniṣad*, which has this well-known verse (III, 18):

> The embodied swan moves to and fro, in the city of
> nine gates and outside, the controller of the whole
> world, of the stationary and the moving.

This tradition of nine is maintained in the *Bhagavadgītā* (V, 13), where the mention of nine gates is commented upon as the two eyes, the two ears, the two nostrils, the mouth, and the two organs (male) of excretion and generation. However, the *Kaṭha Upaniṣad* (II, 2, 1) refers to the city of eleven gates, and the commentary adds the navel and the opening at the top of the skull to the list of nine.

In a native Tibetan work of astrology, the *Dge ldan rtsis* . . . (Sec. Ja) by Mi-pham tshaṅs-sras dgyes-pa'i-rdo-rje, there is a correspondence of orifices and planets which is of interest to mention here simply because the nine differ by inclusion of the navel and omission of the mouth, which at least shows a lack of unanimity on what the nine orifices are when spelled out:

two eyes	—	Sun (right eye) and Moon (left eye)
two ears	—	Mars and Mercury
two nostrils	—	Jupiter and Venus
navel	—	Saturn
urethra, anus	—	Rāhu and Ketu (head and tail of the dragon)

When we pass to the Buddhist Tantras, we find in the Buddhajñānapāda wing of the *Guhyasamājatantra* tradition, in the work of the founder Buddhaśrījñānapāda, his *Dvikrama-tattvabhāvanā-nāma-mukhāgama* (PTT, Vol. 65, p. 8-5 to p. 9-1), this list of nine orifices in explanation of transfer or transit (*saṃkrānti*) by a yogin or through death by way of one or other orifice to an associated external realm: 1. forehead, 2. navel, 3. crown of head, 4. eyes, 5. ears, 6. nostrils, 7. mouth, 8. urethra, and 9. anus. This list includes the eleven of the *Kaṭha Upaniṣad*, reduced in number by counting the eyes, ears, and nostrils, as one each; and then adds the forehead center. The work continues in this manner:

One should understand the forehead as the prognostic of the realm of form (*rūpadhātu*) and birth (there). The navel is the prognostic place of the gods of the realm of desire (*kāmadhātu*) and certainty of birth among them. The crown of head is the prognostic source of the formless realms (arūpyas) and birth therein. If there is transfer of knowledge in the two nostrils, the person is born in the abode of the yakṣas. The two ears are the certain passage to the abode of vidyādharas. The two eyes are the prognostics for birth as a king of men. In the case of transit of knowledge through the mouth, one may understand it as the prognostic of pretas (hungry ghosts). One should take the urethra as the prognostic for prognostics of animals. One should understand the going of knowledge through the anus as the prognostic of the hell beings. Having thus understood the individual aspects for transfer of knowledge, one should do (mantra) placement in the seven upper orifices by means of the syllable of five soundings (*nādita*). One should place SŪṂ in the urethra and KṢUṂ in the anus. Having thus stopped up the seven orifices, when one searches the place through the following sequence with one's own mind, he will certainly go to that very realm.

Before going further, let me summarize that passage:

Orifice	*Prognostic of what place or beings*
forehead	realm of form
navel	passion gods in realm of desire
crown of head	formless realms
nostrils	abode of yakṣas
ears	abode of vidyādharas
eyes	a king of men
mouth	hungry ghosts
urethra	animals
anus	hell beings

Vitapāda's commentary on that work, the *Mukhāgamavṛtti* (PTT., Vol. 65, p. 65-1,2) explains: The six orifices, forehead, etc. are good. The three orifices, urethra, etc. are bad. Therefore, one should understand the prognostic for birth therein by the coming and going of one's own knowledge (*jñāna*) in either the good or bad orifices. (His subsequent comments show that "knowledge" means the yogin's knowledge; hence that the yogin can establish a correlation with a certain realm by centering his knowledge or know-how, in a certain orifice). In the case of the yakṣas, this means birth as Vaiśravaṇa and other yakṣas on Mt. Meru. Vidyādhara (holding the occult science) means becoming a yogin who has *vidyā* and the eight *siddhis* of "eye ointment", etc. The five soundings are HŪṂ, because this is the sounding of the five Buddhas. In the case of SUṂ for the urethra, this is white. KṢUṂ for the anus is yellow. Having stopped up (or plugged) the orifices, one goes to one's own realm of mind (*cittadhātu*). One "searches" by the eight methods of recitation, etc.

In agreement with a portion of these statements, Bhavabhadra states in the *Śrīvajraḍāka-nāma-mahātantrarājavivṛti* (Derge Tanjur, Rgyud, Tsha, 137a-2):

> The text, "From the navel, the gods of the desire realm," means that any perceptual stream (*vijñāna*) that goes forth from the navel orifice, is born among the gods of the desire realm. The text, "With the form of the *bindu*, heaven," means that any such one that goes forth from the orifice in the middle of the forehead is born among the gods of the realm of form. The text, "proceeding upwards," means going forth through the golden door (the Brahmarandhra).

This author, Bhavabhadra, has written a commentary on the Tantra *Ārya-Catuṣpīṭha*, which is also an authority for what are known as the "gates to the intermediate state (*antarābhava*)."

Notice, in short, that the three bad destinies of hungry ghosts, animals and hell beings, are correlated respectively with the mouth, urethra, and anus, which accordingly are the three "bad" orifices; while the two good destinies of men and gods are correlated with the other six, which are the "good" orifices. But notice also that the mouth is included among the seven upper orifices in terms of methods for blocking the orifices. Apparently, the praxis of the yogin to stop or inhibit the passage through the orifices is accomplished by imagining a mantra syllable at each of the orifices.

I also noticed what at first seemed to be a peculiar theory in the *Saṃpuṭa-tantra* about nine orifices, and did not feel confident about including it without consulting the commentaries. Upon referring to the three commentaries in the Tanjur (using the Narthang edition), I did not readily find the place in Indrabhūti's commentary (Toh. 1197, the *Smṛtisaṃdar-śanāloka*), so turned to the explanations—which I quickly located—in Abhayākaragupta's *Āmnāyamañjari* (Toh. 1198) and in Śūravajra's *Ratnamālā* (Toh, 1199). Abhayākaragupta (Narthang Tanjur, Rgyud, Dza, 19b-1, ff.) states that the practice belongs to the Stage of Completion. The use of seed-syllables or of evoked goddesses here seems also to mean plugging or gaining control over respective orifices by imagining seed syllables and goddesses in those places. This tradition employs different syllables than the preceding system, which suggests that the important thing is not the particular syllables employed but rather a consistency or sticking to the same system throughout all the practice. In the *Saṃpuṭa-tantra* tradition, the seed-syllables belong to the eight forms of the goddess Jñānaḍākinī (the Wisdom Dākinī), for which reason the nostrils and ears are counted as one orifice in the correspondence system of eight terms, and are counted as two in order to get the total of nine orifices. Combining the data from the two commentaries, and helped by the *maṇḍala* No. 4 in the *Niṣpannayogāvalī* (edited by B. Bhattacharyya), the following summary is possible (unfortunately, some of the seed syllables are still questionable):

TABLE 11

ORIFICES, AND EMANATIONS OF THE WISDOM ḌĀKINĪ[1]

ORIFICE	SEED-SYLLABLE (*bīja*)	GODDESS
crown of head	of fire—KṢUṂ	Vajraḍākinī
eyes	of earth—HŪṂ	Ghoraḍākinī
nostrils and ears	of wind—YUṂ	Caṇḍālī
tongue	of ambrosial water—SUṂ	Vetālī
neck	purifying delusion—STUṂ	Siṃhinī, the Lion-faced
arms (armpits?)	purifying pain—HAṂ	Vyāghrī, the Tiger-faced
heart	purifying vibration—SMAṂ	Jambukī, the Jackal-faced
navel	of lord of animals (paśupati)—DHUṂ	Ulūkī, the Owl-faced

There are some intriguing features to that table. For one thing, the four elements which the seed-syllables represent are stated in the standard astrological order, because Aries is a fire sign, Taurus earth, Gemini wind, and Cancer water; with the same order repeated for the rest of the zodiacal signs. Reference to the materials in my essay "Female Energy and Symbolism in the Buddhist Tantras" will show that ordinarily the four elements are made to correspond to the element *cakras* navel, throat (=neck), heart, and privities. The present table does not have an entry for "privities" and so there is an implication that "arms" is the replacement for "legs". Because the four elements are not here in the usual location, they must be understood in an extraordinary way, as explicitly stated for water, i.e. "ambrosial water". Again, when the *Saṃpuṭa-tantra* (PTT.

1. Of those eight forms of the Wisdom Ḍākinī, the most famous is the Lion-faced one, and frequently the Wisdom Ḍākinī is identified with this particular form in evocation (*sādhana*) rites. According to the *Niṣpannayogāvalī*, her "heart" mantra is OṂ HRĪḤ SVĀHĀ. This text also singles out the *ḍākinī* Vetālī for a mantra, OṂ VETĀLĪ HŪṂ SVĀHĀ, that is said to be "all-active" (*sarvakarmika*). The *ḍākinī* Vajraḍākinī and presumably the following three are to be identified with the *ḍākinīs* pictured in the collection called *Rin 'bhyuṅ* (see Lokesh Chandra, *A New Tibeto-Mongol Pantheon*, Part 9, Rin 'byuṅ 141). The general type of the *ḍākinī* posture is depicted by the drawing "Buddhaḍākinī" in my chapter on Tantric Ritual.

Vol. 2, p. 246-3-3,4) assigned the "delusion" syllable to the neck, one might have theorized that it would start the usual Buddhist set of "three poisons" (lust, hatred, delusion). When it continued with an assignment of the word "*kleśa*" (the Sanskrit original for the Tibetan *ñon moṅs*) the translation "defilement" (which is the usual Buddhist rendition) would be inapplicable; evidently *kleśa* has here its more literal meaning of "pain". This conclusion is further certified by the next assignment—that of "swinging" (*cala*; Tibetan *gYo ba*) to the heart orifice, so here I adopted the more generalized rendition of "vibration". The "lord of animals" syllable, associated with the navel, recalls the Hindu legend of Viṣṇu, that when he was sleeping upon the cosmic waters a lotus grew from his navel, and on the lotus there arose the creator Brahmā. Dowson, *A Classical Dictionary of Hindu Mythology and Religion*, p. 360, also mentions the epic legend that the destroyer Śiva (or Rudra) sprang from Viṣṇu's forehead. In the present table, this could only concern the crown of the head, associated with fire.

Specialists in Buddhism would probably wish the present writer to comment on the relation with the preceding of the well-known characteristics attributed to the Buddha—and consistently represented iconographically—of the *uṣṇīṣa* at the crown of the head and the *ūrṇā-kośa* in the middle of the forehead. For one thing, the *uṣṇīṣa* protuberance is frequently personified as a goddess, especially Uṣṇīṣavijayā (She, the Victory of the *uṣṇīṣa*); and through the secondary mark, "head umbrella-shaped" (*chattrākārottamāṅga*), Uṣṇīṣa-Sitātapatrā (the White Umbrella Lady of the *uṣṇīṣa*) (see the Frontispiece, George Roerich, *Tibetan Paintings*). In my article on the characteristics in the *Leibenthal Festschrift* (Santiniketan, 1957), I cited Rgyal-tshab-rje's subcommentary on Haribhadra's *Sphuṭārthā*, "His face is adorned with a 'treasure of hair' (*ūrṇā-kośa*). It is between the eye-brows in the location of the 'drop' (tilaka) . . . It has the appearance of a silver lump the size of a seed of emblic myrobalan."

The foregoing materials also associate the crown of head with a goddess, in this case Vajraḍākinī (see the picture in Evans-Wentz, *Tibetan Yoga and Secret Doctrines*), and that place is associated with the formless realms. The forehead—the location of the *ūrṇā-kośa*—is associated with the realm of form. Abhayākaragupta in his *Āmnāya-mañjari* (PTT. Vol. 55, p. 245-2) states: "Likewise, the Tathāgata sees with the *uṣṇīṣa*; likewise, he sees with the *ūrṇā-kośa*; so also with each characteristic." This suggests those characteristics, especially those two main ones mentioned above, to have the functions already described as correlated to external realms by reason of a yogin's knowledge; in short, that they function as "eyes" toward those realms. That same author, Abhayākaragupta, in his *Muni-matālaṃkāra* (PTT. Vol. 101, p. 259-2) cites some scripture, without giving the title: "The enlightenment of the śrāvakas is in his face; the enlightenment of the pratyekabuddhas is in the mid-forehead; the Incomparable, Right-completed Enlightenment is in the *uṣṇīṣa*." The word śrāvaka means "hearer"—hence in the iconography, the long ears of the Buddha; and since the Śrāvaka must practice meditation—also the half-closed eyes and nose for "counting the breaths" and like exercises; such must be the meaning of his enlightenment shown in the face.

Another aspect to the orifices is how they function as entrances; and this topic in the form of entrances to the future parents by a being of the Intermediate State (*antarābhava*), which are the three possible entrances by a *gandharva*, is discussed in my essay "The Five-fold Ritual Symbolism of Passion," later in the present work. There is also the entrance of divinity in the form of the "knowledge being" (*jñāna-sattva*).

A further technique, even more mysterious, is the reputed art of reanimating a fresh corpse. This is called in Tibetan *groṅ 'jug* (entering the city). It is one of the most esoteric teachings of the Marpa-Milarepa lineage, descended from Nāro-pā.

Turning to the topic of passage through the orifices, no matter how much a single researcher collects materials on these topics from various books in the Tibetan canon or elsewhere, he cannot bring together the strands to form a unified picture such as one finds in one of the great Tibetan manuals that have integrated the canonical descriptions with the oral instructions of the *gurus*. Tsoṅ-kha-pa's commentary on the Six Laws of Nāro-pā (the "Yid-ches gsum ldan") is precisely such an integrated work, and fortunately my readings in other works of this author over the years enables me to read his text at this point also, namely his passage explaining the transit (*'pho ba*; Sanskrit, *saṃkrānti*). Just prior to the passage I shall translate (PTT, Vol. 161, p. 10-4-8 to p. 11-2-2)[2] he mentions that a person who is sick, suffering, or old, should not engage in this practice; and after the passage he alludes to some deviate views about it.

* * *

> There are two basic counsels about transit. Of these two, [first] the *purification* (*sbyaṅ ba*) is as follows: The *Vajraḍāka* (i.e. the *Śrīvajraḍāka-nāma-mahātantra*) states: "The alternations (*mtha'*) of the place are to be purified. After their purification one should perform transit of the state of being. Otherwise it would be purposeless." That refers to the alternations, pleasure and pain, of the place, i.e. the body. That is, Bhavabhadra explains that if one transits without having first purified by cultivation of the heat—the *ṅal ba* (yogin's rest) is purposeless. Thus, the prior cultivation of the heat is a distinguished basis for accomplishing the transit. Furthermore,

2. Compare with the rendition of this part of Tsoṅ-kha-pa's text in C. A. Muses, editor, *Esoteric Teachings of the Tibetan Tantra* (Falcon's Wing Press, 1961), pp. 252-55.

the *Vajraḍāka* states: "Upon binding the orifices by means of the 'pot' (*kumbhaka*), the orifice holes become pure." Both the *Catuṣpīṭha* and the *Saṃpuṭa* are consistent with that, because they express the necessity to cultivate the *kumbhaka* of wind with a capacity to compress within the wind that enters the sense organs and other orifices. Now, *kumbhaka* was previously explained to have the three degrees of highest, middling, and lowest; and those many persons who assert that it suffices to have the lowest degree, speak as though they do not understand the meaning of the Tantra. Hence, when one stops the transit of *vijñāna* through the eight orifices, not including the golden gate at the crown of the head, it transits through the golden gate at the crown of the head. And that transit of attainment is the chief basis for the *vidyādhara* (wisdom holder) who practices *mantras*. Such statements of the Tantras are essential; and even though there are (various) visualizations of *vijñāna* (the perceptual stream) departing from the body, it is necessary to complete the characteristic of visualizing it as explained according to those Tantras. There is both brief and expanded subject matter of visualization of the transit according to the fourth *Gdams ṅag śeg dril* and of the transit according to the counsels of the Rṅog school. Here I shall speak briefly using as sources the precepts of the *gurus* who put uppermost the precepts of this school (i.e. that of Rṅog). In this case one may wonder which deity should be contemplated as the basis for purifying the transit. The *gurus* maintain that one should contemplate whatever is one's own tutelary deity. Since the *Saṃpuṭa* and the *Catuṣpīṭha* have stated a method of contemplating the deity especially in this case, that is a reason—if one would succeed—to do it accordingly. As it would take too much space, I shall not go into that matter here.

[Second:] *The "brightness" of oneself as deity and uniting of the winds*. Starting with the realm of contemplating the secret place, or the navel, one imagines a red A at the navel, a black HŪṂ at the heart, a white KṢA at the *brahmarandhra* (the golden gate). Then one vehemently draws up the lower wind, and imagines it pushed to the A-syllable of the navel; and having arrived, pushed to the HŪṂ; and having arrived at the HŪṂ, pushed to the KṢA-syllable. And he imagines it re-descending to the place of the HŪṂ in the heart and to the place of the A in the navel. Now some persons claim that one should contemplate it dissolving in the A and HŪṂ, but doing it the former way (i.e. simply arriving, not dissolving) is better. One should work at it that way as long as the prognostics (*rtags*) have not arisen. The prognostics are an itching sensation, throbbing, etc. at the crown of the head. Then the application to the rite is as follows. One should put the main part of the body in sitting up position, and clasp his two knees with his two hands. One should start with taking refuge and generating the mind of enlightenment. Then from the realm of the "bright" where oneself is the tutelary deity, one visualizes in the space straight up in front of one's head, at a distance from 1-1/2 to six feet at a comfortable level, the *guru* and tutelary deity in inseparable manner. Deeply moved with devotion and faith, one fervently beseeches him. Then, having brightly posited the A of the navel, the HŪṂ of the heart, and the KṢA of the crown of the head; vehemently drawing the lower wind one contemplates that the A itself is within the central vein and while (moving) upward pronounces a group deer-like sound (*khyu ru ru byuṅ nas*) and dissolves in the HŪṂ of the heart; and one recites A-HIK for as many times as necessary. Furthermore, the HŪṂ itself pronounces (while moving) upward, and one recites A-HIK up to twenty times and contemplates that it (the HŪṂ) is pronouncing in the throat. Then one should contemplate the bright KṢA-syllable at the *brahmarandhra*, and that it is pure white, as though the *brahmarandhra* constituted the starry realm; and reciting A-HIK vehemently five times one sees that HŪṂ proceed hastily through the *brahmarandhra* and dissolve in the heart of the inseparable *guru* and tutelary deity. Controlling consciousness that way, he settles it in the realm without discursive thought. That shows in abbreviated form the transit according to the sayings of the *gurus* and the *Catuṣpīṭha*.

* * *

Tsoṅ-kha-pa's passage establishes rather clearly that some of the varying descriptions—for example, some of those already brought forward in this essay—have to do with two separate phases of the praxis. That is to say, the description may concern the phase of purifying the orifices, and this is associated with containing the winds in *kumbhaka*, which is referred to as the "heat",[3] or the description may concern the phase of transit of the perceptual principle (*vijñāna*) through the gate at the crown of the head.

Tsoṅ-kha-pa referred to three degrees of *kumbhaka*, which he treated earlier in the same work. He may well intend the three mentioned in the *Saṃbarodaya-tantra* (PTT, Vol. 2, p. 205-2-7,8): "The lowest amounts to thirty-six; the doubling of that is the medium; the tripling is the great." The text seems to mean the number of times one performs the *kumbhaka*, thereby lengthening it. The "great" kind thus amounts to 108 times.

3. Mircea Eliade, *Yoga; Immortality and Freedom* (New York, 1958), pp. 246-47, shows the relation between the *kumbhaka* yoga, the heat, and the rise of the *kuṇḍalinī* power (to use the Hindu terminology).

That brings us to the question of what is meant by the "pot" (*kumbhaka*). This involves establishing the usual condition of issuance through the orifices and the contrasting abnormal or yoga condition of that issuance.

Concerning what is usually issuing forth from the various orifices, Buddhaguhya states in the *Dhyānottara-ṭīkā* (Derge Tanjur, Rgyud, Thu, 14b-2,3): "*Prāṇa* is the vital air characterized as issuing from, and entering, the eyes, ears, nostrils, mouth, navel, male and female sex organs, the unclean orifice, the pores of head hair and body hair." Buddhaguhya is also the author of the *Tantrārthāvatāra* (Toh, 2501), upon which Padmavajra's *Tantrārthāvatāravyākhyāna* (Toh. 2502) comments (Derge Tanjur, Rgyud, Ḥi, 169b-5, ff.):

> Moreover, we must explain the orifices through which the vital airs of breath issue and how they do so, how to inhibit them, the time of inhibiting them, and illustrations. Among them, through what orifices do they issue? They issue without and within all the (nine) orifices of the body, i.e. mouth, nose, (sex) organs, (etc.) and all the pores. How do they issue? When thought (*citta*) is excited or relaxed, they issue a long ways; and when it is bound fast, they issue a short ways, and subsequently, whatever be their gathering place, enter in a direction straight above the navel. As to how one inhibits them, one gathers them within the "member" (*aṅga*, i.e. body) of tortoise (i.e. holds the breath in, *kumbhaka*), one gathers them within the "member"—seizing in the manner of the tongue's drinking water; and without breathing in, with the small tongue (the uvula) like a calm(?) stream and without straining. Relaxed as though breathing in sleep, one holds and equalizes them. As to the extent of time for restraint: At the outset, when fastening oneself in *samādhi*, one restrains gradually, and does it as long as the *samādhi* and muttering are not finished. The fault of not doing it that way is as follows: the wind whirls, whereupon the heart gets diseased, the body heavy; one is panic-stricken and one's thoughts become tumultuous (i.e. they race). Moreover, if one holds the breath fiercely, a fault occurs in this case: it is taught that upon reverting from that, the *samādhi* is spoiled. When, like an animal, the vital air is not controlled, it is said, "There is no accomplishment of *samādhi*." . . .

One striking fact emerges: In Buddhaguhya's tradition the process of *kumbhaka*, or holding the breath in the body as though it were a pot, does not involve *mantra* placement as we have noticed in some of the foregoing materials. Another thing: *kumbhaka* here is not the ordinary method of taking a deep breath and trying to hold one's breath, but a gradual method of drawing in the breath by imperceptible degrees, with the tongue lapping it up as though it were water drops.[4] Also, implicit to all these discussions is the theory of winds in the body operating in their individual cycles with individual colors and the like, with which the yogin must be familiar.

Tsoṅ-kha-pa's Anuttarayoga treatment involves the central vein of the body, hence the system of three chief veins (in the position of the spine) and implies the system of *cakras*. In this connection, there is the terminology "upper orifice" and "lower orifice". Thus the tantric writer Bhavyakīrti mentions in his *Prakāśikā* commentary on the *Pradīpoddyotana* (PTT, Vol. 61, p. 1-5): "'Arises via the upper orifice' means, via the path of the two nostrils of the face," but the upper orifice is also treated as the neck. The "lower orifice" is at the position of the Hindu Mūlādhāra, the perineum triangle, which in the male is at the root of the penis, the juncture of the three veins. The *Sṅags rim chen mo* (437a-1) cites the *Saṃpuṭa-tantra*:

> The left *nāḍī* (i.e. *lalanā*) starting at the neck
> is She with the Saṃbhogakāya (i.e. the "sister"),
> who rests at the navel, and drips intoxication into
> the lower orifice.
>
> The *nāḍī* (*rasanā*) going upward from the navel is (She)
> likewise dripping in the upper orifice, who rests at the
> neck and is known to drip blood (i.e. She with the
> Nirmāṇakāya, the "daughter").
> The intoxication is explained as moon.
> The blood is said to be sun.

That is rather obscure, but is presented here to contact mystically with some of the foregoing materials and also to add an aspect to the orifices that ties in with subsequent tantric studies in this work.

There are some unanswered questions. For example, what is meant by "the yogin's knowledge" for concentrating in a certain orifice? Here, a curious personal experience may be mentioned. In the year 1946, soon upon returning to Los Angeles after I was discharged from the U.S. Army, an older friend of mine took me along with another friend who had just been discharged from the U.S. Navy to a free public demonstration by an occult-type organization that expected thereby to encourage some of the attendees to enroll for private instruction for which charges were made.

4. See Alain Danielou, *Yoga; The Method of Re-Integration* (London, 1949), especially pp. 58-60, for some Hindu theories of *kumbhaka* practice. This author calls it the "chalice". I use the word "pot" because the idea is to succeed by degrees of attainment to draw in the breath so slowly that the body can be considered a pot that is being filled by water drop by drop, where the "water" is of course the droplets of air.

In this good-sized hall which could easily seat a hundred or more persons, the guide instructed us to meditate on our heart while breathing in unison with the measured sound-beat made by a metronomic instrument (which presumably was set to agree with heart-beat time). In a very short while I experienced a strange shift of consciousness: I was in some mysterious place with a fierce rushing back and forth, and became terrified. Promptly I quit the measured breathing and bounced back to normal consciousness, sitting through the rest of the session without cooperating. At the conclusion of the demonstration I asked the other two friends what they had experienced. Each replied that he had followed the directions but nothing in particular happened. This example shows that by concentrating on a spot of the body in a certain way, controlling the breathing and so on, it is possible to "go there" and it is possible to go to an orifice, and perhaps "through the orifice". Obviously, the person doing this must be prepared for it with a knowledge of how to do it and what to expect, the standard of success and what to do if he is successful. That is the "yogin's knowledge".

Another observation is that the texts cited make no distinction between the male and the female as regards the orifices, although it might be thought that the female has one more than the male. Surely these works are not written with solely the male in mind, and so there must be an explanation for this uniformity. I found a passage that may solve this problem. It is in the *Maṇi-mālā* commentary on the tantric Nāgārjuna's *Pañcakrama* (PTT. Vol. 62, p. 154-2): "Some (sentient beings) fall fearfully into a woman's watery orifice organ and every day are born and die." Hence the text counts the birth channel as the urinary orifice, comparable to the male's urinary passage also used for issuance of semen. Accordingly, the woman's orifices are also nine.

However, in a Hindu tantric text, as discussed by Shashibhuṣan Dasgupta, *Obscure Religious Cults*, pp. 239-40, the terminology "tenth door" is applied to the mouth of the Śaṅkhinī, a curved duct in the head that starts from the moon in the thousand-petalled lotus at the crown of the head. Through this Śaṅkhinī vein passes the ambrosia (*amṛta*) (cf. our previous section on the "Five Ambrosias") which is discharged out of the lower end, called the "tenth door."

Finally, there is no conclusion on whether Maudgalyāyana depended on such orifices for his legendary exploits of visiting the heavens and hells. The fact that the nine gates are mentioned in such ancient works as the *Śvetāśvatara Upaniṣad*, which has a section on *yoga*, suggests that the yogic experimentation with these orifices is of great antiquity. But there is no proof that around the time of Gautama Buddha there was any definite correlation of these orifices with external realms in the well-developed manner of the tantric texts cited herein.

13

TANTRIC TEACHINGS ABOUT THE INNER ZODIAC

Ever since persons have come to believe in personal horoscopy, they have wondered why it should work. Doubtless the same question occurred in India because belief in astrology has been deep seated there for many centuries. The Buddhist Tantras of the Mother Tantra variety in the Anuttarayoga tradition have some theories of an inner zodiac, in all likelihood worked out in conjunction with northern Śaivism, probably Kashmir Śaivism. While these theories, insofar as I have come across them, are not sufficiently elaborated to show a determined rationalization to find an inner equivalent for the outer disposition of planets, etc. of a horoscope, it should be of interest to present these theories as I have found them.

In any case, the theories do not speak of any zodiacal circle hidden in the body, with the sun and other planets circling accordingly. Besides, while traditional astrology classifies the signs into four groups by the elements of fire, earth, wind, water, and has seven planetary rulers, the tantric theories of an inner zodiac use the fifth element "space" (*ākāśa*) which is sometimes translated "ether" and add Rāhu and Ketu (head and tail of the dragon that causes eclipses, i.e. the ascending and descending nodes) as planetary rulers. Furthermore, some theories might be inconsistent; or, perhaps it is better to say that it has not been an easy task to reconcile them. However, all the theories take for granted the tantric theory of three central veins (*nāḍī*) in the position of the spinal column (perhaps to be located in a so-called "subtle body" rather than in the physical body) referred to as right, left, and middle, with their names differing in the Hindu and Buddhist Tantras:

	Right	*Middle*	*Left*
Hindu	Piṅgalā	Suṣumnā	Iḍā
Buddhist	Rasanā	Avadhūtī	Lalanā

Besides, these systems range centers or critical vortexes at various places along this triadic central system. These are usually called "cakras" or "lotuses" (*padma*). The Hindu explanations are well known through the voluminous writings of Arthur Avalon. The Buddhist tantric explanation is available, for example, in S. B. Dasgupta, *An Introduction to Tantric Buddhism* (pp. 160-174). One can also refer to Mircea Eliade, *Yoga: Immortality and Freedom* (pp. 236-45) on these same matters; and there is considerable information in my forthcoming *Yoga of the Guhyasamājatantra.*

The Heart Cakra

The tantric theory of the heart *cakra* can be elucidated by an interesting treatment of the inner zodiac found in Padmavajra's work in the field of Mother Tantra entitled, *Śrī-Ḍākārṇavamahāyoginītantrarāja-vāhikaṭīkā-nāma* (Tōhoku No. 1419; Derge Tanjur, Rgyud, Dza, 286b-3, ff.). On folio 289a, he assigns the zodiacal signs to petals of the heart *cakra.* Here I replace the Sanskrit and Tibetan terms with the standard Western equivalents. A minor correction was made of an obvious text corruption (interchange of Cancer and Aquarius positions), since Aquarius belongs to the Wind Corner; and also because the famous work of Indian astrology, Varāhamihira's *Bṛhat-jātaka*, states in Chap. I, verse 11, that Aries, Taurus, Gemini, and Cancer with their triangular signs (their element families) represent the four quarters commencing from the East. On the facing page is Padmavajra's solution (Observe the clockwise orientation!):

In accordance with Varāhamihira's hint (perhaps he had in mind the inner zodiac), one can take the cardinal direction sign along with the intermediate direction pair to make an individual set (the zodiacal triangle), e.g. Aries in the East along with Leo and Sagittarius (S.E.) as the fire set. This reduction to four quarters would have to be accepted as the more primitive formulation representing the early development of the heart-*cakra.* This is only partially consistent with the explanation in Tsoṅ-kha-pa's *Sṅags rim chen mo* (Peking blockprint, 434b-5, ff.), where five goddesses are shown to be the personifications of four directional veins of the heart as the essence of the elements and of sense objects, with a fifth goddess in the middle (the central vein, the Avadhūtī). The group of four goddesses (their Sanskrit names in the *Hevajratantra*, I, i, 18) are, in the given order, Traivṛttā, Kāminī, Gehā, and Caṇḍikā; while Māradārikā is in the middle. The passages which Tsoṅ-kha-pa cites do not state completely—nor does

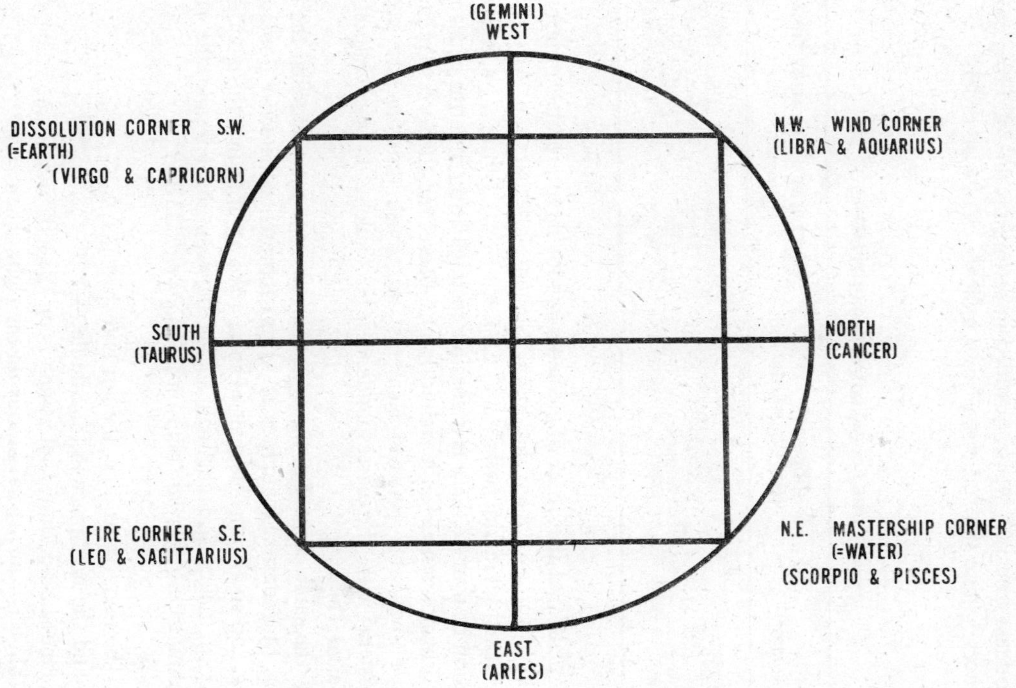

An Astrological Representation of the Heart Cakra

his own commentary—the respective correspondences to the four elements. One passage does say, "earth, etc." But they do state the relation to sense objects; and since the identification with elements of the four main goddesses in the *Guhyasamājatantra* (Chap. XVII) also starts with earth (the goddess Locanā), we are justified in setting up the following correspondences, where the successive rows indicate clockwise order:

TABLE 12

THE FOUR GODDESSES OF THE HEART

GODDESS (*Hevajratantra*)	GODDESS (*Guhyasamājatantra*)	ELEMENT	SENSE DOMAIN
Traivṛttā	Locanā	Earth	Form (rūpa)
Kāminī	Māmakī	Water	Sound (śabda)
Gehā	Pāṇḍarā	Fire	Odor (gandha)
Caṇḍikā	Tārā	Wind	Taste (rasa)

It is plain that the order of elements cannot be interpreted in terms of external astrology, where discordant elements alternate, i.e. Aries (fire), Taurus (earth), Gemini (wind), and Cancer (water). But in my subsequent discussion of transits there is a possible reconciliation in terms of element wind correspondences to the zodiacal signs. Moreover, the correspondences in the above table between elements and sense domains are mostly inconsistent with the correspondences in Table 2 in the chapter on Analogical Thinking.

Now the same context in the *Sṅags rim chen mo* mentions that the fifth goddess Māradārikā (daughter of Māra) represents the sense domain of *dharma*, and so also the element of space (*ākāśa*), and since this goddess is located in the central channel, she is between the left and the right. According to the *Saṃpuṭa* citation in *Sṅags rim*, 437a-6:

> The two "veins", i.e. the left and the right,
> and the birthplace in the middle:—
> One should know that semen is on the left and
> blood (=menstrual blood) on the right. Their
> mutual admixture is the mixture Dharmadhātu.

(This language is related to the Indian theory that the embryo is created from the man's semen and the woman's menstrual blood).

The usage of the term "*dharmadhātu*" in this context is equivalent to another word of this literature, "*dharmodaya*" (source of dharmas). In this tantric context, *dharmadhātu* means a birthplace, but in non-tantric Buddhism, it appears to be described by negatives.[1]

Besides, the *Sṅags rim* (435a-2, ff.) differentiates the middle into three veins (right, left, and middle), to make a total of eight heart veins in this system (five goddesses, and three central veins). Tsoṅ-kha-pa, in the same place, shows that in the conditions of womb the three main veins (called the "three queens") are the basis of all. However, the set of five, representing the five elements as well as the five sense objects, begin operations during the phases of the womb and continue them during life, while the three main veins apparently begin a new function upon the start of a living birth, so they would perhaps be responsible for the astrological true time of birth.

Transits

It should be mentioned that Padmavajra (in the previously cited *Vāhikaṭikā-nāma*, 286b-3, ff.), besides the solution already mentioned, also makes the division of the twelve signs into "right" and "left", associating them with "rise of breath". Here the six right (odd-numbered) ones begin with Aquarius, and the six left (even-numbered) ones begin with Capricorn. In Tsoṅ-kha-pa's collected works (Lhasa ed., Vol. Da, "*Dus 'khor Naṅ le*" —perhaps should read *Khams le*, 22b-1, ff.) we read: "In the same way that outside the sun transits the twelve signs, so inside, the wind transmigrates with twelve transits the lotus veins." In the same work, 36b-4, ff. he mentions that the wind transits the six right petals and the six left petals.

Presumably it is with reference to the Hindu system, interpreted as the solar year, that in Kashmirian Śaivism, Abhinavagupta's *Tantrāloka* (Vol. IV, p. 97) states:

> Arising from the heart in Capricorn, etc., which
> are the six and six intervals, the sun would enact the
> six months of Māgha, etc., and the progress to the North.

Compare with the popular Śaiva classic *Śivasvarodaya*, verses 73-74:

> There are twelve transits (*saṃkrama*) within the day
> and night. Taurus, Cancer, Virgo, Scorpio, Capricorn,
> Pisces, are in the "moon" (i.e. the breath rises in
> the left *nāḍī*). During Aries, Gemini, Leo, Libra,
> Sagittarius, and Aquarius, one ascertains good or bad in the
> rise (of breath) in the right (*nāḍī*).

1. See D. Seyfort Ruegg, "Le *Dharmadhātustava* de Nāgārjuna," *Études tibétaines* (Paris, 1971), especially, p. 466.

Notice the difference in statement: In the case of six and six intervals of the sun (as in Tsoṅ-kha-pa's *Kālacakra* passage and Abhinavagupta's verse), the signs are divided into two groups, with consecutive signs in each group (say from Capricorn to Gemini; and from Cancer to Sagittarius). But in the other arrangement (Padmavajra's "right" and "left", and the *Śivasvarodaya*) the signs are divided into two groups on the basis of their being "right" or "left" oriented.

The allotment of twelve signs to a single *cakra* might be intended by the Hindu Anāhata-cakra, which is a red lotus of twelve petals, situated just below the eight-petalled heart-lotus that faces upward. In the standard representation of this *cakra* (see, for example, Arthur Avalon, *The Serpent Power*), the twelve petals of this heart lotus are arranged in a circle. It is difficult to imagine—if this be the intention—how the same twelve-petalled lotus could function both for two sets of six signs transitted consecutively and for two sets of six signs functioning according to "left" and "right". But the four passages might all be consistent by virtue of the following materials.

A native Tibetan work on astrology in my possession[2] divides the inner signs into two groups by northern and southern progress, in consecutive transits, with the northern group termed "auspicious" and the southern group "inauspicious". This has to do with "element winds", and is undoubtedly the esoteric side of Indian lore that goes with, whether or not it explains, the celebrated passage of the *Bhagavadgītā* (VIII, 24-25):

> Fire, light, day, the increasing phases (of the Moon),
> the six months of the northern path (of the Sun),
> then going forth the men who know the Absolute go to
> the Absolute.
>
> Smoke, night, so also the decreasing phases (of the Moon),
> the six months of the southern progress (of the Sun),
> in them the yogin obtains the lunar light and returns
> (to earth).

That Tibetan work is in fact a commentary on an astrological treatise in the Tanjur, i.e. translated from the Sanskrit, that is probably in the tradition of Kashmir Śaivism. I consulted this Tanjur work (Toh. 4322, the *Yuddhajaya-nāma-tantrarāja-svarodaya-nāma*) in the Narthang edition to get some idea of how much was being added by the Tibetan commentator in the work which I now cite (6a-6b); and can say at the outset that the

2. The Dpal gYul las rnam par rgyal ba'i rgyud don rab tu gsal ba'i ṅag gi bkod pa kun gzigs dbyaṅs 'char chen po śel gyi me loṅ źes bya ba.

native work is most helpful and shows deep study of the subject from different angles, including the *Kālacakratantra* tradition.

> The two paths of sun and moon are explained as the southern and northern progress.
>
> According to the sequence at the time of the left movement, the ākāśa wind descends by the middle (channel). That is the sign of Aries.
>
> The passage of the fire wind from above, is the sign of Taurus; the water wind from below, is Pisces.
>
> The earth wind moving through the post (*ka ba*) (both nostrils), is Aquarius.
>
> The wind moving through the corner (i.e. the side=left nostril) is Gemini.
>
> The five moving on the left, upon being fixed, are the Capricorn sign.
>
> The ones moving on the left are auspicious. Space works for Umā (the consort of Śiva). Fire operates for accomplishment; water achieves ambrosia; earth works for success; wind works for perfection.
>
> Their planetary rulers in sequence are: Rāhu (head of the dragon), Venus, Moon, Mercury, Jupiter. The Tantra did not tell the planetary ruler of *ākāśa* . . .
>
> Then, at the time of moving on the right—the space (*ākāśa*), fire, water, earth, and wind (winds), moving by reliance on the middle, above, below, post, and corner, are respectively, Libra, Scorpio, Virgo, Leo, Sagittarius; and all five upon being fixed are Cancer.
>
> The movements on the right are inauspicious. Space works for terror. Fire operates for death. Water achieves ignorance. Earth yields conflagration. Wind operates for suffering.
>
> Their rulers are, in sequence, Mercury—for space; and Mars, Saturn, Sun, and Ketu (tail of the dragon).

There are a few difficulties or drawbacks with the above native Tibetan verse solution of the Tanjur work (which is also in verse). First of all, since it admits that the Tanjur work did not assign a ruler to "space"—the fifth element that was added to the classical four—fire, air, water, earth—it quite reasonably assigned Rāhu to "space" in the left series, since Rāhu is the planet added to the traditional ones of exoteric astrology. Furthermore, in the Buddhist Tantras the middle channel corresponds to Rāhu, so this agrees. But then, on passing to the right series, the author assigns Mercury to the "space" element wind; and here we should expect, and I must correct it to, Ketu; since Rāhu and Ketu are the head and tail of the dragon, and so Ketu also corresponds to the middle channel and "space". Besides, to take the planetary rulers "in sequence" by the *given order*, which in fact repeats the statement of the Tanjur text—just does not work out. Since the addition of a new planet was necessary to govern the added element, it must be presumed that the basic Tanjur text was intending those other named planets by way of the elements which they govern. Now it is well known in exoteric astrology that the Sun rules a fire sign (Leo) and the Moon a water sign (Cancer) and that the other five classical planets each rule two signs of different elements. Taking this into consideration, it is plain that there is only one solution for both the left series and the right series that allots rulers to the inner zodiacal signs on the basis of elements which those planets govern by reason of a sign in the usual system. This is my summary of the exoteric zodiacal signs contributing the element to the system of inner zodiac:

Left Series	*Right Series*
Venus' earth = Taurus (No. 2)	Saturn's earth = Capricorn (No. 10)
Moon's water = Cancer (No. 4)	Mars' water = Scorpio (No. 8)
Jupiter's fire = Sagittarius (No. 9)	Sun's fire = Leo (No. 5)
Mercury's wind = Gemini (No. 3)	Mercury's wind = Gemini (No. 3)

In summary, this would use up from among the twelve traditional signs, Nos. 2,3,4,5; 8,9,10. This suggests a theory of this tradition that the classical seven planets have each their chief rulership in a given sign from among those seven of the summary. In fact, this agrees with the Western astrologers who now assign newly discovered planets to other signs, i.e. Uranus to Aquarius (No. 11), Neptune to Pisces (No. 12). Then, in consideration that Indian astrology adds the head and tail of the dragon as planets, but preserves the planetary rulership according to the Greek system, it would follow that only by these features of esoteric astrology could we continue this assignment to the remaining signs, with Rāhu going with Aries (No. 1) and Ketu with Libra (No. 7). Then only Virgo (No. 6) is left over. But enough of speculation!

Then, no matter how the planets are assigned to the signs of the inner zodiac, the chief elements of those astrological verses can be tabulated as follows:

TABLE 13

Element Winds and Transit of Inner Zodiacal Signs for Fruits

ELEMENT WIND	NORTHERN PROGRESS (left movement)	SOUTHERN PROGRESS (right movement)
(All five fixed=Solstice)	Capricorn	Cancer
Earth	Aquarius (success)	Leo (conflagration)
Water	Pisces (ambrosia)	Virgo (ignorance)
(Middle space=Equinox)	Aries (Umā, the goddess)	Libra (terror)
Fire	Taurus (accomplishment)	Scorpio (death)
Wind	Gemini (perfection)	Sagittarius (suffering)

By "all five fixed" is meant of course, all five element winds, which are fixed at the time of "solstice". Presumably on these grounds Capricorn works for a blend of the other five fruits (success, etc.), while Cancer works for a blend of the other five (conflagration, etc.).

Furthermore, the meaning of left and right is clarified by the *Sṅags rim* (437b-4) with citation of the *Samvarodaya*:

> Having entered by the left,
> the right is its path of leaving.

Tsoṅ-kha-pa quotes the commentary: "Because the *vijñāna* which 'has entered.' departs by way of the right and takes a sensory domain, thereupon, riding on the wind, enters by way of the *lalanā* (left vein)." This shows the meaning of left as auspicious because there is entrance of breath, and right as inauspicious because there is exit (expiration) of breath, as will be mentioned later by citation of Tsoṅ-kha-pa's *Sbas don*. Naturally, *vijñāna* will enter or leave in some zodiacal sign or other, in the preceding sense of the inner zodiac.

The Tanjur work, the *Yuddhajaya* . . . (Narthang, Vol. Go, 45b-5) states that the northern and southern progression is a movement in five *maṇḍalas*. The context shows that the five mean the four element *maṇḍalas*, plus the element "space" counted as a "*maṇḍala*" even though it represents the "central channel" (Suṣumnā or Avadhūtī). Materials in my subsequent essay "Female Energy and Symbolism in the Buddhist Tantras" show that the earth vortex (*maṇḍala*) is in the privities; the water vortex in the heart; the fire vortex in the throat; and the wind vortex at the navel. The extended treatment in the *Sṅags rim chen mo* shows that the initial activity of the elements in the heart "vein" spreads out to the other centers. It appears that there is a "left" and a "right" for each *cakra* of the fourfold group of elements, while "space" (*ākāśa*) in the central channel has instead a downward and upward movement.

The Sixteen Digits of the Moon

Returning to the directional orientation with Aries in the East, this is consistent with Padmavajra's exposition (again the *Vāhikaṭika-nāma*, 309a-1 to 309b-4) about the sixteen digits (*kalā*) of the Moon as yoga experiences. His remarkable passage is now translated in full:

> Accordingly, he increases his own ocean of knowledge, as do the digits of the moon, because he cultivates the praxis. The cultivation of praxis will be explained here. By contemplating the letters of glorious He-ru-ka in the cakras belonging to the moon, i.e. the mind (*manas*), they arise as the sixteen joys. Their establishment by digits of the Moon will be here set forth as they are. The text says, "first of all," and so on; the transits (*'pho ba*) number sixteen; first of all arises joy. As to "knowledge" (*jñāna*), it belongs to the yogins who apprehend the *Aries transit*; this is to be known; when one is truly aware of it, there is knowledge. By entering the second one, the *Taurus transit*, he has a body which proceeds in the sky, that is, he rightly proceeds with a body made of wind. By the third one, *Gemini*, he arises in the form of that mind, like the shaft of an arrow, as though incorporeal. In the fourth, *Cancer* "image of the target," he penetrates the mind, that is, he opens up all entities. In the fifth one, the *Leo transit*, he with the nature of the five peaks, that is, with the nature of *cittavajra* pleasure, penetrates the five aspects, to wit, recollects the five strands of desire, form, sound, etc. In the sixth, *Virgo*, called "origination of the six elements," with the mind of enlightenment he arouses the joy of the Great Person. In the seventh, *Libra*, he is said to have the form of the ocean; this means those in the middle of the ocean, who have the ocean of knowledge, as previously explained in the chapter on characteristics of (the goddess) Lāmā. In the eighth one, the *Scorpio transit*, named "Lotus," he has the form of joy of those very eight spaces of the heart lotus, and arises together with the moving and non-moving (worlds). In the ninth, *Sagittarius*, called "elixir (*rasāyana*)," because he refrains from laboring in the nine veins (probably the nine orifices), all the elements of the body get the elixir along with ecstasy. In the tenth one, *Capricorn*, called "desire of the Capricorn Moon," he has the nature of all the ten (intra-uterine) states, superior to them with the conatal body (*sahaja-deha*). In the eleventh, *Aquarius*, called "tranquil form," he has the distinguished joy of arising in the form of liberation, transcending the fourth (i.e. as Śiva). Having entered the twelfth, the *Pisces transit*, called "form of the wheel," his mind has the form

> of the Viṣṇu lineage, which means the seed of enlightenment from the enduring form of all joys. In the thirteenth, he is in the food of the rising Sun (the solar vein). In the fourteenth, he is in the food of the rising Moon (the lunar vein). In the fifteenth, by praxis of Rāhu (the eclipse planet) all the quarters melt into the Avadhūtī. The sixteenth is called "bindu-nāma" for which reason it is said to be "free from time," and so it is called "introspection," and so on. One should understand all those characteristics.

It is not possible here to fully explain all that is meant by that passage, which seems to intend all possible yoga experience in terms of these sixteen transits. However, a few indications of the meaning can be drawn out in a way that shows how the author builds up the theory by allowing to each zodiacal sign its numerical value.

The first transit suggests the "sameness knowledge" of Buddhism, because the transit into Aries is the Equinox. The second transit, in Taurus, involving a body made of wind, in fact requires both "wind" and "mind-only"—as will be shown in my *Yoga of the Guhyasamājatantra*—hence two things. The third transit, in Gemini, shows the hypostasis of the divine into the human by the three elements—the divine mind, its ray (like an arrow shaft), and the yogin brought into conformity.

The fourth transit, in Cancer, covers what in non-tantric Buddhism is called the four states of penetration (*nirvedha-bhāgīya*), which are "warmth," "summits," "forbearances," and "supreme mundane natures." This is an ancient category going back to early Buddhism. In Tantra (see *Mkhas grub rje's*, pp. 28-31), there is the *mantra*, CITTAPRATIVEDHAṂ KAROMI ("I perform mind penetration.").

In further explanation of the fifth, sixth and seventh yoga transits (in Leo, Virgo, and Libra), we may cite Indrabhūti (Derge Tanjur, Rgyud, Ca, 134b-7, ff.), commenting on the *Saṃpuṭatilaka*, 1st kalpa, 2d chap.:

> Now there are the thirty-seven natures ancillary to enlightenment. Here, the natures of enlightenment are the five personality aggregates (*skandha*), the five elements (*dhātu*), the five sense organs (*indriya*), the five sense objects (*viṣaya*); likewise the five organs of action (*karmendriya*) and their five actions (*karma*). In this case, the sixth is the aggregate of knowledge (*jñāna*), the element of knowledge, the organ of knowledge, the knowledge object; likewise the knowledge organ of action and its action. The thirty-seventh one pervades those (thirty-six); this means the knowledge realm as *dharmin* (possessor of the natures). Accordingly there are thirty-seven natures—those natures as ancillary, explained as members (*aṅga*); those members are of three kinds and of many kinds.

That passage shows that in this system of Mother Tantra, to the fivefold groupings, a sixth element of knowledge is added (Padmavajra: "with the mind of enlightenment"), and finally a seventh, the possessor knowledge realm (Padmavajra: "who have the ocean of knowledge").

The eighth transit, in Scorpio, requires an explanation that is accessible in the Father Tantra tradition of the *Guhyasamājatantra*, and available in Sanskrit in the tantric Nāgārjuna's *Pañcakrama* (Abhisambodhi-krama, verses 25-27), as translated with further explanations in my *Yoga of the Guhyasamājatantra* (forthcoming):

> The disciple who has secured the precepts then applies himself unremittingly to *yoga* of two sorts: by the sequence of "contraction" as well as by "expansion".
> Drawing (the winds) from head down, and from feet up, into the heart, the yogin enters *bhūtakoṭi* (the true limit): this is called "contraction".
> Having first rendered the stationary and the moving life into the Clear Light, he then renders that into himself: this is the stage of "expansion".

Since this is the mystical experience of "death" it agrees with Scorpio's fruit (death) as shown in the Table.

There is no point in dilating upon the ninth transit, because I have devoted a whole essay to the theory of nine orifices. Skipping to the eleventh and twelfth transits, the same Tibetan astrological work cited in my Nine Orifices essay (the *Dge ldan rtsis*), presents in the section called *Rtsis 'grel* the series of numerical correspondences; the elevenfold are the names of forms of Śiva, and the twelvefold the names or forms of Viṣṇu. In the case of Śiva, he is said to have transcended the fourth, meaning that he is beyond the four states of consciousness, waking, dreaming, dreamless sleep, and the fourth. In the case of Viṣṇu, it is his wheel with twelve spokes that is emphasized, because Pisces as the last month completes the twelve spokes.

The thirteenth, fourteenth, and fifteenth transits are respectively in the right channel (of the Sun), the left channel (of the Moon), and the middle channel (of Rāhu). There is this verse in the *Śivasvarodaya* (v. 100):

> During the flow of the Moon, poison is destroyed; during that of the Sun, there is control over the powerful. During Suṣumnā, liberation is obtained. One *deva* stands in three forms.

Reverting to the tenth transit, in Capricorn, it is useful to compare this with the sixteenth, "free from time." The yogin in the tenth transit is proceeding through the intra-uterine states (the ten lunar months) but in extranormal fashion with the co-natal body (*sahaja-deha*); however, this yogin is not "free from time." Rather, his time is called "inconceivable," as is clear from Tsoṅ-kha-pa's commentary (the *Sbas don*) on the *Cakrasaṃvara-tantra* (PTT. Vol. 157, p. 15-1), where he cites a commentary to the effect that there are three kinds of time—good time, bad time, and inconceivable time. When the breath comes in the nostril, that is good time; when it goes out the nostril, that is bad time. When those two are unified (either as holding or withholding the breath), that is the inconceivable time. (Since the embryo does not inhale and exhale, the ten states have inconceivable time). Besides, good time ("coming") is the time of the three joys (*ānanda*, *paramānanda*, and *viramānanda*; cf. *Hevajra-tantra*). Bad time ("going," i.e. emission) is when the mystic drop (*bindu*) is emitted. Avoiding the two times (good and bad), one has the inconceivable time, with the co-natal joy (*sahajānanda*). All that is an explanation of certain initial words of the Tantra, to wit, *ekasmin samaye* ("on a certain occasion"), now to be understood as the inconceivable time. Tsoṅ-kha-pa gives a further explanation, which in our present context means avoiding the thirteenth and fourteenth transits (the channels of the Sun and Moon), and using only the central channel, hence the fifteenth transit (Rāhu's channel), with cultivation of the mystic heat; hence also the inconceivable time. Thus, only the sixteenth transit can be characterized as "free from time."

I close with the Tibetan expression of good wishes,

> / Oṃ bde legs su gyur cig /
> Oṃ. May there be happiness and good fortune!

14

FEMALE ENERGY AND SYMBOLISM IN THE BUDDHIST TANTRAS

Introductory Considerations

The worship of divinity under sexual emblems is very ancient ir 'ndia, presumably as old as the Mohenjo-daro civilization, which is usually held to be pre-Aryan. The Buddhist Tantras have numerous references to male and female dieties; and the latest class of that literature, called the Anuttara-yoga-tantra is pervaded with sexual symbolism. This is true both of the traditional scripture (*āgama*) and the later commentaries. We should know that these works and the associated practices were evolved among peoples who took the spirit world for granted, believed that human beings could develop supernormal powers granted by deities, and assumed that in certain esoteric groups the appropriate procedures for such ends has been handed down from time immemorial.

Since the Tantric literature, Hindu as well as Buddhist, is often abruptly dismissed as unworthy of serious attention, we should consider its possible worthiness as a topic of study.[1] There are two preeminent fields in which

1. In each case I shall give (preceded by "Toh." for "Tohoku University") the catalogue numbers as found in the two catalogues published by Tohoku University: the one on the translated canon (Hakuju Ui, Menetada Suzuki, Yenshô Kanakura, and Tôkan Tada [eds.], *A Complete Catalogue of the Tibetan Buddhist Canons* [Sendai, Japan, 1934]) having numbers from 1 to 4569; the one on native Tibetan works (Yenshô Kanakura, Ryujo Yamada, Tôkan Tada, and Hakuyu Hadano [eds., *A Catalogue of the Tohoku University Collection of Tibetan Works on Buddhism* [Sendai, Japan, 1953]) having numbers from 5001 to 7083. Unless otherwise mentioned, all folio number references to the former refer to the Derge edition; and references to the latter refer to Lhasa editions.

intelligence may be focused: the open or public, and the closed or private. This division involves no necessary value judgment. For example, the form of man and the form of woman are two superficial commonplace aspects that according to the Tantras conceal two mysteries of heightened consciousness. These two forms are not less worthy than their two mysteries and to the extent that a society realizes this worthiness, indeed sacredness, that society is civilized, removed from the brutes. In the same sense, the Buddhist Tantric literature is neither more nor less worthy of study than non-Tantric Buddhism. It should be recognized that Tantrism falls in the domain of the esoteric.

The esoteric is also of two kinds: natural and intentional. In illustration of the first kind, a man may have a great talent which to his distress is unnoticed by the world: it remains hidden, perhaps through what the Chinese philosophers called *Li*, the principle of things. Also the Buddhists claimed that the twelvefold formula of Dependent Origination is profound and therefore not easily understood: it eludes solution by its intrinsic difficulty. In illustration of the second kind, there are those numerous government documents stamped "confidential" and "secret." And there are the secrets of the Tantras. In his great commentary on the fundamental Yoga-tantra called *Tattvasaṃgraha*, Ānandagarbha writes: "'This secret' means dwelling in [or upon] the disk of the full moon; . . . that is secret because it is not proper to be taught to all persons."[2] In addition, some Tantric materials are naturally esoteric.

The present article consults the small number of Buddhist Tantric texts that have been edited in the original Sanskrit. Among the commentaries, originally in Sanskrit, some important passages have been taken from the Tantric authors Saraha, Indrabhūti, Candrakīrti, and Nāgārjuna, as found in the Tibetan translations of their chief works. Moreover, the native Tibetan works are often of superlative value, especially because they integrate the former written traditions (translated canon) with the oral precepts of the line of teachers (*guru*). Among these, I employ the works of Tsoṅ-kha-pa (1357-1419 A.D.), founder of the Gelugpa school, and of his disciple Mkhas grub rje.[3]

The Prajñā

Modern scholars have been somewhat confused on this subject by wholesale use of the term *śakti* ("power") in reference to Buddhist goddesses. This term, general in Hindu Tantras, seldom occurs in the Buddhist Tantras, which actually employ the following generic words for the goddesses or females: *prajñā* ("insight"), *yoginī* ("female *yogin*"), *vidyā* ("occult science" or "know-how"—"wisdom" in its historic mean-

2. Toh. 2510, the *Tattvālokakarī*, Tanjur, Li, 228a-3.
3. See n. 1.

ing including all academic learning), *devī* ("goddess" or "queen"), *mātṛ* ("mother"), *mātṛkā* ("mother" or "letters"), *ḍākinī* ("fairy"), *dūtī* ("female messenger"), *śurī* ("heroine"), and *mudrā* ("seal" or "gesture").

The word *prajñā* is especially important because in both Tantric Buddhism and in non-Tantric Mahāyāna Buddhism it contrasts with the term *upāya* ("means," "approach"). A certain Tantric tradition holds that after the fall from Paradise the phase involving division into male and female constituted a separation of "means" from "insight": henceforth men were a source of means and women of insight.[4] But the means are various and insight is one: so in non-Tantric Buddhism Prajñāpāramitā ("the Perfection of Insight") is called "mother of the disciples (*śrāvaka*), self-enlightened ones (*pratyekabuddha*), and Buddhas," who have diverse fathers or approaches (*upāya*).[5] This is a sort of mystical polyandry that curiously parallels the well-known Jungian thesis about the man's shadowy anima (his unconscious female) and the woman's shadowy animus (her unconscious males), because Jung states: "A passionate exclusiveness therefore attaches to the man's anima, and an indefinite variety to the woman's animus."[6]

According to Buddhist metaphysical treatises, an element of *prajñā* occurs as one of the momentary ingredients in every idea we have.[7] But as long as human beings (whether male or female) are enveloped in lust, hatred, and delusion, this *prajñā* element can be called "impure."[8] Such is the historically foisted condition of *prajñā*. But some persons become monks, restrict their worldly activities, withdraw their grasp upon the world. Becoming in a sense more like women, they alter the environment of *prajñā* and specialize it out, so to say, ultimately gaining its perfection (*prajñāpāramitā*). What is at issue here is not the obvious, but the subtle—those potentialities of human beings that in the manner of seeds hide their natures until nurtured.

These natures—whether of men or women—are fostered like plants raised in hothouses when the person withdraws from society. In Jung's

4. A Tibetan account of this view is presented in my "Buddhist Genesis and the Tantric Tradition," in *Oriens Extremus*, Vol. 9, No. 1 (1962), one of the articles as a memorial of the late F. D. Lessing, reprinted herein.

5. See my chapter "Perfection of Insight: Buddhist Tantra Within Mahāyāna Buddhism."

6. *The Basic Writings of C. G. Jung*, ed. Violet S. de Laszlo (New York: Modern Library, 1959), p. 180 (from: *The Relations between the Ego and the Unconscious*).

7. Technically, *prajñā* in this context is one of the ten *mahābhūmikas;* cf. Louis de la Vallée Poussin, *L'Abhidharmakośa de Vasubandhu, Premier et Deuxième Chapitres* (Paris and Louvain, 1923), pp. 153-56.

8. Hence the entry *ḥchal baḥi śes rab*, glossed as *śes rab ñon moṅs can*, "corrupted insight," in the native Tibetan dictionary by Dge-bśes-chos-kyi-grags-pa (Chinese ed., 1957), p. 283.

language: "Isolation by a secret [? alchemy] results as a rule in an animation of the psychic atmosphere as compensation for loss of contact with other people. It causes an activation of the unconscious, and this produces something similar to the illusions and hallucinations that beset lonely wanderers in the desert, seafarers, and saints."[9] The extreme limit of such isolation is illustrated by the experience of Gautama Buddha beneath the Tree of Enlightenment. In traditional accounts of Māra's onslaught, we find the future Buddha beset by hosts of demonic beings and tempted by the three daughters of Māra.[10] Somewhat as a tormented liver motivates a snake dream, the besieged foundation of human nature objectifies a malicious panorama. Gautama is *unmoved* by this vivid display: he knows it is all an illusion. Then the Earth Goddess, Mother of the World, *moves*: shaking [literally: earth-quaking] in six different ways she disperses the hosts of Māra.

This celebrated encounter suggests a number of considerations:

1. Indian symbolism does not necessarily assign to male the active, to female the passive role.

2. The proposition "All mental objects (*dharmāḥ*) are an illusion" has one meaning for the ascetic, another for the metaphysician. For the *yogin* who has developed the intense visualizing power called eidetic imagery—natural to many children in certain years prior to puberty—the proposition is the rule of mental health. For the metaphysician, unliberated from discursive thinking, the proposition is the basis of an impractical world denial.

3. It is one matter to recognize something as an illusion, another matter to get rid of that thing. This contrast is the topic of a simile in the *Kāśyapa-parivarta-sūtra*, as quoted in Tsoṅ-kha-pa's *Lam rim chen mo*: "Kāśyapa, thus for example, when two trees are rubbed together by the wind, and fire arises [from the friction], [that fire] having arisen burns up the two trees. In the same way, Kāśyapa, by reason of the most pure discrimination [analyzing mental objects], the power of noble insight (*ārya-prajñā*) is born; and [that Fire] having been born, burns up that most pure discrimination."[11] Elsewhere in the *Lam rim chen mo*, this "discrimination" (*pratyavekṣaṇa*) is treated as a form of *prajñā*. It is *prajñā* on the intellectual level; the *prajñā* born from it is of a mystical nature and eliminates both discrimination and its object, which by "rubbing together" during intense concentration, have given birth to that *prajñā*. Hence Dayal is not quite

9. C. G. Jung, *Psychology and Alchemy*, trans. R. F. C. Hull ("Bollingen Series," Vol. XX [New York, 1953]), p. 49.

10. For some data on the three daughters, including their names, cf. E. H. Johnston, *The Buddhacarita, or Acts of the Buddha* (Calcutta, 1936), Part II, p. 188.

11. Toh. 5392, Tashilunpo ed., 476a-4. The Sanskrit is not extant in Stael Holstein's edition of the *Kāśyapa-Parivarta Sūtra*.

right in saying: "The two great Mahāyānist schools of Buddhist philosophy do not agree in their interpretation of *prajñā*. The *Vijñāna-vādins* (*Yogācāras*) explain *prajñā* in a positive manner. . . . The Mādhyamika philosophers have interpreted *prajñā* in a negative sense."[12] The latter *prajñā* is the one sometimes called the "eye of *prajñā*," which sees nothing (the void),[13] but as it springs from the intellectual *prajñā* ("knowing things as they really are") stressed by the Vijñāna-vādins there is no essential disagreement in the alternate explanations of the term. The real difference is in the emphasis, and there is no denying the importance of this factor. However, the feature of ascending levels of *prajñā* is a doctrine of Buddhism prior to the rise of Mahāyāna: there is the insight consisting of hearing or learning (*śruta*), the insight consisting of pondering (*cintā*), and the insight consisting of cultivation [in one's own life] (*bhāvanā*). In the third case, one no longer hears or ponders: one is that thing formerly heard and pondered and hence no longer "sees" it.

4. In the myth, the illusion-destroying power is a Woman, the Earth Goddess; in non-mythic language this power is *ārya-prajñā*. In the myth, this Woman is external to the future Buddha; in non-mythic language it is a power produced in himself. In the myth, the future Buddha is seated beneath the Tree of Enlightenment touching Earth with his right hand, and Earth (the World Mother) shakes. In the Order (*saṃgha*) founded by Gautama Buddha the monk is not allowed to touch a woman. Besides, the Indian Buddhist reformer Atīśa (eleventh cent.) writes that in final meaning (*nītārtha*) one does not need to go to the Bodhi tree considered as an external tree in order to achieve Enlightenment (*bodhi*).[14]

5. But why is the Earth Goddess represented mythically as an Other when in more prosaic terms "she" is an interior power? The question confronts us with the mystery of all mythic composition. On this point, Eliade properly emphasizes that the myth is detached from profane time; it provides an entry into the "Great Time, the sacred time."[15] The non-mythic Buddhist description of impending Enlightenment provides the intellect with technical terms. The scholar can "grasp" it; he may think he understands it. Still, the description is profane and likewise the understanding.

12. Har Dayal, *The Bodhisattva Doctrine in Buddhist Sanskrit Literature* (London, 1932), pp. 236-37.

13. Edward Conze, *Selected Sayings from the Perfection of Wisdom* (London, 1955), p. 80.

14. Toh. 3948, the *Bodhimārgapradīpapañjikā-nāma* (catalogued with the author's alternate name, Dīpaṃkaraśrījñāna), Tanjur, Dbu ma, Vol. Khi. Atīśa is commenting on verses (8b.-9, in my numbering) of his *Bodhipathapradīpa* (Toh. 3947).

15. Mircea Eliade, *Myths, Dreams and Mysteries*, trans. Philip Mairet (London, 1960), p. 23.

Reverting to that Tantric tradition about the separation of "means" and "insight," it, of course, constitutes a rationale for (re)uniting those two along with the merit and knowledge collected since the original fall. Both the Tantric and non-Tantric Buddhist purposes are colored by the "nostalgia for Paradise" discussed by Eliade in consideration of both archaic societies and Christianity.[16] In the non-Tantric tradition the "means" are usually explained as these five Bodhisattva perfections (*pāramitā*): giving, morality, forbearance, striving, and meditation. In the Tantras, the "means" may also be explained as the *maṇḍala* or consecrated circle in which initiation takes place.[17] This *maṇḍala* may be the initiate's body. But while the "means" is associated with men, and "insight" with women, this by no means implies that ordinary human marriage unites the "means" and "insight" in either the non-Tantric or Tantric sense. Indeed, that type of marriage generally confirms the loss of Paradise.

This is not to deny the legitimacy of the literal interpretation sometimes made by the Tantras, to wit, that they teach salvation through sexual union. But this symbolism by its very nature is capable of multiple interpretations, and thus separates the *mahātmans* ("great-souled ones") from the *alpātmans* ("small-souled ones") as well as from those in between. This view of ours is borne out by Eliade's remark while considering Hindu and Buddhist sexual Tantric statements: "We have already noted that the tantrics are divided into two classes: the *samayins*, who believe in the identity of Śiva and Śakti and attempt to awaken the *kuṇḍalinī* by spiritual exercises, and the *kaulās*, who venerate the Kaulinī (=*kuṇḍalinī*) and employ concrete rituals."[18] Of course the classical commentators could not avoid this issue and used expressions preserved in Tibetan translation as *sgra ji bźin pa* and *sgra ji bźin ma yin*, the Sanskrit originals for which were *yathāruta* and *na-yathāruta*. The former means "standard terminology", the latter "non-standard terminology." Thus, Jñānākara discusses these terms and mentions that in the standard terminology the "sixteen-year old girl" (*prajñā* aged sixteen) refers to the concrete sixteen-year-old girl, while in the non-standard terminology that aged girl refers to the sixteen voids.[19] Again, using the generic term *mudrā*, the two kinds are called the *karmamudrā* ("seal of action") and *jñānamudrā* ("seal of knowl-

16. *Ibid.*, pp. 59-72.

17. Atīśa mentions that in the Tantras the "means" is the *maṇḍala;* this in his *Bodhimārgapradīpapañjikā-nāma* (n. 14, above), while commenting on verse 42 (my numbering) of his *Bodhipathapradīpa*, which states: "Hence, in order to eliminate all the obscuration of defilement and the knowable, the yogin should continually cultivate *prajñāpāramitā* together with the means."

18. Eliade, *Yoga: Immortality and Freedom*, trans. Willard R. Trask ("Bollingen Series," Vol. LVI [New York, 1958]), p. 262.

19. Toh. 3719, the *Mantrāvatāravṛtti*, Tanjur, Rgyud, Tsu, 204a-b.

edge"): "The *karmamudrā* has breasts and hair, is the basis of pleasure in the realm of desire (*kāmadhātu*) . . . involves transient pleasure (*kṣara-sukha*). . . . The *jñānamudrā* is imagined by one's mind . . . is the basis of pleasure in the realm of form (*rūpadhātu*) . . . involves contact pleasure (*sparśasukha*).[20]

The problem is whether the syncretism of Buddhism with Tantric lore giving rise to the Buddhist Tantras is consistent with non-Tantric Buddhist traditions. My own solution involves an interpretation of the "dissoluteness" of the *prajñā* or "woman" frequently mentioned in certain Tantric texts. Thus, with reference to the Tantric consort called the outcast (*ḍoṃbī*), Eliade cites Kāṇha's line, "O *ḍoṃbī!* no woman is more dissolute than thou!"[21] We are not denying that some of the Tantric authors may denote a concrete woman by their *ḍoṃbī* when we hold that there scarcely could have been a more appropriate symbol for the inner faculty of *prajñā* than the dissolute outcast.

This "woman" is the initiatress of the *yogin*, and for this function had best be "dissolute." For in the world we know the man is initiated sexually by a woman who is temporarily dissolute—however moral she may be at other times. Besides, woman is the initiator par excellence: she obviously ushers one into life and, obscurely, into death. Indian mythology reminds us of this with the stark figure of Kāli, the World Mother as destroyer. Hence also, that *ḍoṃbī* as "insight" initiates one into knowledge, whether mundane or divine, commonplace or awesome.

This *prajñā* is found in all circumstances, foul and pure, as an ingredient of every idea. We do not have the introspective power to trace the ordinary *prajñā* to the glorious state free from the three psychological poisons, because just as that point is reached our discrimination, itself a form of *prajñā*, would vanish according to the *sūtra* citation. We only assume it is the same *prajñā* (or is it an alter ego?) that is the Perfection of Insight as dissolute as ever, for she consorts as freely with giving, morality, forbearance, striving, and meditation, as her wicked elder sister does with lust, hatred, and delusion. And she discloses the same ultimate truth to all the spiritual heroes.

So we can present our solution of the problem: if that dissolute woman the Tantras talk about is really an interior power and is represented externally as an Other in purely mythical language, this may well be consistent with non-Tantric Buddhism, for that woman may be no other than the Earth Goddess who shook in six ways (whether or not she was rising through six *cakras* of the body). And if that woman is the kind we

20. Mario E. Carelli (ed.), *Sekoddeśaṭikā of Naḍapāda* (*Nāropā*) (Baroda, 1941) p. 56.
21. Eliade, *Yoga*, p. 261.

would call a woman in profane time, when time is added to a place, such Tantric interpretations have little in common with the teaching of Gautama Buddha.

The Three Meanings of "E-vaṃ"

The remarks in the preceding section about *prajñā* and *upāya* suggest that the Tantras do not bring up in isolation the subject matter involving female symbolism. Usually male symbolism occurs side by side, especially in the discussion of *evaṃ*, the word which begins both the non-Tantric sermons called Sūtras and the esoteric literature called Tantras. The opening lines, setting the occasion for the work, are called the *nidāna*, a word which means "fundamental cause," "theme of the discourse," "introduction," "introductory chapter," and so on. The numerous commentaries on Buddhist Sūtras and Tantras naturally afforded no end of opportunity for the learned commentators to expand on the meaning of the *nidāna* according to their respective schools. No matter how the *nidāna* would subsequently diverge in the various works, its standard form for the first sentence was: *evaṃ mayā śrutam ekasmin samaye*, which interpreted as words in an ordinary sentence means "Thus by me it was heard on an occasion." Brough challenges the modern punctuation established by the Pāli school, which interprets the adverbial phrase *ekasmin samaye* with the meaning "on one occasion" as inaugurating the second sentence to add a time to the place where the Bhagavat dwelt (*vijahāra*).[22] When the adverbial phrase goes with the first sentence it adds a time to the "hearing," which might have occurred "all at once" in Great Time. Insofar as the present writer has inspected several Mahāyāna commentaries, they agree with Brough's indications; and one may refer to the *Mahāprajñāpāramitāśāstra* for confirmation.[23]

The Tantric commentaries also employ an interpretation not found in non-Tantric works: they comment on the *nidāna* as composed of individual syllables. The Tantric commentary summarizes the teaching of the whole work as will be shown extensively in the rest of its commentary by arbitrarily assigning meanings to the syllables of the *nidāna*, interpreted as the "theme of the discourse," starting with the initial *e* of *evaṃ* down through the *ra* of *vijahāra* ("dwelt"). For example, the work *Hevajrapiṇḍārthaṭīkā* identifies the first six syllables with six goddesses, in order, Locanā, Māmakī, Pāṇḍarā, Tārā, Vajradhātvīśvarī, and Prajñāpāramitā. The next six syllables are the six Buddhas, the usual five and Vajrasattva, who here represent the six personality aggregates (*skandha*), the usual five and a sixth

22. John Brough, "Thus have I heard . . . ," *BSOAS*, XIII, No. 2 (1950), 416-26.
23. Lamotte (trans.), *Le Traité de la grande vertu de sagesse* (Louvain, 1944), I, 56 ff.

not specified here but probably *jñāna-skandha* (the aggregate of knowledge).[24] This particular syllabic commentary on the *nidāna* continues down through *vijahāra* and thus announces the main deities as well as indicates the sixfold nature of the correspondence system.

In effect, the Tantric commentaries on the Anuttara-yoga-tantra literature interpret the language of the basic Tantra in two ways: as words having the meanings that they seem to have; and as words having arbitrarily assigned meanings, especially when the words are decomposed into syllables. In illustration, *evaṃ* has its ordinary meaning of "thus," and has two syllables each with their arbitrary meanings as assigned in a particular Tantric tradition.

Perhaps the appearance of the letters *e* and *va* in certain Indian alphabets suggested their use for symbolizing the female and male principles, as is done in the *Guhyasamāja-tantra* cycle. Following this tradition, Tsoṅ-kha-pa writes: "states three meanings of E-vaṃ: (1) the E-vaṃ of the fruit to be attained; (2) the E-vaṃ of the path of attainment; (3) the E-vaṃ as "signs" guiding that [path]."[25] He goes on to illustrate the three meanings:

1. *E* is the secret place for teaching the doctrine (*dharma*), such as the sky, the *bhaga* ("female organ," metaphorical), the *dharmodaya* ("source of natures"), the lotus, and the lion's seat. Vaṃ is whoever the Tantra sets forth as the Teacher, be he Vajradhara, Heruka, and so on, who dwells in the *bhaga*, lion's seat, and so on. (These deities symbolize the inseparable union of the void and compassion.)

2. *E* is "insight" (*prajñā*), "voidness" (*śūnyatā*). *Vaṃ* is "means" (*upāya*), "great compassion" (*mahākaruṇā*). Together they constitute the *bindu* (T. *thig le*).

3. *E* is the mother's *bhaga* place (*ādhāra*) (*yum gyi bha-ga rten*). *Vaṃ* is the father's *vajra* ("male organ," metaphorical) placed (*ādheya*) therein

24. Toh. 1180, *Hevajrapiṇḍārthaṭīkā*, Tanjur, Rgyud, Ka, 7a-5 ff. The author, *Vajragarbha (T. Rdo rje sñiṅ po), gives six goddesses, representing elements, for the syllables of *evam mayā śrutam;* six Buddhas, representing *skandhas*, for those of *ekasmin samaye;* six goddesses, representing sensory objects (*viṣaya*), for those of *bhagavān sarvata-* and six *bodhisattvas*, representing sense organs (*indriya*), for those of *-thāgatakāyavāk-*, these two groups of six constituting the twelve sense bases (*āyatana*); six fierce goddesses and six fierce gods, ordinarily located in twelve spots of the body, such as the limbs, for the syllables of *-cittavajrayoṣidbhageṣu vijahā-;* and finally Vajrasattva, the chief one, thirty-seventh, who is *prajñā* and *upāya*, for the syllable *-ra*. For purposes of this arbitrary interpretation of the syllables, amounting to the cast for the *Hevajra* drama, the author has not hesitated to omit the word *hṛdaya* which appears among the opening words in the Sanskrit text of the *Hevajra-tantra*. His repetition of Vajrasattva is quite normal; this deity is playing two roles, one as a Buddha and another as the central deity. In the Mother Tantras, such as the *Hevajra*, the correspondence systems generally go by sixes. The usual way of increasing the elements and the *skandhas* to six is to add "knowledge" (*jñāna*), i.e., *jñāna-dhātu* and *jñāna-skandha*.

25. Toh. 5284, *Collected Works*, Vol. Ca, *Mthaḥ gcod*, 64b-3.

(*de la brten paḥi yab kyi rdo rje*). This again is of two kinds: (*a*) the external *E-vaṃ* as "signs," the union with the "seal" (*mudrā*); (*b*) the internal *E-vaṃ* as "signs," the guiding agent for the path of piercing the vital centers of the *cakras* (the "wheels" imagined along the spinal column). "Here, 'signs' means signs of the genitals in the sense of shape."[26] These shapes associated with the *cakras* are the triangle and the circle.

Tsoṅ-kha-pa's treatment enables us to add some information to each of the three.

1. The first meaning of *e-vaṃ* is the literal meaning of the *nidāna* of the Tantra. Both the *Guhyasamāja-tantra* and the *Hevajra-tantra*, as edited in Sanskrit, begin with two sentences that can be rendered as follows: "Thus by me it was heard on an occasion. The Bhagavat dwelt in the *bhagas* of the diamond ladies who are the essence of the Body, Speech, and Mind of all the Tathāgatas." These *bhagas* belong to the four goddesses Locanā, Māmakī, Pāṇḍurā, and Tārā, who are respectively associated, in this stage, with the *cakras* of navel, heart, neck, and head.[27]

2. The second meaning of *e-vaṃ* is the union of "insight" and "means," or in alternate terminology, the union of "void" and "compassion." As discussed in our preceding section, this union involves aspects of the male and of the female but is not the union of ordinary marriage. The union, as mentioned above, constitutes the *bindu*. This is the mystical androgynous element composed of the white (male) and red (female) elements, whose ordinary function is to rise and descend in the central channel of the body (imagined to be in the spinal column), causing, as we shall soon point out, the states of consciousness. Tsoṅ-kha-pa in his *Guhyasamāja* commentaries often refers to the *bindu* as composed of the winds and mind-only (*vāyu* and *cittamātra*); and instead of "mind-only" the word "perception" (*vijñāna*) is sometimes used. In this terminology apparently the winds are in the "means" category and the mind-only or perception in the "insight" category. The *bindu* is also called *bodhicitta* ("mind of enlightenment"). The second meaning of *e-vaṃ* concerned with the path, as well as the third meaning concerned with the signs along the path, is made explicit by the arbitrary commentarial explanations of the syllables of the *nidāna*.

3. The external *E-vaṃ* as "signs" may mean the symbolic Father-Mother (*yab-yum*) unions of a god and goddess frequently depicted in Tibetan art. The internal *E-vaṃ* as "signs" is explained by Tsoṅ-kha-pa in this passage: "Thus that work [the *Saṃpuṭa*] explains the meaning of the E-vaṃ with locus in the shape of the *cakras* of head and navel—the shape of the E-triangle; as well as in the shape of the *cakras* of heart and

26. *Ibid.*, 66a.
27. That initial passage is elaborately explained in my *Yoga of the Guhyasamāja-tantra*.

neck—the shape of the Vaṃ-circle."[28] When Mkhas grub rje describes these *cakras* in his commentary on the *Hevajra-tantra* he especially clarifies the emphasis on four *cakras* for the Tantric manipulation of the "winds":

> The *cakra* of the navel with triangular shape faces upward; the *cakra* of the heart with circular shape faces downward; and the former has 64 petals (or "veins"), the latter 8. The *cakra* of the neck with circular shape has 16 petals and faces upward; the *cakra* of the head with triangular shape has 32 petals and faces downward. The total of those "vein" petals of the four *cakras* is 120; and since they form the support for the winds and perception, they are explained to be the 120 chief "veins."[29]

We can appreciate these symbols somewhat better by noticing what Tsoṅ-kha-pa says in a different work: "Among those, the *cakras* of navel and neck are *prajñā* with the shape of the E-triangle; and the *cakras* of heart and head are *upāya* with the shape of the Vaṃ-circle."[30] The neck and head *cakras* are now assigned shapes differently than in the two foregoing citations. However, Tsoṅ-kha-pa is here following the *Guhyasamāja* (Father Tantra) tradition, whereas the *Saṃpuṭa* and the *Hevajra* are in the Mother Tantra tradition. It follows that these tantrics do not believe that there are triangles and circles in the respective places. Those signs are meditative props imagined at those centers to facilitate concentration; and it is only important that the symbolism be consistent in a particular Tantric tradition. In agreement with this conclusion, Indrabhūti writes: "For the reason that the consonants are *upāya* and the vowels are *prajñā*, there are four *cakras*. There is the combination of *upāya* with *prajñā*, the combination of *upāya* with *upāya*, the combination of *prajñā* with *prajñā*, and the combination of *prajñā* with *upāya*. Hence four kinds are stated."[31]

When these Buddhist Tantras deal with seven *cakras*, one is added at crown of head in the position of the *uṣṇīṣa* with four petals; and two below, one at the sacral place (*gsaṅ ba*) with thirty-two petals and another, the lowest of all, at the "tip of the jewel" (*nor buḥi rtse*) with eight petals.[32] This system of seven *cakras* is obviously parallel to the Hindu Tantra series named, in order from top to bottom, Sahasrāra, Ājñā, Viśuddha, Anāhata, Maṇipūra, Svādhiṣṭhāna, and Mūlādhāra. The fundamental

28. *Mthaḥ gcod* (*op. cit.*), 66a.
29. Toh. 5483, *Collected Works*, Vol. Ja, *Brtag ḥgrel*, 68b-6.
30. Toh. 5292, *Collected Works*, Vol. Cha, *Rdor bzlas*, 21b-1.
31. Toh. 2472, the *Ratnacakrābhiṣekopadeśakrama*, Tanjur, Rgyud, Zi, 151a.
32. According to Abhayākara's *Āmnāya-mañjari* (Toh. 1198,) as quoted and explained in the *Sṅags rim*, 436b.

group of four *cakras* of the Buddhist Tantras therefore corresponds to the Ājñā, Viśuddha, Anāhata, and Maṇipūra *cakras* of the Hindu systems, although there are some differences in the respective descriptions. The *cakra* of the head, sometimes called the *Mahāsukha-cakra*, thus corresponds to the Hindu Ājñā *cakra* in the head between the eyebrows, hence in the position of the *ūrṇā-kośa*, one of the main characteristics of the Buddha. It is of interest to observe that in the Hindu Tantras much is said about the goddess Kuṇḍalinī, who lies sleeping in the lowest *cakra*, the Mūlādhāra; whereas the equivalent goddess in the Buddhist Tantra system, called Caṇḍālī or Nairātmyā, is at the navel *cakra*.

It may be noted that while the *Hevajrapiṇḍārthaṭīkā*, above cited, sets forth six basic goddesses for the first six syllables (*evaṃ mayā śrutaṃ*), the basic Tantra of the *Hevajra* gives only the first four goddesses, Locanā and so on (*evaṃ mayā*).[33] This is consistent with the *Guhyasamāja-tantra* cycle, which has an Explanatory Tantra entitled *Caturdevīparipṛcchā* ("Questions of the Four Goddesses"); and in Tsoṅ-kha-pa's commentary on this work we learn that a chapter is devoted to the questions of each goddess, Locanā, and so on, with the same names and same order as above.[34]

The primacy in this system of four *cakras* for physiological manipulation in ascetic practices may well go back to the old Upaniṣadic theories of the four states of consciousness. The *Brahmopaniṣad*, one of the Saṃnyāsa Upaniṣads, later than the early Upaniṣads but preceding the Tantric literature as we now have it, teaches that the Puruṣa has those four states when dwelling in the four places, namely, waking state in the navel, sleep (i.e., dream) in the neck, dreamless sleep in the heart, and the fourth, Turīya, in the head.[35] In agreement, Tsoṅ-kha-pa writes:

> When one has gone to sleep, there is both dream and absence of dream. At the time of deep sleep without dream the white and red elements of the *bodhicitta*, which is the basis of mind, stay in the heart, so mind is held in the heart. At the time of dreaming, those two elements stay in the neck, so mind is held in the neck. At the time when one is not sleeping, they stay at the navel, so mind is held there. When the male and female unite, those two stay in the head.[36]

This passage shows a belief that the orgasm or climax of ordinary coitus

33. Snellgrove (ed.), *op. cit.*, I, 49, or II, 4.
34. Toh. 5285, *Collected Works*, Vol. Ca, *Bźis źus*.
35. Eliade, *Yoga*, p. 128.
36. Toh, 5301, *Collected Works*, Vol. Cha, *Yig chuṅ*, 65a-5 ff.

yields a fleeting experience of a fourth state. At least the Anuttarayoga-tantras seek to bring about this pleasure-void (*sukha-śūnya*) experience in a non-fleeting form (*akṣara*), whereupon it is called "great pleasure" (*mahāsukha*), hence the name of the forehead *cakra*. It is the sexual union not of a man and woman but of a god and goddess. It is more prolonged in certain states of religious exaltation, mystical climax, and heightened consciousness in general, than it is in human orgasm. Moreover, if this fourth state be understood as all three of the waking, dreaming, and dreamless sleep states taken together, it becomes comprehensible that one could be in this fourth state and at the same time be emphasizing one or other of those ordinary three states. Another way of stating this proposition is that, once the mind has attained the fourth state, it could then evolve from this state in a more or less prolonged experience of an extraordinary type of waking, dream, or dreamless sleep. Along these lines, the Tantras speak of three light or void stages that evolve from the fourth, the Clear Light. According to our next section, "The Female, Male, and Androgyne," the *form of woman* is a symbol of the heightened state of consciousness that emphasizes the waking state, the *form of man* is a symbol of such a state that emphasizes the dreaming state, while the theoretical *form of androgyne* is a symbol of such a state that emphasizes the dreamless sleep state. Moreover, employing the terminology of "pleasure-void" (*sukha-śūnya*), Tsoṅ-kha-pa says: "Among them, 'means' is Spread of Light: 'insight' is Light; neutral (or androgyne), the merger of those two, is Culmination of Light. Among pleasure and void, Light is predominantly the cognition of void; Spread of Light is the reverse of that; and Culmination of Light has the two in equal proportion."[37] This statement implies that the secret state of mind during a woman's climax and other exalted states of consciousness of the same nature, however achieved, are predominantly the cognition of voidness among the two factors of pleasure and void. There are similar implications for the secret states of mind typically male and androgyne.

Another late Hindu text, the *Ṛgvidhāna*, speaks of the yogin's attempt to raise *manas* (the mind) from the navel to the heart, then to the neck, to the place between the eyes, and finally to the skull, whereupon to make the *manas* revert to the navel.[38] The last state in the ascension is the one usually referred to as "beyond the fourth" (*turyātīta*); and in the Hindu system the Sahasrāra *cakra* is beyond the body comparable to the *uṣṇīṣa*, which is depicted in Buddhist art as emerging from the top of the head. Some Buddhist Tantras also speak of this final state as corresponding to a fifth body. Thus in the commentary on the *Mañjuśrī-nāma-saṃgīti* by Ñi-maḥi dpal-ye-śes (*Sūryaśrījñāna) we read: "He has the nature of the five

37. *Mthaḥ gcod* (*op. cit.*), 49b-2.
38. Eliade, *Yoga*, p. 137.

bodies by reason of waking, dream, dreamless sleep, the fourth, and beyond the fourth."[39] The text goes on to explain this person as the Pervading Lord (*vibhu*, T. *khyab bdag*) who possesses the five knowledges. Later on, the same text mentions that the symbol of five tufts of hair on the head (*pañcaśikha*) stands for the five states.[40] The Buddhist *uṣṇīṣa* may be a variant of this symbol; and in any case, the corresponding state in Buddhism is Complete Enlightenment, according to Tantrism when the Goddess Caṇḍālī ascends to the crown of the head. If this Pervading Lord or Complete Buddha then descends to teach, he as the union of "insight" and "means," the second meaning of *E-vaṃ*, is the *Vaṃ* and wherever he teaches is the *E* of the first meaning of *E-vaṃ*. In this section the female symbolism is portrayed within sets of threefold correspondences, especially involved with the three syllables *Oṃ*, *Āḥ*, *Hūṃ*. This treatment is expected to lead to some important considerations concerning a table, "The Great Time." but first we must lay the groundwork by citation of a number of passages of threefold correspondences. Indeed, the analogical way of thinking is basic to the Tantras.

Among the correspondences to the triad of male, female, and androgyne, there is the set of body, speech, and mind, as well as the set of three *guṇas*, *sattva*, *rajas*, and *tamas*; but inconsistencies appear in the respective correspondences. For example, Mkhas grub rje in his commentary on the *Hevajra-tantra* quotes from the *Saṃpuṭa* that *sattva* is the intrinsic nature of body, *rajas* that of speech, and *tamas* that of mind;[41] while Tsoṅ-kha-pa in his commentary on the *Caturdevīparipṛcchā* says: "*Tamas* is the thunderbolt of body (*kāyavajra*); *rajas* is the thunderbolt of speech (*vāgvajra*); *sattva* is the heart, the intrinsic nature of mind (or the *cittavajra*)."[42] These inconsistencies can be resolved for the most part by placing the textual passages containing the correspondences in two groups labeled the basic time (*gżi dus*) and the fruitional time (*ḥbras dus*), or profane time and Great Time. The Tibetan terminology of the two times is mentioned this way in Tsoṅ-kha-pa's discussion of the *Kālacakra-tantra*: "The twelve members of the basic time are the twelve [members of Dependent Origination, viz.] unwisdom (*avidyā*) and so on, and the twelve transits of the wind. The twelve members of the fruitional time are [stoppage of Dependent Origination, viz.] stoppage of unwisdom, and so on, and the stoppage of the twelve transits."[43]

The tantric Nāgārjuna presents many of the threefold sets near the

39. Toh. 1395, the *Amṛtakaṇika-nāma āryanāmasaṃgīti-ṭippaṇī*, Tanjur, Rgyud, Pha, 60b-2.
40. *Ibid.*, Pha. 73a-3.
41. *Brtag ḥgrel, op. cit.*, 67a-5, 6.
42. *Bzis zus, op. cit.*, 32b-2.
43. Toh., 5381, *Collected Works*, Vol. Na, *Brjed byaṅ*, 49b-5.

beginning of his commentary on the *Guhyasamāja-tantra*. But at least there he does not speak of a division into two groups, and he does not clarify the respective order in which a number of the sets of three things correspond to each other. Fortunately, the writings of Tsoṅ-kha-pa on the *Guhyasamāja* cycle provide the necessary further information, but for every topic it proves best to compare with what he says in another one or more of his works.[44]

Nāgārjuna writes concerning the three syllables *Oṃ*, *Āḥ*, *Hūṃ*: "By reason of the nature of the three syllables, the yogin should dispose them in the head, the neck, and the heart, and then mutter them in the thunderbolt manner."[45] He mentions that the vowels have the nature of *prajñā*, the consonants the nature of *upāya*, and the semi-vowels, *ya*, etc., the nature of both. "For that very reason, they are the nature of female, male, and androgyne. Hence *Āḥ*, which condenses the vowels, is the intrinsic nature of *prajñā*. *Hūṃ*, which condenses the consonants, is the intrinsic nature of *upāya*. *Oṃ*, which condenses *ya*, *ra*, *la*, *va*, is the intrinsic nature of the androgyne."[46] Nāgārjuna continues with further identifications: "Those three syllables are also the three elements; the nature of body, speech, and mind; the nature of moon, sun, and fire; the intrinsic nature of inspiration and so on; and the intrinsic nature of the three transitional experiences, death and so on."[47]

By "inspiration" Nāgārjuna means inspiration of the breath. Tsoṅ-kha-pa explains these correspondences as follows: "Here one should recite in the sequence of drawing in the wind with an *Oṃ*, holding the wind inside with an *Āḥ*, and exhaling with a *Hūṃ*; and recite in a manner that does not violate the ancillaries of *dhāraṇī* (incantation) muttering."[48] The disposition in head, neck, and heart concerns the movement of the four lord (*nātha*) winds that are *upāya* (*thabs mgon po bźiḥi rluṅ*) along with their four [fractional] queen (*devī*) winds that are *prajñā* (*śes rab lha mo bźiḥi rluṅ*) from their ordinary locations during basic or profane time in extraordinary combinations within those three centers during fruitional or Great Time. Tsoṅ-kha-pa explains these mixtures of winds this way (in my summation): *Oṃ*, the *prāṇa* wind of the heart *cakra*, the *udāna* wind of the neck *cakra*, and the *bindu* in the position of the *uṣṇīṣa*, is the thunderbolt of body at the Mahāsukha-cakra of the forehead. *Āḥ*, the initial *prāṇa* of the heart *cakra*, the *apāna* wind of the sacral center, along with the *udāna* of the neck center, is the thunderbolt of speech at the neck *cakra*. *Hūṃ*,

44. These correspondences are presented elaborately in Giuseppe Tucci, *Tibetan Painted Scrolls* (Rome, 1959), pp. 240-41.

45. Toh. 1784, *Śrīguhyasamājatantrasya tantraṭīkā-nāma*, Tanjur, Rgyud, Sa, 8a-4.

46. *Ibid.*, 9b.

47. *Ibid.*, 9b.

48. *Rdor bzlas*, *op. cit.*, 63a-2, 3.

the *apāna* wind of the sacral center, the *udāna* wind of the neck center, and the pervasive *prāṇa* normally in the forehead, is the thunderbolt of mind at the nave of the heart lotus. And the winds mixed that way dissolve the knots (*mdud*) of those centers.[49] Moreover, Tsoṅ-kha-pa writes: "Thus, the three syllables are made into body, speech, and mind as follows: *Oṃ* is made into body, *Āḥ* into speech, *Hūṃ* into mind. They are made into the three bodies in the same order as follows: posited as the Nirmāṇa-kāya, the Sambhoga-kāya, and the Dharma-kāya."[50] By the three transitional experiences, Nāgārjuna means death, birth, and the intermediate state. Tsoṅ-kha-pa associates death with the Dharma-kāya, the intermediate state with the Sambhoga-kāya, and birth with the Nirmāṇa-kāya.[51] Again, he explains that *Oṃ* is the secret "heart" (*hṛdaya*) incantation of Vairocana, the Body of all the Tathāgatas; *Āḥ* likewise of Amitābha, the Speech of all the Tathāgatas; and *Hūṃ* likewise of Akṣobhya, the Mind of all the Tathāgatas.[52] The three elements are the red, the white, and the *bodhicitta*; and Tsoṅ-kha-pa gives the correspondences for these as well as for a number of other sets of three.[53] Without further citation of these passages, I shall present my solution of the two groups of correspondences.

The first group (basic time) has correspondences to the right, left, and middle "veins" of the body; the second group (fruitional time), to sequences of lights or voids. The first group involves the usual rhythm of breaths or winds in the various *cakras*. The second group involves a Tantric manipulation of those winds in a succession of wind mixtures to engender a controlled sequence of photism experiences. In both groups, and customarily in other contexts of the Tantras, the sequence of imagining and muttering the three syllables is *Oṃ*, *Āḥ*, *Hūṃ*. The contrast between the two groups will be clearer by placing some essential elements in brief tabular form (Table 14).

The basic or profane time correspondences are more fully stated as follows: Androgyne, the semi-vowels, mind, *bodhicitta* or *bindu*, [in some texts: Râhu,] or *tamas* among the *guṇas*, is in the central "vein," called the Avadhūtī. Prajñā, the vowels, speech, the red element, the sun, or *rajas* among the three *guṇas*, is in the left "vein," called the Lalanā. Upāya, the consonants, body, the white element, the moon, or *sattva* among the *guṇas*, is in the right "vein," called the Rasanā. The meaning of the

49. *Ibid.*, folios 70-71.

50. Toh. 5316, *Collected Works*, Vol. Ña, *Sbas don*, 152a-3.

51. Toh. 5290, *Collected Works*, Vol. Cha, *Don gsal*, folio 25a-b, as cited in my "Buddhist Genesis and the Tantric Tradition," reprinted herein.

52. *Rdor bzlas*, *op. cit.*, 51b.

53. E.g., in *Sṅags rim*, 437a-3 ff.; in *Bźis źus*, 32b-2 ff. Some of these correspondences are already in my "Notes on the Sanskrit Term *Jñāna*," *JAOS*, LXXV, No. 4 (October-December, 1955), 258 ff. My studies in that article constitute a decisive step toward my present understanding.

TABLE 14

BASIC TIME CORRESPONDENCES

MIDDLE VEIN	LEFT VEIN	RIGHT VEIN
Oṃ	*Āḥ*	*Hūṃ*
Mind	Speech	Body
Androgyne	Prajñā	Upāya
Tamas	*Rajas*	*Sattva*

FRUITIONAL TIME CORRESPONDENCES

LEFT	RIGHT	MIDDLE
Oṃ	*Āḥ*	*Hūṃ*
Body	Speech	Mind
Prajñā, form of woman	Upāya, form of man	Form of Androgyne
Tamas	*Rajas*	*Sattva*

sequence *Oṃ*, *Āḥ*, *Hūṃ* (Androgyne, Prajñā, and Upāya) is shown in part in Mkhas grub rje's great commentary (*Ṭīk chen*) on the *Kālacakra-tantra*:

> During the first five (lunar) months of the womb, developing the five personality aggregates and the five elements, under the power of *tamas*, in the state of dreamless sleep which has no manifestation of discursive thought (*vikalpa*), there is the *bodhicitta* of the Jina (i.e., the Bhagavat) which is the diamond (*vajra*) Dharmakāya. During the sixth and seventh, under the power of *rajas*, experiencing "objects" (*viṣaya*) like a dream, in the state of dream, there is the Saṃbhoga-kāya. Then, from the beginning of the eighth month up to birth, under the power of *sattva*, in the waking state, there is the Nirmāṇa-kāya.[54]

Now, various Buddhist Tantric texts identify the four basic *cakras* (cf. our preceding section) with the Buddha bodies, that is, the *nirmāṇa-cakra* is at the navel, the *dharma-cakra* at the heart, the *saṃbhoga-cakra* at the neck, and the *mahāsukha-cakra* at the head.[55] Combining this information with the data in Mkhas grub rje's passage, we see that the heart *cakra* with eight "veins" develops first, the neck *cakra* with sixteen "veins" develops second, inferentially the forehead *cakra* with thirty-two "veins" and the navel *cakra* with sixty-four "veins" develop last. The inference requires the

54. Toh. 5463, *Collected Works*, Vol. Ga, *Ṭīk chen*, Naṅ le, 18a-6 ff. For some further information on what develops during those ten months, see my "Studies in Yama and Māra," *Indo-Iranian Journal*, III (1959), 70-72.

55. For example, Snellgrove (ed.), *op. cit.*, I, 49.

Nirmāṇa-kāya to be associated with the head and navel. As a matter of fact, when Mkhas grub rje in the same *Kālacakra-tantra* commentary mentions the positional correspondences of the Buddha bodies, he associates the Dharmakāya with the heart and the Saṃbhoga-kāya with the neck, but places the *bindu* generating the waking state, and accordingly also the Nirmāṇa-kāya, at the level of the forehead (*dpral ba*).[56] The correspondences of basic time associate the Nirmāṇa-kāya with the navel, but the correlation with the forehead *cakra* in fruitional time is referred to when Dasgupta writes: "It is said that when the Bodhicitta is produced in the navel region the goddess Caṇḍālī is also awakened, as it were, in the *Nirmāna-cakra*. When she is awakened the moon situated in the forehead begins to pour nectar and this nectar rejuvenates and transubstantiates the body of the Yogin."[57] We may assume that upon birth as an ordinary male or female, the World Mother goes to sleep by the navel, which is then the *nirmāṇa-cakra* in place of the forehead *cakra*, hence given a different name, *mahāsukha-cakra*. One of the chief aims of the tantrics is to reawaken the forehead *cakra* as the *nirmāṇa-cakra*. We shall touch upon more matters related to the basic time in our next section, "The Groups of Four and Five."

Passing now to fruitional time correspondences, this sequence is initiated by the *Oṃ* at the forehead, where the moon is said to melt when Caṇḍālī at the navel blazes, with the dissolution of the four elements, which are Locanā and so on, and the dissolution of the five personality aggregates, which are the five Tathāgatas or Buddhas.[58] This event signals the end of profane or basic time. The dissolution of the elements is associated with certain signs or appearances. According to a Tsoṅ-kha-pa commentary on the *Guhyasamāja* cycle, the dissolution of the earth element into water yields an appearance like a mirage (*marīci*), of water into fire an appearance like smoke (*dhūma*), of fire into wind an appearance like fireflies (*khadyota*), of wind into the three Lights an appearance like a lamp (*pradīpa*), and of the Lights into ultimate nature an appearance like a cloudless sky (*nirabhragagana*).[59] However, the three Lights are also distinguished as being like moonlight, sunlight, junction of day and night;[60]

56. *Ṭīk chen*, Naṅ le, 30a-b.
57. S. B. Dasgupta, *An Introduction to Tantric Buddhism* (Calcutta, 1950), pp. 189-90.
58. Snellgrove (ed.), *op. cit.*, I, 50.
59. Toh. 5286, *Collected Works*, Vol. Ca, *Ye rdor*, 15a-2. Tsoṅ-kha-pa says he is following the *Sgron gsal* (Candrakīrti's *Pradīpoddyotana*, Toh. 1785). The Sanskrit terms come from the *Sekoddeśaṭīkā*, text 39.28, in comparison with the Tibetan translation, Toh. 1351, Tanjur Rgyud, Vol. Na, 252b-7 ff. The *Sekoddeśaṭīkā* reverses the order of the first two appearances, taking smoke as the first sign. Cf. also the *Śvetāśvatara Upaniṣad* (II, 11).
60. Cf. my "Notes on the Sanskrit Term *Jñāna*," *op. cit.*, p. 260; in *Mthaḥ gcod*, *op. cit.*, Tsoṅ-kha-pa says that the moonlight is white, the sunlight is red or yellow-red (54a-4 ff.).

so now we can understand better Nāgārjuna's set of moon, sun, and fire. In fact, the *Oṃ* corresponds to the first of the three Lights and hence assumes the preceding appearances of mirage, smoke, and fireflies.[61] Let us proceed to the table of fruitional time correspondences (Table 15), of which several lines were already given.

TABLE 15

THE GREAT TIME

OṂ	ĀḤ	HŪṂ
Prajñā, the form of woman	Upāya, the form of man	Androgyne
8-petalled lotus	5-pronged thunderbolt	
Moonlight	Sunlight	Fire
Night	Day	Juncture of day and night
Left	Right	Middle
Waking	Dream	Dreamless sleep
Void	Further Void	Great Void
Light	Spread of Light	Culmination of light
Body	Speech	Mind
Vairocana	Amitābha	Akṣobhya
Birth	Intermediate State	Death
Nirmāṇakāya	Saṃbhogakāya	Dharmakāya
Tamas	*Rajas*	*Sattva*
Head	Neck	Heart
Inspiration	Retention	Expiration

However, the Fire listed under *Hūṃ* probably means here "the fire of time" (*kālāgni*), that is, the fire superior to time, because it puts an end to the cosmic eon and hence brings even Great Time to an end, ushering in the Clear Light, the Fourth Void, from which the other three evolve; whereas the dragon Rāhu in basic time only temporarily eclipses the sun and moon. It is of interest that the set of moon, sun, and fire is also found in the Hindu Tantras.[62]

Our chief intention is to expose the female symbolism, but it is possible to do this only within a larger framework of symbolism. In basic time, Speech is female—a bit of symbolism prominent in Indo-European mythology; and in fruitional time, Speech is male. In the former time, Body is male; in the latter time, Body is female. In both times, Mind is androgyne or neutral. The correspondences in basic time exactly agree with the genders of the Sanskrit nouns: *vāc*, feminine (speech); *kāya*, masculine (body); and *citta*, neuter (mind). An alternate word for mind, *manas*, is also neuter. We note that the correspondences of sun and moon to *prajñā*

61. *Mthaḥ gcod, op. cit.*, 51a.
62. Eliade, *Yoga*, 238.

and *upāya* are also reversed when passing from the former to the latter time. This shift seems to coincide beautifully with the contentions about a recessive male in the human female and a recessive female in the human male, or the animus and the anima of Jung's system. That is to say, when the *yogin* attains the Great Time his recessive female becomes actualized; when the *yoginī* attains this time her recessive males become actualized. This casts a flood of light on the sexual symbolism of mystical visions. Almost all of the Buddhist scriptures were composed by men, as far as is known. Hence these works speak so much about attaining *prajñā*, the void, the state of waking, and light. Hence that large body of scriptures entitled *Prajñāpāramitā* ("The perfection of insight"), and the personification of *Prajñāpāramitā* as the "Mother of the Buddhas." These men were seeking to externalize or objectify what is referred to by our first column of the Great Time under *Oṃ*. When successful, they achieved a more or less prolonged state of mystic consciousness, without reliance on a sexual partner, that is the birthright of all earthly women, who achieve a transitory experience of this secret state of thought in a climax with the aid of a sexual partner. But women are always representing this state by means of body. Hence the correspondence to body in fruitional time. Those conclusions imply that if women had been writing the books, the titles and contents would have diverged considerably. If they renounce earthly men and seek fulfilment in an exalted mystical consciousness, when successful they realize what is suggested by the *Āḥ* column in the Great Time, as Briffault describes it: "The primal function of the primitive religious magic of generation is re-echoed throughout the long line of female votaries of the Divine Bridegroom, in the lascivious ecstasies of a St. Theresa, of a St. Catherine, of a Madame Guyon."[63] But Briffault evinces no evidence in his essay that he understands the true state of affairs: men ordinarily attain transitory experiences of this consciousness of predominant pleasure (*sukḥa*) and negligible void (*śūnya*) through their sexual conquests. And generally men represent this state by means of speech. Anyway, such is the outcome of the table; the reader may judge for himself or herself whether the above statements are true in fact or simply a forcing of issues to make the columns "come out right." The Tantric procedure is to master the techniques of passing through the three Lights to the experience of the Clear Light, to thus carry away the three bodies of a Complete Buddha; and Tsoṅ-kha-pa teaches that if one does not know how to proceed with skill he simply has momentary experiences of all these states when dying, passing through the intermediate state, and being reborn.[64]

63. Robert Briffault's "From Sex to Love in Religion," in A. M. Krich (ed.), *The Anatomy of Love* (Laurel Edition [New York, 1960]), p. 45.

64. E.g., in his *Ye rdor*, *op. cit.*, 17b-4 ff.

The Groups of Four and Five

A fine summary statement of the goddesses considered as consorts in the *Anuttara-yoga-tantra* is given by the Tibetan author Kloṅ-rdol bla-ma:

> The "means path" of another's body is the four families of "seals" (*mudrā*), namely: Padminī, Śaṅkhinī, Hastinī, and Mṛgī. Moreover, each of those has the three varieties "together-born female" (*sahajā*), "field-born female" (*kṣetrajā*), and "incantation-born female" (*dhāraṇījā*). The "together-born female" enables one to attain the illusory body and the Goal Clear-light. The "field-born female" enables one to attain the Symbolic Clear-light with the arcane state of body, of speech, and of mind. The "incantation-born female" is the *yoginī* at the final limit of the "stages of production" (*utpatti-krama*). The families (*kula*) are explained as follows: the butcher maiden belongs to Akṣobhya's family; the washerman maiden to Vairocana's; the necklace-stringer maiden to Ratnasambhava's; the dancer maiden to Amitābha's; the artisan maiden to Amoghasiddhi's.[65]

The four terms, Padminī and so on, derive from the Hindu *kāmaśāstra* literature. They represent a classification of women. However, the explanation in *Kāmasūtra* (chap. ii) of the three terms Mṛgī, Vaḍavā, and Hastinī, is not applicable here. The set of four terms have explanations according to Apte's dictionary[66] somewhat along the lines of the "characteristics of maidens" (*kanyālakṣaṇam*) in Varahamihira's work on omens, although the latter author does not use such terms as Padminī.[67] These expressions (sometimes with *citriṇī* in place of *mṛgī*) have been adopted by the Buddhist Tantric authors, and not necessarily with the same meanings as in the former literature. Lva-va-pa says: "Padminī belongs to the Deva family: Hastinī has the lineage of Yakṣas; Śaṅkhinī is known among the humans; Citriṇī is in the Preta family."[68] This passage could be interpreted to mean that all four have human form, while Śaṅkhinī is really human. Another interpretation is that none are human, while Śaṅkhinī is a fairy that has assumed a human form. And perhaps Lva-va-pa has something else in mind. However, Tsoṅ-kha-pa writes:

65. Toh. 6534, *Collected Works*, Peking ed., Vol. Ga, 31a-7.

66. Vaman Shivram Apte, *The Practical Sanskrit-English Dictionary* (Bombay, 1924). The definition of Padminī on p. 585 is from the *Ratimañjarī*.

67. V. Subrahmanya Sastri, *Varahamihira's Brihat Samhita* (Bangalore City, 1947), II, 578-84.

68. Toh. 1401, *Sādhananidāna-śrīcakrasaṃvara-nāma-pañjikā*, Tanjur, Rgyud, Ba, 38a-6.

> The object to be summoned is (*a*) the god maiden (*surakanyā*), (*b*) the demi-god maiden (*daityakanyā*), (*c*) the four kinds of human maidens—Padminī, Śaṅkhanī, Hastinī, and Mṛgī. They on all circles (*maṇḍala*) of earth, are summoned from everywhere. The first is summoned from above the earth; the second, from beneath the earth; the third, from upon the earth.[69]

Tsoṅ-kha-pa is following a tradition more consistent, literally speaking, than Lva-va-pa's with the Hindu meaning of the four terms. Indrabhūti also places the gods above earth, men on earth, and the demi-gods (*asura* or *daitya*) beneath earth.[70]

Whatever the meaning of this classification into Padminī and so on, the fourfold group leads immediately to the fivefold group, or vice versa. This is because four entities are naturally arranged in a square, implying a "center" of a "squared circle" (*maṇḍala*) with the implied or given fifth entity in the middle. This is not to say that the group headed by Padminī is to be equated with the fivefold group headed by the butcher maiden. If all nine were included in one "squared circle," the group of five would be in the cardinal directions and the center, the group of four in the intermediate directions.

The one in the center depends on the correspondence system. Thus, the correlation to "space" (*ākāśa*) among elements or to "Knowledge of the Natural Realm" (*dharmadhātujñāna*) among divine knowledges determine the center.[71] When the system takes Vairocana as the chief Buddha, then the washerman maiden (*rajakī*) in this set of correspondences is regarded as an embodiment of the central goddess.

The fourfold group usually represents the situation of basic time, as portrayed in the preceding section, while the fifth entity either involves fruitional time or suggests it. We should also recall that various important non-Tantric five-termed sets divide into a four and a one. The five personality aggregates (*skandha*) include four on the side of "name" (*nāma*) and one on the side of "form" (*rūpa*). The "form" aggregate in turn consists of the four elements and their evolutes. While Buddhism, consistent with Hindu systems, includes the five elements of wind, and so on, in one group, calling them "realm" (*dhātu*), Buddhist metaphysics does not include the fifth element, space, among the "great factors of becoming" (*mahābhūta*). A certain treatise of this category explains that wind, fire, water, earth, are both "great" (*mahā*), that is, pervasive, and "factor of becoming" (*bhūta*).

69. *Bźis źus, op. cit.*, 41b-1.

70. *Toh.* 1413, *Śrīcakrasaṃvaratantrarājasambarasamuccaya-nāma-vṛtti*, Tanjur, Rgyud, Tsa, 30a-7.

71. Cf. my "Totemic Beliefs in the Buddhist Tantras," Table 2, and discussion, note.

Space is just *mahā* in the pervasive sense, and the *nāma* personality aggregates are just *bhūta*.[72]

The four-and-one symbolism is used for the eaved palace (*kūṭāgāra*) described as having a single courtyard (*ekapuṭa*) and as follows in a verse: "Having four corners, four entrances that are ornamented with four portals, as well as four balconies that are resplendent with nymphs (*apsaras*) and with garlands and other decorations."[73]

Already in the biography of the Buddha called the *Lalitavistara* one finds this verse about the Tree of Enlightenment: "The ornamented 'essence of Enlightenment' (*bodhimaṇḍa*) is therefore distinguished by four 'divinities of enlightenment' (*bodhidevata*) like the paradise tree (*pārijāta* in heaven."[74] The Tibetan translation interprets *bodhidevata* as "goddesses of the Tree of Enlightenment."[75] According to Dowson in *A Classical Dictionary of Hindu Mythology*, the Pārijāta kept in Indra's heaven is the delight of the nymphs of heaven. Also, the four daughters of Sakkā (Indra) seem to be connected with this tree.[76] In these cases four goddesses make up the fourfold group. The word *maṇḍa* ("core," "essential part") substituting for "tree" (*vṛkṣa*) especially shows that the tree represents the central or fifth entity.

To illustrate the case of goddesses in both cardinal and intermediate directions, we may refer to the "Maṇḍala of the Diamond Realm" (*vajradhātu-maṇḍala*). The Indo-Tibetan form of this *maṇḍala* is interpreted in the Yoga-tantra literature class, and the Sino-Japanese Tantric school elaborates it into a highly complex *maṇḍala* that is one of the two main ones of the Shingon sect of Japanese Buddhism.[77] There are four female deities belonging to the inner sanctum (*garbhakūṭāgāra*) who are located in the four intermediate directions (south-east, southwest, northwest, northeast) and called, respectively, Wanton Movement (Lāsyā), Garland (Mālā), Song (Gītā), and Dance (Nṛtyā). A commentary of the Yoga-tantra class, while discussing this very *maṇḍala*, calls these four the secret goddesses (*gsaṅ baḥi lha mo rnams*).[78] According to the *maṇḍala* text, they

72. Toh. 4365, *Arthaviniścayaṭīkā* (no author catalogued), Tanjur, Sna-Tshogs, Ño, 13a-6, 7.

73. *Sādhana-mālā*, No. 239, text 459.11.

74. Lefmann edition, p. 281.

75. Toh. 95, *Ārya-Lalitavistara-nāma-mahāyānasūtra*, Kanjur, Mdo-sde, Vol. Kha, 138b-7.

76. Odette Viennot, *Le culte de l'arbre dans l'Inde ancienne* (Paris, 1954), 79 (cf. Malalasekera, *Dictionary of Pāli Proper Names*, II, 964, for their names—Āsā, Saddhā, Hirī and Sirī. These names signify, in the respective order, "hope," "faith", "shame," and "splendor").

77. Benoytosh Bhattacharyya (ed.), *Niṣpannayogāvalī of Mahāpaṇḍita Abhayākaragupta* (Baroda, 1949), introductory section, pp. 54-56.

78. Padmavajra's *Tantrārthāvatāravyākhyāna* (Toh. 2502), Tanjur, Rgyud, Vol. Ḥi, 225a-5.

belong, respectively, to the Buddha families, Akṣobhya, Ratnasambhava, Amitābha, and Amoghasiddhi. Of a different type are the four goddesses on petals of the first circle of the same *maṇḍala*, who are located in the cardinal directions starting with east: Sattvavajrī ("Diamond of Sentient Being"), Ratnavajrī ("Diamond of Jewels"), Dharmavajrī ("Diamond of the Law"), Karmavajrī ("Diamond of Ritual Acts"). The text states that they belong respectively to the same four Buddha families as do the other fourfold group. In the present case, however, three of the names directly show this relationship. Ratna is a standard name of the Ratnasambhava family, and Karma of the Amoghasiddhi family. Dharma in the sense of enunciation of the doctrinal syllables is usually correlated with Amitābha in this literature. Hence, these four represent a definite female essence of family, and their names could not have been formulated until after the theory of the five Buddhas (the four now in point and Vairocana) had arisen.

Since the text already relates the two fourfold groups by means of four Buddha families, it is feasible to relate the individual entities under headings as follows:

BUDDHA FAMILY	ABSTRACT GODDESS	SENSUOUS GODDESS
Akṣobhya	Diamond of Sentient Being	Wanton Movement
Ratnasambhava	Diamond of Jewels	Garland
Amitābha	Diamond of the Law	Song
Amoghasiddhi	Diamond of Ritual Acts	Dance

In the Anuttara-tantra terminology, since the fourfold group beginning with Padminī and the fivefold group beginning with the butcher maiden seem both to refer to types of concrete women, we may theorize, for want of noticing in the texts an explanation which may be restricted to oral precepts, that the former group refers to the concrete "femaleness" going with four of the latter group, all five of which are identified with the "Mothers" or the *prajñās* of the five Buddha families. This would involve an interpretation of this literature which the present writer feels is consistent both with Hindu *kāmaśāstra* usage and the general tenor of the Anuttara-tantras, namely, that what the world considers to be the signs and characteristics of femaleness is in fact the phenomenalization of the "Mothers" of the Tantric families and hence falls into distinct types. Of course, similar statements could be made for the signs of maleness. Such ideas are consistent with the world outlook prevalent in the old Vedic period when different deities were in charge of the departments of nature, and with the later Indian astrological texts which identify the various parts of the body with the twelve zodiacal signs or with the nine planets. The Tantric formulations simply carry out the identification by classifying under one or another of the Buddha families: all things are invested with the sacredness of Buddha nature, and this may be a mental preparation for initiation into the Great Time.

The four "great factors of becoming" are identified with goddesses who are the "Mothers" of the families: "Locanā is said to be earth, Māmakī held to be the realm of water, Pāṇḍarā known as fire, Tārā proclaimed wind."[79] Here elements do not mean the gross ones with which we are ordinarily familiar, but pure forms of the elements. Johnston shows that these elements are already regarded as divine forces in Upaniṣadic literature.[80] The four in the standard order of wind, fire, water, earth, are symbolized this way: "He should see the *maṇḍalas* of the four 'great factors of becoming' each next one upon the preceding one; blue, red, white, yellow; a bow (i.e., a semi-circle), a triangle, a circle, a square; the transformations of the syllables *Yaṃ*, *Raṃ*, *Laṃ*, *Vaṃ*."[81] In the same order the elements are associated with navel, throat, heart, and privities; and, if the correspondences are mutually consistent, Tārā, Pāṇḍarā, Māmakī, and Locanā would be the consorts, respectively, of the Buddhas Amoghasiddhi, Amitābha, Akṣobhya, and Ratnasambhava. This is the logical consequence of the identification of Amoghasiddhi and so on with the various winds having their bases in certain centers of the body.[82] These particular correspondences are the ones in this Tantric passage on the four bases of magical power (*ṛddhi-pāda*):

> The certainty regarding the four bases of magical power:—(1) Rightly situated as the heart-based [wind, i.e., *prāṇa*] with the magical power of *Māmakī*, belonging to the water-wind Vajra Lord (i.e., Akṣobhya); (2) Said to be in the neck as *udāna* with the magical power of Pāṇḍarā belonging to the fire-wind Padma Lord (i.e., Amitābha); (3) mentioned to be in the sacral region (or privities) as *apāna* with the magical power of Buddhalocanā belonging to the earth-wind Ratna Lord (i.e., Ratnasambhava); (4) in the navel as the wind-*maṇḍala*, the *samāna* along with the fire [of the sleeping goddess Caṇḍālī], with the magical power of *devī* Tārā belonging to the family of the Karma Lord (i.e., Amoghasiddhi). Each one of the four goddesses belonging to each [family Lord] is mentioned with the force of magical power along the channel [of

79. *Guhyasamājatantra*, chap. xii, p. 137.
80. E. H. Johnston, *Early Sāṃkhya* (London, 1937), p. 20.
81. *Sādhana-mālā*, No. 251, text pp. 490-91. This is the usual three-staged evocation after attaining the void: (1) germ syllable (*bīja*), (2) emblem (*cihna*), (3) body of deity (*kāya*). Hence, the *Yaṃ* is transformed into a bow, the latter into a blue wind; and likewise with the others.
82. Cf. Table 2, and note thereto, this work.

the body] equipped with the four *maṇḍalas* [of the "factors of becoming"].[83]

However, as was pointed out in the section "The Three Meanings of *E-vaṃ*." the order, Locanā, Māmakī, Pāṇḍurā, and Tārā (*evaṃ mayā*) represents an association with the *cakras* of navel, heart, neck, and head. As compared with the preceding correspondences, this moves up Locanā from the sacral region to the navel and Tārā from the navel to the head. The section "The Female, Male, and Androgyne" touches upon the mysterious communication between the navel and the head which may explain this shift of Tārā's position.

Moreover, one finds some difference in relating these "Mothers" to Buddha families in the Ārya school of the *Guhyasamāja*, the *Kālacakra-tantra*, and in the *Hevajra-tantra*.[84] The association of the green Tārā, also called Samayatārā, with Amoghasiddhi is standard. The next most frequent agreement is that Pāṇḍarā, or the white-dressed red Tārā, goes with Amitābha. However, the Māmakī and Locanā associations differ considerably. The reason is that the correspondence of four goddesses to five Buddhas always leaves out one Buddha. This is the chief Buddha of the particular Tantra, and this Buddha is placed in the center when one has a "squared circle." The corresponding realm is space or ether (*ākāśa*), which Lva-va-pa equates with the "Diamond Sow" (Vajravārāhī),[85] who is also called "Queen of the Diamond Realm" (Vajradhātvīśvarī) and "Fairy of Divine Knowledge" (Jñānaḍākinī).[86] In *maṇḍala* representation of the Buddha pentad the central Buddha is usually Vairocana or Akṣobhya, and this particular emphasis causes one or more of the "Mothers" to be assigned an association apparently inconsistent with other Tantras.

The goddesses as "great factors of becoming" are regarded as multiplying factors of the Lord winds, the male aspects of the elements. Thus Tsoṅ-kha-pa writes: "Regarding 'Pāṇḍarā and so on,' the wind of the Lotus Lord (i.e., Amitābha) is dominated by 225 winds each of fiery Pāṇḍarā of fire, windy Tārā of fire, earthy Locanā of fire, and watery

83. Toh. 453, the *Advayasamatāvijaya*, Kanjur, Rgyud, Vol. Cha, 148a-5. For our identification of the navel fire with the sleeping goddess Caṇḍālī, cf. Toh. 2330, Tilli-pa's *Saddharmopadeśa-nāma*, Tanjur, Rgyud, Vol. Źi, 270b-1: / lte bar tsa-ṇḍā-lī yi me / "at the navel the fire of Caṇḍālī."

84. For the *Guhyasamāja* Ārya school the correspondences are in Nāgārjuna's commentary (already cited, nn. 45-47 above), 26b and following folios. For the *Kāla-cakra*, cf. Bhattacharyya (ed.), *op. cit.*, p. 77. For the *Hevajra*, cf. Snellgrove (ed.), *op. cit.*, I, 128.

85. In his *pañjikā*, *op. cit.*, Ba, folio 43.

86. Bhattacharyya (ed.), *op. cit.*, Sanskrit text, p. 79.

Māmakī of fire; and the same goes for the other three [Lord winds]. This amounts to twenty-four divisions of 'watches' according to the *Amnāyamañjari*."[87] Hence there is the fiery Pāṇḍarā of fire, of wind, of water, and of earth. As each of the four goddesses regularly rotate as consorts of each of the Buddhas in the aspects of the winds or purity of elements, it seems a matter of convention for a certain Tantra to associate one of these goddesses with a certain Buddha as though it were always the case. Nevertheless, in the phase when a goddess is involved with the particular Buddha of her own element, when, for example, Pāṇḍarā goes with Amitābha, this appears to be a special case of juncture.

The Three Grades

The cited passage of the Kloṅ-rdol bla-ma mentions three varieties for each of those four kinds of females, Padminī and so on. This type of language is found in the "Mother Tantras," of which the most important is the *Śrīcakrasaṃvara-tantra* and associated literature. When that passage speaks of the illusory body as well as the Goal and Symbolic Clear Lights, it is employing terminology found especially in the "Father Tantras," of which the most important is the *Guhyasamāja-tantra* and associated literature. Because the passage incorporates materials derived from those two major classes, it becomes possible to clarify the meaning somewhat by using both commentarial traditions. It will perhaps be a modest step toward this understanding to demonstrate the following equivalences in alternate terminology of the two great divisions of the Anuttara-yoga-tantra:

GRADE	MOTHER TANTRA LANGUAGE	FATHER TANTRA LANGUAGE
Highest	Together-born female	Mother
Intermediate	Field-born female	Sister
Lowest	Incantation-born female	Daughter

Thus Indrabhūti is following "Mother Tantra" tradition when he writes: "The location is the circle of 'women,' namely together-born, field-born, incantation-born; and the butcher maiden, she of great power, the dancer maiden, the washerman maiden and so on."[88] In his commentary on the third chapter of the *Saṃpuṭa* he says: "In regard to the passage, 'All women . . .,' 'all women' means all the goddesses. They are the illusory goddesses field-born, incantation-born, and together-born,

87. *Sṅags rim*, 442a-3, 4.
88. The *Ratnacakrābhiṣekopadeśakrama*, *op. cit.*, Zi, 147b-1.

the yoginīs located in the locations and secondary locations."[89] Tsoṅ-kha-pa quotes Lva-va-pa: "Highest is the together-born female; middling is the field-born female; lowest is the incantation-born female."[90] Accordingly, Tsoṅ-kha-pa writes: "Then, having taken recourse to the power of the incantation-born, one moreover achieves the assembling of the field-born [ones]; taking recourse to the latter, one is able to exhort the together-born and make the latter the consort."[91]

Furthermore, these goddesses called "messengers" (*dūtī*) are held to grant occult powers, as the same writer comments: "The passage 'Occult power (*siddhi*) is speedily produced' means that the speedy production of the occult power is attained by taking recourse to the 'messenger.'"[92] Tsoṅ-kha-pa goes on to compare the female messenger with the sharp edge of a sword. To take proper recourse to either object one must be fearless. In the case of the *dūtī* one would then achieve the *siddhi*. However, "If there is a fault in the recourse, one achieves not the benefit but rather no end of great troubles."[93]

Now let us turn to the "Father Tantra" *Guhyasamāja*:

> The adept who carnally loves the "mother," "sister,"
> and "daughter"—
> Achieves the extensive *siddhi* at the true nature of
> the Mahāyāna summit.[94]

The tantric Candrakīrti comments on this by citing an unnamed *āgama*, in fact an Explanatory Tantra of the *Guhyasamāja* cycle, which relates these three grades of women to the graded Buddha bodies:

> He should love by the non-dual *yoga* of thusness the Prajñā-woman, who is the Perfection of Insight called "devoid of intrinsic nature", the "Mother" identical to the Dharmakāya.
> He, equipped with the *yoga* of his own presiding divinity should love just that one referred to as "sister", engendered equal to the Sambhogakāya. But, by (his) incantation body, the performer should contemplate that "daughter" with the form of the Nirmāṇa (kāya).
> The yogin of this kind, loving the "mother," "sister," "daughter,"

89. Toh. 1197, *Śrīsaṃpuṭatilaka-nāma-yoginītantrarāja-ṭikāsmṛtisaṃdarśanāloka-nāma*, Tanjur, Rgyud, Ca, 152b-2.
90. *Sbas don*, *op. cit.*, 145b-1.
91. Toh. 5320, *Collected Works*, Vol. Ta, *Ḥdod ḥjo*, 132a-6.
92. *Sbas don*, *op. cit.*, 136b-4.
93. *Ibid.*
94. Chap. v, p. 20.

attains the extensive *siddhi,* i.e. the supreme dharma-nature of Mahâyâna.[95]

While Kloṅ-rdol bla-ma's passage provides the basic data for correlating the symbolism of the two traditions, we are able to take advantage of his remarks only by correlating the Tantric theory of initiation (*abhiṣeka*) attainments. Tsoṅ-kha-pa writes: "The initiation of the flask accomplishes the Nirmâṇakâya, the secret initiation the Saṃbhogakâya, the insight-knowledge initiation the Dharmakâya; the Saṃbhogakâya here mentioned is also explained as the illusory body."[96] Mkhas grub rje states that the initiations of the flask (*kalaśa-abhiṣeka*) are conferred in the initiation phase of the "stages of production" (*utpatti-krama*).[97] The secret initiation (*guhya-abhiṣeka*) involves the three arcane states of body, speech, and mind, the insight-knowledge initiation (*prajñājñāna-abhiṣeka*) is associated with together-born joy, and both these initiations are conferred during the "stages of completion" (*saṃpanna-krama*).[98] Except for the apparent disagreement regarding the placement of the illusory body, it follows immediately that the "daughter" is the incantation-born female, the "sister" the field-born female, and the "mother" the together-born female. However, this "solution" has perhaps brought up more difficult points than it has solved.

According to Tsoṅ-kha-pa, the *yogin*'s body developed in the "stages of production" is the incantation body (**mantra-deha*); while the one developed in the "stages of completion" is the knowledge body (**jñāna-deha*), which is of two kinds: the impure illusory body and the latter body purified in the Clear Light.[99] The illusory body (*māyā-deha*) is the one formed of the winds and mind only (*rluṅ sems tsam*) and said to be the body of Vajrasattva.[100] According to Nâgârjuna's *Pañcakrama*, it appears like an image in a mirror, and may well be the "body made of mind" (*manomaya-kāya*) of non-Tantric Buddhism.[101] Reference to Table 2 will clarify somewhat the *Vajrajāpa-krama* of the *Pañcakrama*. Recitation of the *Oṃ, Āḥ, Hūṃ* is called "thunderbolt muttering" (*vajrajāpa*), or arcane speech, and involves visualization of the *mantras* (*mantranidhyapti*). Along with this muttering there is Tantric manipulation of the winds. On this

95. Toh. 1785, *Pradīpoddyotana-nāma-ṭīkā*, Tanjur, Rgyud, Ha, 36b-2 ff. The translation follows my *Yoga of the Guhyasamāja-tantra* (forthcoming).

96. *Sṅags rim*, 314b-5.

97. The initiation phase is made explicit in the formulation of these stages with six members; cf. my "Totemic Beliefs in the Buddhist Tantras," *op. cit.*, p. 90, note.

98. Toh. 5489, Mkhas grub rje's *Collected Works*, Vol. Ña, *Rgyud sde spyi rnam*. Now published as *Mkhas grub rje's Fundamentals of the Buddhist Tantras*, tr. by F. D. Lessing and Alex Wayman (1968).

99. *Sṅags rim*, 410b.

100. *Ibid.*, 406b.

101. As discussed in my "Studies in Yama and Māra," *op. cit.*, p. 120.

foundation, one proceeds to the *Cittaviśuddhi-krama*, namely to visualization of the mental substance (*cittanidhyapti*) as the three light stages or three voids, the arcane mind. The arcane body or illusory body consisting of the winds and that mental substance is the topic of the *Svādhiṣṭhāna-krama* (stage of personal blessing). Stationed in the illusory-like *samādhi* (*māyopama-samādhi*), one enters the Clear Light with the illusory body by means of the two simultaneous meditations called "contraction" (*piṇḍa-graha*) and "expansion" (*anubheda*), described in the *Abhisambodhi-krama*. The *Yuganaddha-krama* then describes the non-dual knowledge of a Manifest Complete Buddha who proceeds downward through the three light stages in a manner that carries off the three bodies.[102] For this the Tantras speak of a Fourth Initiation, yielding the maturation for the fruitional attainment of the three bodies, while the previous three initiations make this possible for those bodies. Hence we can add further correspondences to Table 2 by placing under *Oṃ* the initiations of the flask as well as the "daughter," under *Āḥ* the secret initiation as well as the "sister," under *Hūṃ* the insight-knowledge initiation as well as the "mother." But what is the meaning of the "carnal love" for those three classes of "women"? They must be separately discussed.

1. *The incantation-born female.*—She is called a *vidyā* and is evoked by a *vidyā-dhāraṇī*. The male deity can be called a *mantra* and the incantation evoking him is called a *mantra-dhāraṇī*.[103] Lva-va-pa, when speaking of the five initiations of the flask, says:

> Those five initiations which have the nature of the five Tathāgatas (i.e., Buddhas) are also referred to by the expression "wisdom initiation" (*vidyā-abhiṣeka*)—because they accomplish the five "wisdom knowledges" (*vidyā-jñāna*) whose natures are the transmutation of the five unwisdoms (*avidyā*), and because in every case the initiation is conferred by the *vidyā* goddess, Buddhalocanā and so on.[104]

The meaning of this last remark is clarified in Mkhas grub rje's treatment of the initiations of the flask. He states that when the hierophant (*vajrācārya*) sprinkles the disciple with the "diamond water" (*vajra-udaka*) of the Victorious Flask (*vijaya-kalaśa*) it is imagined that in reality the *vidyās*, Locanā and so on, hold the flask and pour the initiatory water.[105]

102. This summary of the *Pañcakrama* is based on the *saṃpanna-krama* section of Tsoṅ-kha-pa's *Sṅags rim*, esp. 405a, where he quotes and discusses three verses of the *Vajrajāpa-krama* (4-6).

103. This is shown in my previous treatment (Chap. 7) on "The Meaning of Initiation."

104. Toh. 1444, *Śrīcakrasambaramaṇḍalavidhiratnapradīpoddyota-nāma*, Tanjur Rgyud, Wa, in a passage beginning 365b-3.

105. In *Mkhas grub rje's;* see n. 98 above.

Furthermore, these *vidyās* such as Locanā can be identified with the maidens mentioned in the Kloṅ-rdol bla-ma's passage, using the same or other names. Thus Saraha writes: "Locanā is the brahmin maid (Brahmaṇī); Māmakī is the outcast (Ḍombī); Pāṇḍarā is the dancing girl (Nartī); Tārā is the washerwoman (Rajakī)."[106] Of course, when incantation-born, they are not concrete.

2. *The field-born female.*—The expression "field-born" refers first of all to those located in fields and secondary fields (*kṣetra* and *upakṣetra*) which are eight in number, as Indrabhūti states: "Now, so as to teach the families of the eight field-born yoginīs. . . ."[107] The intention of the number eight is to describe the fields rather than the *yoginīs*. Besides, the expression "field-born" indicates a larger group of *yoginīs* who are headed in lists by the eight field-born groups. These *yoginīs* are usually placed in locations (geographical or in the body itself) numbering twelve, twenty-four, or thirty-two. Various Anuttara-yoga-tantras belonging to the "Mother Tantra" category and the commentarial literature describe the characteristics of these *yoginīs*, place them in locations, and group them under families of Buddhas, whether five, six, or seven.[108] From a Sanskrit manuscript of one of these works, the *Abhidhānottara*, Bagchi cites "They are faithful to their true religion and brave sisters (*saddharmaratā nityaṃ vīrabhoginyaḥ*)."[109] This is said in reference to one kind of the goddesses named *lāmā*, but the appellation "sister" is of interest as being consistent with our previous identification of the "field-born" with the "sister." These *yoginīs* are of course non-human. This is not only shown by some of the descriptions, but also follows from the fact that they can coalesce with the *yogin*'s body in the sense of becoming located in different spots. The descriptions indeed amount to a classification of the fairy world. The implication is that the *yogin*, upon developing the illusory body, becomes aware of a world whose nature is compatible with that body. Nāgārjuna writes in his *Pañcakrama* (*Cittaviśuddhi-krama*, vs. 36):

> Of all illusions, the illusion of woman is supreme.
> Just here, the variety of three knowledges is clearly marked.[110]

106. Toh. 1652, *Śrī-Buddhakapālatantrapañjikā-jñānavatī, nāma*, Tanjur, Rgyud, Ra, 137a-2.

107. The *Smṛtisaṃdarśanāloka, op. cit.*, Ca, 123a-6-7.

108. Among these works of great importance is a Continuation Tantra of the basic *Cakrasaṃvara Tantra* (Toh. 368) entitled *Abhidhāna-uttaratantra* (Toh. 369). Among the Tanjur texts there is, e.g., Indrabhūti's work, just referred to. There is a great deal of information in Tsoṅ-kha-pa's *Ḥdod ḥjo, op. cit.*, n. 91. See Snellgrove, *The Hevajra-tantra*, I, 66-70, and his annotations.

109. Prabodh Chandra Bagchi, *Studies in the Tantras* (Calcutta, 1939), p. 59.

110. This verse is quoted in the *Sṅags rim*, 313b-2, during Tsoṅ-kha-pa's discussion of the three Higher Initiations (the secret one, insight-knowledge, and the fourth).

The expression "three knowledges" means the three lights, Light, Spread of Light, and Culmination of Light, constituting the arcane mind.

3. *The together-born female.*—Candrakīrti in his commentary on the *Guhyasamāja* cites this verse about her:

> The great goddess located in the heart,
> Causing the yogin's *yoga*—
> The Mother of all the Buddhas—
> Is called Vajradhātvīśvarī (Queen
> of the Diamond Realm).[111]

As the incantation-born female yielded a predominance of void, the field-born female a predominance of pleasure, so now the together-born female yields the experience of pleasure-void (*sukha-śūnya*) in equal measure. This pleasure-void involves a sequence of four joys (*ānanda*), produced by the melted white element in the central channel of the body.

The "carnal love" for these respective females who initiate the male called the *yogin* takes four forms in accordance with the initiation, as Snellgrove translates: "The first is represented by a smile, the second by a gaze, the third in an embrace, and the fourth in union."[112] The *yogin* smiles at the "daughter," gazes at the "sister," embraces the "mother," unites with the latter in the Clear Light, and must stay united upon emerging from the Clear Light and proceeding through the three light stages in the reverse order so as to hold onto the three bodies of the Buddha associated with those three stages. The wife was a daughter, a sister, and a mother.

Their Ages

The many textual references to these goddesses in terms of their ages are not particularly calculated to give assurance regarding their true nature. Especially is this the case with the most complete list of ages noticed by the present writer. Saraha associates five ambrosias (*amṛta*) with *prajñās* of five different ages. The first kind issues from the eye of the eight-year-old Kumārī. The second, from the hollow vein (*rtsa khoṅ stoṅ*) of the twelve-year-old Śālikā. The third, from the union with the sixteen-year-old one who flowers (*puṣpavatī*, woman with menses), called Siddhā. The fourth, from the union with the twenty-year-old one who has menses for the first time, called *Bālikā. The fifth is the (?)menses (*kha ba*, perhaps corruption of *khrag*, "blood") of *prajñā*, the semen of *upāya*, or the burnt fat of

111. *Pradīpoddyotana*, *op. cit.*, Ha, 36a-7. The translation follows my *Yoga of the Guhyasamāja-tantra*.

112. Snellgrove, *op. cit*., I, 95-96.

prajñā, whichever be the case, of the twenty-five-year-old one, named *Bhadrakapālinī (*thod bzaṅs can ma*).[113]

Besides the maiden, these texts also speak of a lad. Thus the *Guhyasamāja* has a verse about the maiden aged twelve and the lad aged twelve.[114] The same work has a verse:

> When he sees the delightful daughter of the gods replete
> with all ornaments, the lad, [or] the maiden,
> He gains the occult power (*siddhi*).[115]

Candrakīrti explains that he, the *yogin*, attains the mundane occult powers (*laukika-siddhi*),[116] usually eight in number. This is indeed a "fairy tale." Jung might have explained that masculine consciousness has come "face to face with its feminine counterpart, the anima."[117] The material of our preceding section suggests that the *yogin* now sees a "sister" or "brother."

It will help our control of the data to organize it into classes of meaning, whether concrete or figurative, already illustrated in an earlier section by the interpretation of the sixteen-year-old girl as the sixteen voids. But it is doubtful that such organization of textual data can yield a native understanding that one has through having been born and reared in a country whose usages are commonplace and subconsciously noticed, while startling to the foreigner. The usual way to be a native in this case is to have gone through it all.

A. Ages of the Yoginīs belonging to Buddha families

Bhavyakīrti writes: "Among them, the butcher maiden, aged twelve, is the *mudrā* belonging to the yogin of Akṣobhya's family. The washerman maiden, aged twenty, is the *mudrā* belonging to the yogin of Vairocana's family. The dancer maiden, aged sixteen, is the *mudrā* belonging to the yogin of Amitābha's family."[118] The passage by the Kloṅ-rdol bla-ma earlier cited contains such expressions as "butcher maiden." We may assume that either the necklace-stringer maiden or the artisan maiden,

113. The *Jñānavatī*, *op. cit.*, n. 106, Ra, 129a-1 ff. In this passage the name of the twelve-yeared female is written *śa-ri-ka*. In Toh. 1654, Abhayākaragupta's *Śrī-Buddhakapālamahātantrarājaṭīkā-abhayapaddhati-nāma*, Ra, 190a-5, the name is transcribed *śā-li-ka;* and Ra, 193a-6, transcribed *śā-li-kā*.

114. Chap. xv, pp. 100-101.

115. Chap. xv, p. 108.

116. *Pradīpoddyotana*, *op. cit.*, Ha, 154a-2-3.

117. Violet S. de Laszlo (ed.), *Psyche and Symbol: A Selection from the Writings of C. G. Jung* (Anchor Original [New York, 1958]), p. 96; in Jung's essay, "The Phenomenology of the Spirit in Fairy Tales."

118. Toh. 1793, *Pradīpodyotanābhisaṃdhiprakāśikā-nāma-vyākhyāṭīkā*, Tanjur, Rgyud, Khi, 41b-6, 7.

or both, is more than twenty years old. Saraha's list has a lower age of eight and a higher one of twenty-five.

However, Candrakīrti's commentary on the *Guhyasamāja* which is followed by Tsoṅ-kha-pa does not entirely agree with Bhavyakīrti. When Candrakīrti comments on a verse of the *Guhyasamāja* (chap. xvi, p. 125) about the sixteen-year-old maiden, he says: "The practice to be practiced by the yogin of Vairocana's family is together with the *mudrā* aged sixteen years."[119] Here the *mudrā* is the goddess Locanā. Candrakīrti agrees that the butcher maiden is aged twelve; but when he comments on a *Guhyasamāja* verse (chap. xv, p. 94) about the dancer maiden, he does not mention the latter's age.[120] Candrakīrti's position, insofar as he did give ages, and Tsoṅ-kha-pa's as well, is consistent with the sizes of *maṇḍalas* in the *Guhyasamāja-tantra*. According to Tsoṅ-kha-pa, "The *Guhyasamāja* states that the *maṇḍalas* of mind, body, and speech in that order have 12 *hastas*, 16 *hastas*, and 20 *hastas*."[121] This data is not all in one place in that Tantra. Thus, chapter iv (p. 18) shows that the *maṇḍala* of mind (*citta*), which normally is associated with Akṣobhya, has twelve *hastas*. Chapter xvi (pp. 113-14) show that the *maṇḍala* of body, associated with Vairocana, has sixteen *hastas*, and that the *maṇḍala* of speech, associated with Amitāyus (=Amitābha), has twenty *hastas*. Unfortunately, no *maṇḍala* sizes are set forth for the categories of merits (*guṇa*) or acts (*karma*), the superintendence going with Ratnasambhava and Amoghasiddhi, respectively.[122]

B. The number of years to the magical power ("Siddhi")

According to Mkhas grub rje, "Certain scholars say that if the *bindu* oozes at the end of sixteen years, the together-born joy occurs directly, and that it (i.e., the *bindu*) is called the together-born body (*sahaja-kāya*)."[123] This interpretation of "age" agrees with these remarks by Indrabhūti: "One's own pleasure generated at the end of the death obtained from the father is precisely the pleasure experienced in the phase of the oozing. At the end of sixteen years a man practices by himself. At the end of twelve years a woman practices by herself."[124] This "oozing" refers to the melted white element in the central channel of the body. The white element is the father element; and the phase of oozing corresponds to dreamless sleep and to death in the correspondences in Table 15.

119. *Pradīpoddyotana*, *op. cit.*, Ha, 173b-4.
120. *Ibid.*, Ha, 136a-5 and Ha, 137a-6.
121. *Sṅags rim*, 160a-2.
122. Cf. Table 2, this work.
123. *Ṭīk chen*, Naṅ le, *op. cit.*, 30a-1.
124. The *Smṛtisaṃdarśanāloka*, *op. cit.*, Ca, 134b-1.

In partial agreement, Candrakīrti quotes this verse, from an Explanatory Tantra of the *Guhyasamāja* cycle:

> The peace abiding in the unborn, whose name would be 16-yeared by differentiation of time starting with a moment, is determined as the "lady" (*yoṣit*).[125]

During his exposition of the secret initiation, Tsoṅ-kha-pa cites this from the *Mahāmudrātilaka*:

> If one does not obtain a twelve-yeared, or sixteen-yeared female, adorned with good features, long eyes, attractive figure and youth, then a twenty yeared one is proper.
> Other "seals" (*mudrā*) above twenty put the occult power far off.
> One should offer his sister, daughter, or wife to the "master" (*guru*).[126]

Tsoṅ-kha-pa is concerned in this context with the method of the secret initiation and does not stop to explain the symbolism of the ages. Since the symbol is multi-valued, the present writer may be spoiling it by presenting a one-valued interpretation, namely, that it means the number of years elapsed when *siddhi* is attained since someone turned his back on worldly affairs to practice yoga—an event as memorable to him as is the marriage contract to worldly persons. But the fact that "seals" over twenty put the *siddhi* far off does lend weight to our interpretation. Concerning the "master," there are both inner and outer kinds.[127]

The problem still remains of why the numbers increase by fours, starting from age eight in Saraha's list, and so continuing to age twenty, then jumping over twenty-four to twenty-five. There seems to be involved an idea that the *yogin* can attain the goal in certain definite numbers of years.

C. The vowels and voidnesses

Previously we have referred to Jñānākara's interpretation of the sixteen-year-old girl as the sixteen voids. The sixteen Sanskrit vowels are identified with the sixteen voidnesses in the *Śrī-Rāgarāja-tantrarāja*:

> A is the voidness of inner and outer, Ā is the voidness of voidness, I is great voidness, Ī is the voidness of ultimate reality, U is the voidness of constructed things, Ū is the voidness of the un-

125. *Pradīpoddyotana*, *op. cit.*, Ha, 34a-2. The translation follows my *Yoga of the Guhyasamāja-tantra*, where the original Sanskrit is given.
126. *Sṅags rim*, 281a-1.
127. See my chapter "Divinity according to the Buddhist Tantras."

> constructed, Ṛ is the voidness of the limitless, Ṝ is the voidness of the beginningless and endless, Ḷ is the voidness of the undeniable, Ḹ is the voidness of ultimate nature, E is the voidness of all natures, AI is the voidness of individual characteristics, O is the voidness of the unobserved, AU is the voidness of the non-existent, AṂ is the voidness of intrinsic nature, AḤ is the voidness of the intrinsic nature of the non-existent.[128]

This Tantra continues: "The seed syllable (*hṛdaya*) of the Saṃbhoga-kāya at the neck is *Oṃ*; the *prajñā* is the sixteen void 'veins.'"[129] Also, Ghandha(?) writes: "At the left side of the yogin is the *prajñā* vowelled sixteen."[130]

Tsoṅ-kha-pa cites an unnamed *āgama* as it was quoted in a Tantric commentary which mentions the sixteen spots of the body where one contemplates the sixteen vowel letters, beginning with A at the base of the thumb.[131] In the same context he shows that one disposes the sixteen letters on the right side of the body for *upāya*, and again on the left side for *prajñā*, the total of thirty-two yielding the thirty-two characteristics (*lakṣana*) of the great person (*mahāpuruṣa*). The idea here is that the sixteen vowels are the sixteen parts of the *bodhicitta* which is the union of *prajñā* and *upāya* as the red and white elements, hence a total of thirty-two sub-parts.[132]

The Tantric texts have comparable remarks for the twelve-year-old girl. Thus, Saraha says: "Those *yoginīs*, adorned with various ornaments, having the form of youth, aged twelve, are accomplished from the twelve vowel letters and in this Tantra are called 'the *prajñā* aged twelve.'"[133] In the *Catuṣpīṭhatantra*, according to Bhavabhadra's commentary, one arrives at the twelve vowels by leaving out "the two neuters" (*ma niṅ gñis*), explained to be Ṛ, Ṝ, Ḷ, and Ḹ.[134]

The present writer has not noticed in these texts the method of applying the vowels to *prajñās* aged eight, twenty, or twenty-five. Presumably one could leave out further vowels for the lesser age or could repeat certain vowels for the two greater ages. For the twenty-year-old maiden, one might apply the standard list of twenty voidnesses.

128. Toh. 405, Kanjur, Rgyud, Ga, 241-4 ff. Cf. T. R. V. Murti, *The Central Philosophy of Buddhism* (London, 1955), pp. 350-51, for the list of twenty voidnesses, which minus Nos. 1, 2, 17, and 20, amounts to the present list of sixteen voidnesses. Murti points out that the standard list of eighteen voidnesses leaves out Nos. 17 and 20.

129. *Śrī-Rāgarāja-tantrarāja, ibid.*

130. Toh. 2404, *Ālikālimantrajñāna-nāma*, Tanjur, Rgyud, Zi, 28b-7.

131. *Sṅags rim*, 380b-6.

132. *Ibid.*, 381a-5.

133. The *Jñānavatī, op. cit.*, Ra, 121b-2, 3.

134. Toh. 1607, *Śrīcaturpīṭhatantrarājasmṛtinibandha-nāma-ṭīkā*, Tanjur, Rgyud, Ha, 149a-2.

D. The transits of body winds

Indrabhūti states:

> The females aged sixteen and so on,
> The "sixteen-yeared female"—
> This has a purport explained otherwise,
> Expressed as the sixteen transits.
> Thereby the *yoginī* wanders—
> As to place, namely—onto sixteen places,
> Onto the wheel's spokes numbering sixteen,
> Onto all of them, the vital winds wander.[135]

Ratnarakṣita says, "The wind has sixteen member transits in a single day."[136] One may arrive at this figure by the winds in eight watches along the right and left channels. It is of interest that sometimes the age of sixteen is expressed as twice eight, as in the case of the goddess Kurukulle, who is colored red and is twice-eight years.[137]

Padmavajra's detailed explanation of the sixteen transits as the sixteen digits (*kalā*) of the moon is too long to translate here. In short, the first twelve transits are of the twelve interior zodiacal signs, starting with Aries (S. *meṣa*, T. *lug*). The thirteenth through the fifteenth concern the right and left channels in whatever order (not specifically mentioned) as well as the middle channel (specifically mentioned), symbolized respectively as the "food of solar manifestation," the "food of lunar manifestation," and the demon Rāhu (who causes eclipses). The sixteenth has the name *bindu* ("the drop").[138] Obviously, one can arrive at the number twelve here by leaving out the last four transits. This gives the number of transits in Tsoṅ-kha-pa's passage, cited in the section on "The Female, Male, and Androgyne," which in fact also refers to transits through the twelve interior zodiacal signs.

Concluding considerations

Since the Tantras were traditionally handed down in esoteric circles, for many centuries they were read only by persons who had a genuine interest in understanding the subject and would spend the necessary time and

135. The *Smṛtisaṃdarśanāloka*, *op. cit.*, Ca. 169b-6.
136. Toh. 1420, *Śrīsaṃvarodayamahātantrarāja-padminī-nāma-pañjikā*, Tanjur, Rgyud, Wa, 24a-2.
137. *Sādhana-mālā*, No. 183, Sanskrit text p. 381.
138. Toh. 1419, *Śrī-Ḍākārṇavamahāyoginītantrarājavāhikaṭikā-nāma*, Tanjur, Rgyud, Dza, 309a-1 to 309b-4. (This passage is translated in its entirety in my essay "Tantric Teachings about the Inner Zodiac.")

endeavor under a *guru*'s direction to achieve maturity. The candidates had to adhere to various vows and pledges. If this symbolism is drawn out of context and presented to the general public in a mutilated, ignorant fashion, these works reap much scorn and condemnation. Even so, the Tantric adepts like Saraha would probably not regret the aversion of the "moral" person. The morality prerequisite for the Tantras in the reform of Atiśa (the Indian *paṇḍit* who came to Tibet around A.D. 1040), a reform revived by Tsoṅ-kha-pa three centuries later, is far too lofty for most persons. This reform requires the Bodhisattva vow to precede the vows and pledges of the Tantras, referred to in brief as the "*mantra* vow." And the reform requires the morality of the Prātimokṣa (non-Tantric Buddhist morality) to precede the Bodhisattva vow.

Our study shows that much of the female symbolism of the Anuttara-yoga-tantra is derived from the human experience of sexual union—meaning both the physical and the mental state. Just as the morality or immorality of this union is independent of the act itself but is derived from the circumstances in which it is conducted, so also the symbolism based thereon is per se amoral but properly or improperly assessed by persons according to their mental orientation.

Finally, one may wonder about the truth of certain strange ideas of this literature, but the Tantras have been scarcely touched by modern scholarship. It is premature to dismiss the Tantras as sheer superstition, as some have done, content to begin with certainty and spared the sleepless night of deepening insight.

15

THE FIVE-FOLD RITUAL SYMBOLISM OF PASSION*

Introduction

A preeminate *sādhana* ("evocation of deity") sequence in the Buddhist Tantras, occurring innumerable times in the *Sādhana-mālā* and similar literature, is the order (1) realization of the void (*śūnyatābodhi*); (2) imagining there a germ syllable (*bīja*); (3) from that generating a hand symbol (*cihna*)—the emblem of the deity; and (4) from that accomplishing the body of the deity.

The present paper treats this *sādhana* formula in a more generalized form, together with its symbolic values, and signals the non-tantric Buddhist progression which the Tantras claim to quicken. Our exposition embodies some surprises, showing in Part I a comparison of Mañjuśrī's arrows with Kāmadeva's arrow attack on Śiva, leading to a comparison of the Greco-Roman tradition with the *skandha*-centers of the body; and then in Part II, introducing the relation with the famous "Heart Sūtra' (*Prajñāpāramitāhṛdaya-sūtra*); the *bodhisattva* preparation, path, and fruit; the Abhidharma theory of basic and conditional causes and of rebirth after death and the intermediate state; and the Buddha Bodies.

Indeed, the 'voidness' referred to in the first step of the usual Buddhist Tantric *sādhana* means the standard non-tantric meditations known as "selflessness of personality" (*pudgala-nairātmya*) and "selflessness of

* This article first appeared in *Studies of Esoteric Buddhism and Tantrism*, edited by Koyasan University, 1965, which may be consulted for Tibetan passages omitted in this reprint.

natures" (*dharma-nairātmya*). So, into the void personality aggregates (*skandha*) the officiant plants germ syllables, and does the same in the void *dharmadhātu* or *dharmodaya* triangle.

The writer wishes to emphasize that the expression "passion" (*anurāga*) is not to be construed as implying that this paper is preoccupied with sexual topics extracted from the Buddhist Tantras. It is true that some of these Tantras employ sexual symbolism; and we regard a symbol as a semantic unit capable of multiple interpretations. When a sexual symbol is employed, a gross person will understand it one way, a refined person in another way. And perhaps the original writer has something else in mind! Such is the case as well with the Śiva *liṅga*. The *Hevajra-tantra* (Snellgrove edition) states (I, ix, 19A): "By whatever thing the world is bound, by that the bond is unfastened." The *Ḍākinī-vajrapañjara*, as is cited in *Subhāṣita-saṃgraha* (Bendall edition), states: "By passion the world arises; down-cast by passion, it goes to its end. By thorough knowledge of the diamond passion, the mind becomes *vajrasattva*." (*rāgeṇotpadyate loka rāgākṣepāt kṣayaṃ gataḥ / vajrarāgaparijñānād vajrasattvo bhaven manaḥ*). It is easily understood that much that is worthwhile in the world has been achieved by passion. The incredible mastery of self attained by Gautama Buddha was hardly possible without an abundant amount directed toward the goal of Enlightenment. It might be objected that his passion was not the kind which leads men to vulgar deeds. But the Tantras claim that the difference is not in the passion, but in the part of the body which preempts its power. This is because the Tantras inherit the viewpoint that man is a microcosm corresponding to the macrocosm. From this standpoint, the head is the highest and best member; and the passion located there or in other upper centers such as the heart works "higher", i.e. to a superior end, than the passion below the navel.

Another reason for the Tantric use of the expression "passion" stems from the old Buddhist term *pañcakāmaguṇa* (the five strands of desire), which stands for the five sensory objects constituting the "knowables" (*jñeya*) that unexamined for what they are, also constitute the "obscuration of the knowable" (*jñeya-āvaraṇa*), the last impediment to Enlightenment. So in native Tibetan literature there occurs the abbreviated expression *spaṅs-rtogs*. *Spaṅs-pa* means "elimination" (of defilements, *kleśa*, such as lust, hatred, delusion); *rtogs-pa* means "realization" (of the knowables, such as forms). They respectively eliminate the obscurations of defilement and the knowable. After purifying the defilements from one's nature, it is still necessary before Enlightenment to face the "five strands of desire". That is the significance of the Māra vision by Gautama under the Bodhi Tree.

We cite a number of works by Tsoṅ-kha-pa (1357-1419 A.D.), founder of the Gelugpa school of Tibetan Buddhism. Material on the arrows used in Part I comes from his Mchan-bu commentary on the *Pradīpoddyotana* in the Japanese Photo. edition, Vol. 148. Our main textual source for Part II is his *Sṅags rim chen mo*. This work which we employ in a separate Peking blockprint (references by "S" plus folio number) contains an elaborate discussion of both the Stage of Generation and the Stage of Completion of the Anuttara-yoga-tantra, stipulated as necessary and in that order. The *Sṅags rim chen mo* shows that both Stages may be expressed with six members (*ṣaḍaṅga*). These two sets of six members are exposed above, Tables 4 and 5.

While five-fold symbolism is ubiquitous in the Buddhist Tantras, we are concerned now with this symbolism in the 2nd member of the Stage of Generation, that of "passion" through Vajrasattva. Furthermore, even here there are two ways of setting forth the five-fold symbolism, namely (a) as a five-part rite (*vidhāna*, *cho ga*); and (b) as a five-membered evocation in terms of germ syllables and hand symbols. The latter is set forth in Part I of this paper, together with a sketch of literary history and doctrine. The former is set forth in Part II, especially following Tsoṅ-kha-pa's exposition of the "passion" member (S 365b-6 to S 366a-6; S 379b-6 to S 388a-2) along with those important doctrinal parallels suggested by his wide treatment beginning S 379b-6 (*rten pa lha bskyed pa*, "generation of the deities as residents").

I. The five arrows of Kāmadeva, the five arrows of Mañjuśrī, and the five *skandhas*

The Hindi work *Vaidik Koś*[1] mentions the *Atharva Veda* (3. 25. 1) as the early occurrence of love's (*kāma*'s) arrow (*iṣu*): "The arrow of love which is terrible—with that I pierce you in the heart."[2] That reference work cites ancient Vedic synonyms of *iṣu* ("arrow"): śaru, śarya, śārī, bāṇa. When classical treatises of astronomy and other subjects began to employ ordinary words to signify numbers, the word "arrow" was regularly employed for the number "5". Sirkar[3] cites for this purpose the synonyms bāṇa, śara, sāyaka, iṣu, viśikha, kalamba, mārgaṇa. In the Mahābhārata *kāma* is personified as a deity (Kāmadeva) represented as releasing flowery arrows from his bow.[4] The *Amarakoṣa* includes *pañcaśaraḥ* "five-arrowed" as a name of Kāmadeva.

1. Sūryakānta, *Vaidik Koś* (Banāras Hindu University, 1963), p. 90.
2. *iṣuḥ kāmasya yā bhīmā tayā vidhyāmi tvā hṛdi.*
3. D. C. Sirkar, *Indian Epigraphy* (Motilal Banarsidass, Delhi, 1965), p. 231.
4. cf. Ram Karan Sharma, *Elements of Poetry in the Mahābhārata*, University of California published in Classical Philology, Vol. 20 (Berkeley, 1964), p. 25.

A Hindi work *Bhāratīya Pratīk Vidyā*[5] mentions four metaphorical kinds of "five arrows". It quotes what it calls the *sthūla-rūpa* (gross form) of the five arrows (*pañcabāṇa*) from the *Kālīvilāsatantra*, namely Kāma, Manmatha, Kandarpa, Makaradhvaja, and Mīnaketu, which are precisely chief traditional epithets of Kāmadeva in his *mūrti* or embodied form.[6] According to Indian mythology, after Kāmadeva's body was burnt up by the fire from Śiva's third eye, Kāmadeva was revived with the epithets Anaṅga (bodiless) and Smara (mindfulness or memory). That Hindi work continues with the *sūkṣma-rūpa* (subtle form) of the five arrows as cited from the *Tripurātāpiny-upaniṣat*, namely, hrī, klī, ai, blū, and strau, which are evidently *mantras*; and this interpretation is certain by the discussion of *sūkṣma-rūpa* in the Tripurā section of the same work.[7]

This work cites only the Amarakoṣa for the list of five flowers of which the arrows are composed, called *bāhyaprakṛtimaya* (made of external substance), and for the list of five arrows by their results, called bhāvanāmaya (produced by imagination). The five flowers are: aravinda, the white lotus; the Aśoka flower; cūta, the Mango flower; navamallikā, jasmine; and nīlotpala, the blue lotus. The five arrows by their results, in fact the usual arrow names, are: unmādana, tāpana, śoṣaṇa, stambhana, and saṃmohana. However, the two *Amarakoṣa* verses in point are interpolations in the original text and are not found, for example, in the *Bibliotheca Indica* Sanskrit-Tibetan edition of the *Amarakoṣa*.[8]

Kālidāsa's *Kumārasaṃbhava* treatment of the Kāmadeva arrow attack on Śiva's mind to arouse love for Gaurī or Umā mentions only the one unfailing (*amogha*) arrow called *Saṃmohana*. This account may be based on the *Matsya Purāṇa* (Ānandāśrama ed., 154. 245)—or an equivalent portrayal in some other *Purāṇa*—where the great arrow (*mahāśara*) released by Makaradhvaja (i.e., Kāmadeva) is called *mohana* and pierces in the heart of Śiva, followed by Śiva's burning up of Kāmadeva. The partial translation into Tibetan of Subhūti Candra's *Amaraṭikā-kāmadhenu* contains a commentary on the Kāmadeva verses of the *Amarakoṣa*. Here a tradition is followed that Kāmadeva shot in sequence five arrows at Śiva, of which the first two missed his thoughts, the second two did no more than enter his mind, and the fifth struck the target and upset Śiva's austerity. The Tibetan terms for the five arrows match the five Sanskrit terms, but are

5. Janārdana Miśra, *Bhāratīya Pratik Vidyā* (Patna, 1959), p. 169.

6. S. Sorensen, *An Index to the Names in the Mahābhārata* (Reprint Motilal Banarsidass), p. 378, furnishes these synonyms of Kāma: Anaṅga, Jagatpati, Kandarpa, Makaradhvaja, Manmatha, Manobhava, Samkalpaja, Smara.

7. Miśra, *op. cit.*, pp. 218-19.

8. Satis Chandra Vidyābhūṣaṇa, ed., *Amarakoṣa*, Bibl. Ind., N. S. 1294 (Calcutta, 1911), p. 8. The two verses are included, for example, in the Nirnaya Sagar Press edition of the *Amarakoṣa* with brief commentary, 1950 edition p. 6.

given in the order unmādana (myos byed), tāpana (sreg byed), saṃmohana (yaṅ dag rmoṅ(s) byed), śoṣaṇa (skyem byed), and staṃbhana (ḥchi byed).[9] This commentary does not specifically name the fifth or successful arrow.

"Five arrows" are also mentioned in the Buddhist *Guhyasamāja-tantra*, Chap. XVI, p. 121:

> The "knower of mantras" should contemplate in the middle of the Diamond Sky an adamantine Mañjuśrī of great power; he should recollect his projecting point with the praxis of five arrows, and make them fall, in the manner of the formidable thunderbolt, in five spots.

Candrakīrti's commentary called *Pradīpoddyotana*, as glossed in Tibetan by Tsoṅ-kha-pa,[10] explains the term "five arrows" with expressions that diverge from the standard list in this order with interpretations as follows: (1) *madana*, sexual frenzy; (2) *mohana*, dazzle; (3) **niḥsmaraṇa*, bewitchment; (4) *mūrcchana*, swoon; (5) *niśceṣṭīkaraṇa*, unconscious rigidity. Tsoṅ-kha-pa's annotation (*mchan bu*) explains that the five arrows belong to the ruler of the Paranirmitavaśavartin gods of the Kāmadhātu—therefore the Buddhist equivalent of Kāmadeva.[11] The *Pradīpoddyotana* states that the officiant—the "knower of mantras"—should contemplate in the Clear Light (=Diamond Sky, *khavajra*) an adamantine Mañjuśrī of great power. The annotation explains that one contemplates in the realm of the void a red Mañjuśrī whose dress and all ornaments are red; holding in his right hand a red lotus the opening bud of which has the five arrow shafts; and holding in his left hand a bow. According to the *Pradīpoddyotana*, the *prayoga* (yoga practice) of the five arrows means that one exhorts the arrows or furnishes targets to them by means of *mantra-nyāsa* (placement of *mantra* letters) in five spots of the body, namely, in the heart, the head (i.e. forehead), the navel, the secret place (standing for the neck), and the feet. The annotation mentions the respective *mantra* to be deposited in the five spots intended to attract the respective arrows.

Given the preceding data, it follows that a popular symbol—Love's arrow—continued to be employed in Indian literature starting with the

9. Satis Chandra Vidyābhūṣaṇa, ed., *Amara-ṭīkā-kāmadhenuḥ*, Bibl. Ind., N. S. 1348 (Calcutta, 1912), p. 23.

10. Tokyo-Kyoto photo reprint of the Tibetan Tripitaka, Peking edition; Tsoṅ-kha pa Bkaḥ-hbum, Pa, extra Vol. No. 158, p. 144. Since the *Pradīpoddyotana* Bihar Ms. is here utilized the five arrow names are definite, except for the tentative form *niḥsmaraṇa.

11. cf. Étienne Lamotte, *Le traite de la grande vertu de sagesse* (Louvain, 1944) I, p. 25, (note), where we learn that the ruler of those gods is called Vaśavartin and is the Buddhist Māra (the tempter). Also in the *Buddhacarita*, XIII, 2 ff. Māra is flower-arrowed, has 5 world-deluding arrows; and Aśvaghoṣa knows the legend of Kāma's arrow attack on Siva.

Atharvaveda, down into the Epic, Purāṇic, Tantric, lexical, and scientific works. In classical times, the arrow became fivefold. The ramification might be related to an idea expressed by the old Buddhist term *pañcakāmaguṇa* (the five strands of desire), referring to the five sensory objects. The adoption of the symbol in the Buddhist Tantras, where iconography of Mañjuśrī frequently depicts him with an arrow in his right hand, a bow in his left, especially in the case where he has four or more hands,[12] shows again the syncretic character of the Tantras[13]—as an example of their wholesale borrowing of symbols, which are turned to purposes of the particular Tantras. In the early Śaivitic account, the yogin seeks to ward off the arrows of Kāma, or not present himself as a target, while in this Buddhist Tantra context, the officiant seeks to attract five arrows. It is reasonable to take this Tantric employment of the symbol as another borrowing of Śaivitic terminology—this borrowing being more obvious in the Avalokiteśvara-Amoghapāśa cult.[14] The appeal of the symbol to the authors of the Buddhist Tantras probably derives from the preference for five-fold terminology and symbolism in Buddhism. Thus, the Ta Chih Tu Lun (*Mahāprajñāpāramitāśāstra*) according to Lamotte's translation raises the question of why the Buddha preferred to reside at Rājagṛha. An answer is given that Rājagṛha has five Vihāra—at the spots Veṇuvana, Vaibhāravana, Saptaparṇaguhā, Indraśailaguhā, and Sarpaśuṇḍikaprāgbhāra.[15] It is noteworthy that the bodhisattva Mañjuśrī was popularly held to have his favorite haunt in China at the mountain Wu-tai-shan, the mountain of five peaks; and that Mañjuśrī has the epithets pañcaśikha and pañcacīra.[16]

So far, we can see why the *Guhyasamāja-tantra* would associate Mañjuśrī in particular (by the expression *mañjuvajra*) with five arrows aimed at five spots (*pañcasthāna*) in the officiant's body. The problem remains of why the Buddhist Tantra is doing this at all: that is, we wonder what this Tantra intends to achieve by this imagination that a deity up in the sky is shooting arrows into five spots of the body. The answer is suggested by the *Guhyasamaja-tantra*, Chap. XVII, p. 137: pañcaskandhāḥ samāsena pañcabuddhāḥ prakīrtitāḥ / "The five personality aggregates (*skandha*) are, in short, the five Buddhas." The process of effectuating these identities is

12. cf. Benoytosh Bhattacharyya, *The Indian Buddhist Iconography* (Firma K. L. Mukhopadhyay, Calcutta, 1958), Chap. III, Bodhisattva Mañjuśrī.

13. cf. Louis Renou et Jean Filliozat, *L'Inde classique* (Payot, Paris, 1947), I, 423 ff.

14. This borrowing is evident through much of the "Lotus family" of the Buddhist Tantra, especially for Amitābha, Avalokiteśvara, and Tārā; cf. A. Wayman, "The Twenty-One Praises of Tārā, A Syncretism of Saivism and Buddhism", *Journal of the Bihar Research Society*, 45: 1-4, 1959, pp. 36-43.

15. Lamotte, *op. cit.*, I, pp. 179-181.

16. Franklin Edgerton, *Buddhist Hybrid Sanskrit Dictionary*, p. 315.

called *anurāga*, attraction of deific essence.[17] That the *skandhas* are being aimed at is indicated by the *Pradīpoddyatana* context and Tsoṅ-kha-pa's annotation, because the five mantras deposited in body spots are standard germ syllables (*bīja*) of the five Buddhas, and because those five spots are allocated respectively to the five *skandhas* in another passage by Tsoṅ-kha-pa in his *Ḥdod ḥjo* ("Wishing cow") commentary on the *Śrīcakrasaṃvara-tantra*, a passage which I translate from Tibetan as follows:

> The *Viśeṣadyota* (Toh. 1510) explains that since the aggregate of forms (*rūpa-skandha*) is the basis of seeds, the chief place of the *rūpa-skandha* is the middle of the head; and explains that the forehead is the place of the *bindu*: hence one contemplates it (i.e. the *skandha* of forms) there. Because the aggregate of feelings (*vedanāskandha*) depends on warmth, its chief place is the navel. Because ideas (*saṃjñā*) arise concomitantly with the six perceptions (*vijñāna*) based on the eye, etc. (i.e. based on the five outer senses and the mind) and because the neck is the central place for the senses, the place of *saṃjñā* is the neck. Since the aggregate of motivations (*saṃskāra-skandha*) is the wind-basis of *mūlaklésa* and *upakleśa-caitasika-s*, its place is both feet beneath the ankle bone. Because the aggregate of perceptions (*vijñāna-skandha*) is the *prāṇa*-wind-basis of consciousness (*citta*) and located in the heart, the place of the *vijñāna-skandha* is explained as the heart.[18]

This passage taken together with the *Pradīpoddyotana* commentary, as well as the standard correlation between the five germ syllables, five Buddhas, and five *skandhas* enables us to set up the five-fold *anurāga* process in tabular form (Table 16).[19]

This location of *skandhas* in body spots invites a comparison with Greco-Roman concepts. According to Onians, the Greek ψυχή, the life spirit active in procreation, was believed to be in the head; the Romans had as analog the *genius*, for which the forehead was considered sacred, and believed that the head was the source of seed and concerned in procreation.[20] Note that the *rūpa-skandha* is placed in the head for the same reason. Again, in Greek thought the liver was the inmost spring of deeper

17. The *anurāga* phase is part of the Stage of Generation, as set forth extensively in Tsoṅ-kha-pa's *Sṅags rim chen mo*. This is of utmost importance in determining the difference between the Stage of Generation and the Stage of Completion.

18. Tsoṅ-kha-pa, Bkaḥ-ḥbum, Lhasa ed., Vol. Ta, "*Hdod ḥjo*", f. 27 a-b, ff.

19. cf. the correspondences presented by Shashi Bhusan Dasgupta, *An Introduction to Tāntric Buddhism* (Univ. of Calcutta, 1950), p. 97.

20. R. B. Onians, *The Origins of European Thought about the Body, the Mind, the Soul, the World, Time, and Fate*, p. 129.

TABLE 16

"THE FIVE-ARROW CORRESPONDENCES"

ARROW NAMES (anurāga process)	MANTRA-NYĀSA (germ syllable and where deposited)	SKANDHA THERE LOCATED	BUDDHA THUS EXHORTED
1. sexual frenzy	Hūṃ in heart	vijñāna (perceptions)	Akṣobhya ("Unmoved one")
2. dazzle	Oṃ in head	rūpa (forms)	Vairocana ("The Sun")
3. bewitchment	Svā in navel	vedanā (feelings)	Ratnasaṃbhava ("Source of Jewels")
4. swoon	Āḥ in neck	saṃjñā (ideas)	Amitābha ("Immeasurable Light")
5. unconscious rigidity	Hā in feet	saṃskāra (motivations)	Amoghasiddhi ("Unfailing Success")

emotions.[21] This agrees with locating the aggregate of feelings (*vedanā-skandha*) at the navel. For the Greeks and Romans, the heart—more generally the chest—was the seat of consciousness and the seat of breath; and consciousness was naturally identified with the breath.[22] This concept agrees perfectly with the Tantric location of *vijñāna* in the heart as the wind basis of object consciousness. It is remarkable that three of the Buddhist *skandhas* can be so closely identified with Greco-Roman attributions of functions to corporeal centers. The Tantric location of *saṃjña* in the neck and *saṃskāra* in the feet has no obvious Greco-Roman parallel, although Onians does discuss the role of the feet.[23] *Saṃjñā* is placed in the neck probably because, as Johnston has pointed out, *saṃjñā* is the naming function;[24] and so associated with the neck as the seat of speech. Regarding the placement of *saṃskāra-skandha*—as a center of corruptions or afflictions (*kleśa*)—in the feet, this agrees with the Hindu correlation of the lower part of the body with the underworlds (*pātāla*); and the Mongolian Lama Dilowa Gegen Hutukhtu once told me that the feet are the location of Yama, the Lord of Death, and his sister Yamī.

It is noteworthy that Indian thought consistently placed in the heart the function of perception. Hence, the arrow of love was aimed at this target and said to pierce "in the heart" (*hṛdi* in the *Atharvaveda*; *hṛdaye* in the *Matsya-Purāṇa*); and the five arrows were made to fall "in five spots" (*pañcasthāneṣu* in the *Guhyasamāja-tantra*) beginning with "in the heart".

21. *Ibid.*, p. 85.
22. *Ibid.*, pp. 40 ff. and p. 49.
23. cf. his appendix, pp. 524 ff.
24. E. H. Johnston, *Early Sāṁkhya* (London, 1937), p. 21.

I use the word "perception" advisedly. The plan of Kāmadeva was to make Śiva perceive Umā or Gaurī, make Śiva conscious of her as an object, aware of her as the paragon of female sensuous appearance. Therefore, the arrow was aimed at the heart, where Buddhism places *vijñāna*; and therefore I regularly translate *vijñāna-skandha* as "aggregate of perceptions".[25]

The above considerations support what is already well known, namely that religious practices of India in classical times take for granted the Vedic corpus. In addition, there is a suggestion of Greco-Roman tie-ups with the Buddhist Tantras, which merits further investigation.

II. The five-fold rite

In his annotation to the *Pradīpoddyotana* passage about the five arrows, Tsoṅ-kha-pa (Photo ed., Vol. 158, Pa, 355 a-b) rejects the position of some lamas that this evocation occurs in the yuganaddha phase of the Saṃpanna-krama. He concludes that it represents a high capability of service in the Utpatti-krama and is meant for a person of sharp senses who can achieve success (*siddhi*) in seven days.

Since the procedure of arrow imagination must pertain to the 2d *aṅga* of Utpatti-krama, it is of interest that Tsoṅ-kha-pa does indeed mention five syllables (*yi ge lṅa*, S 387 a-5) without listing them, but (S 385a-3) also mentions the *nāda* which comprises the three syllables, again not listing these, which are usually Oṃ, Āḥ, Hūṃ. Moreover, he brings up (S380b-6ff.)—but in a different connection—the standard terminology of sixteen Sanskrit vowels deposited in different parts of the body, and of thirty-four Sanskrit consonants coordinated with the five elements. Furthermore, some of Tsoṅ-kha-pa's materials on the 2d member apply more easily to the five-syllable evocation than to the restriction to three syllables or to *nāda*. This is certainly the case when explaining (S 385a-1, 2) the symbolism of the five-pronged thunderbolt as representing the five limbs (two legs, two arms, and head from neck up), the five fingers and toes on each of hands and feet, or the five senses in the head. For it is easy to see that the five arrow shafts held by Mañjuśrī as Vajrasattva correspond to the five-pronged thunderbolt. Therefore, "three syllables" may be taken as the abbreviated reference to the five syllables, and the distinction between

25. The above translations of all five *skandhas* follow rather closely Th. Stcherbatsky, *The Central Conception of Buddhism*, (reprint, Susil Gupta, Calcutta, 1961), pp. 5-6. My observations of numerous passages about the *skandhas* in Buddhist literature support Stcherbatsky's renditions except for his rendering of *vijñāna* as "pure sensation" or "general consciousness" and *rupa* as "matter", both correct but too vague. Vijñāna—like the other *nāma-skandhas*—is indeed consciousness, for in the case of *vijñāna* there is consciousness of an object, in a word: "perception". *Rupa* is indeed matter, but that matter which is perceived, so the literal sense of *rupa* as "form" is more appropriate.

nāda, the three syllables, and the five syllables may involve the difference between ordinary and superior candidates, as suggested by Tsoṅ-kha-pa.

There are two *āgama* passages cited for the five-fold rite. The first, quoted (S 365b-6) from *Gur* (S. *Pañjara*),[26] shows the method of generating deity by exhortation with mystic song (*źu ba glus bskul nas skyed tshul*, discussed S 382b-3, ff.):

> One should contemplate the five aspects:—
> (1) First imagining a man;
> (2) Then the emanation of the fairy circle (*dākinī-cakra*);
> (3) The entrance of the *gandharva* exhorted by the directional goddesses mindful to petition (it) (by mystic song) to descend;
> (4) After exhortation the guidance by that circle as follows: depositing the three *vajras* of *moha*, etc., in three spots, the eye, etc.;
> (5) Then the *vajra* "passion" causing the *jñāna* element to enter.

The second, quoted (S 380a-1) from the third *brtag-pa* of *Kha-sbyor* (S. *Saṃpuṭa*),[27] shows the method of generating deity by means of the five Abhisaṃbodhi (*mṅon byaṅ lṅas skyed tshul*, discussed S 379 b-6, ff.):

> (1) The moon, having the "mirror-like" knowledge;
> (2) Likewise (=the 2d moon), having the "equality" knowledge;
> (3) The germ syllable (*bīja*) and (4) the hand symbol (*cihna*) of one's god, called "discriminative" (knowledge), and all those into one, (called) "procedure-of duty" (knowledge);
> (5) The pure and perfect image (*bimba*) (having *dharmadhātu* knowledge).

According to Tsoṅ-kha-pa (S 386b-2) in order to understand either of these two formulations of the rite, one must associate them with the three states of birth, death, and the intermediate state (*skye ḥchi bar do gsum*). Indeed (S 383b-4, 5) the very name Utpatti-krama ("stage of generation") is used because it is analogical to the life cycle of being born from a womb, amassing *karma*, dying, being an intermediate state being in a womb, and then taking birth again, thus becoming a son or daughter.

The rationale for applying this terminology to yoga experience is the well-known Buddhist meditation to negate the ordinary view of the

26. *Gur* abbreviates the Tibetan title equivalent to *Arya-Ḍakinīvajrapañjarāmahātantrarājakalpa-nāma* (Tohoku No. 419).

27. *Kha-sbyor* abbreviates the Tibetan title equivalent to *Saṃputa-nāma-mahātantra* (Tohoku No. 381). The passage occurs in the Peking edition, Tokyo reprint, Vol. 2, p. 254, 5th folio.

personality aggregates (*skandha*). In early Buddhism, the *skandhas* were seen by similes such as "forms (*rūpa*) are like a lump of foam." In the *Prajñāpāramitāhṛdayasūtra*, the *skandhas* are each identified with voidness. If these aggregates are to be so profoundly affected and transmuted, such a successful meditation must be comparable to death, because Buddhism teaches that such a drastic nullification of the *skandhas* occurs at death. So Tsoṅ-kha-pa writes (S 384 a-3,4): "Then the contemplation of voidness is comparable to death; because, by deciding the *skandhas* which are the foundation for adhering to "I" and "mine" to be devoid of intrinsic nature, and nullifying their manifestation—is comparable to abandoning the wornout *skandhas*." When the *skandhas* are seen as void, and this is to be regarded as a Symbolic Death, it follows that there is for the yogin also a Symbolic Intermediate State and a Symbolic Rebirth.

Therefore, both *āgama* passages are to be understood as a *sādhana* rite of Symbolic Death, Intermediate State, and Rebirth. But, admittedly, the two passages cannot, obviously, be so construed. In the case of the five Abhisambodhi, the first two (cf. S 386a-4, ff.), namely the moon and the second or red moon (=sun), constitute the *hetu-vajradhara*, while the last, the perfect image, is the *phala-vajradhara*. Now, the *phala-vajradhara*, being the fruitional spiritual rebirth, must. according to Buddhist dogmatics, be the result of the being which died, and so the *hetu-vajradhara* is the Symbolic Death. That leaves the intermediate two Abhisambodhis—the germ syllables and hand symbols—to represent the Intermediate State and this is the way they are treated. So (S 384b-2); "Having entered the syllables of the Intermediate State . . ." (*bar srid kyi yi ge źugs nas . . .*); (cf. S 384b-4) that is why (3) germ syllable and (4) hand syllable are taken together in the *āgama* passage; and so (S 385a-1) "the five pronged thunderbolt generated as the hand symbol from the germ syllable". That the 3rd and 4th aspects in the rite represent the Intermediate State as the sojourn in the womb is partly born out immediately by the formulation in the former *āgama* passage involving mystic song. There the 3rd aspect involves the entrance of the gandharva. Wijesekera points out on the basis of Pāli Buddhism that in the Mahātaṇhāsaṅkhaya Sutta the presence of the *gandhabba* (Skt. *gandharva*) is required in order that coitus of parents may lead to a conception; and that Buddhaghosa explains the term "*gandhabba*" in this case as "the being about to enter the womb . . . being driven on by the mechanism of Kamma / =karma /." Wijesekera also notices that in the *Amarakoṣa* the term *gandharva* is explained as "*antarābhavasattva*"—which of course is the Sanskrit for "Intermediate State Being".[28] Again, the two *āgama* passages agree on the fourth aspect because the "three *vajras* of *moha*, etc." are hand symbols, the *vajra* being

28. O. H. de A. Wijesekera, "The Concept of Vijñāna in Theravāda Buddhism," *Journal of the American Oriental Society*, 84: 3 (July-Sept. 1964), p. 256.

the thunderbolt symbol, and "*moha*, etc." stand for the three Buddhas, Vairocana, Akṣobhya, and Amitābha, heading the Moha, Dveṣa, and Rāga families—who are generated from the three germ syllables.

Depositing three thunderbolts is comparable to introducing five arrows as in the Mañjuśrī episode, by exhortation of five germ syllables.

The relation to non-tantric Buddhism is further shown by introduction of the terminology of the *bodhisattva*'s five paths.[29] For these correlations Tsoṅ-kha-pa cites the *Man sñe* (S. *Mañjari*)[30] starting at S383b-6. The *bodhisattva*'s Path of Accumulating Merit (*saṃbhāra-mārga*) took place prior to the experience of Symbolic Death: it is in the phase of *pūrvakālabhava* (*ḥdas paḥi srid pa*), defined by *Abhidharma-kośa* III 13c-d as "subsequent to the moment of birth and prior to the moment of death" (*sa punar maraṇāt pūrva upapattikṣaṇāt paraḥ*). Furthermore, according to the *Pitāputrasamāgama*—as quoted in *Sikṣāsamuccaya*, "And immediately after the cessation of that 'first perception' (*prathama-vijñāna*) pertaining to birth, a contiguous matching 'stream of consciousness' proceeds. Among those, the cessation of the 'last perception' (*carama-vijñāna*) is counted as 'death' (*cyuti*) in this case; the emergence of the 'first perception' is counted as 'birth' (*upapatti*) in this case."[31]

Symbolic Death

"Death" is here explained (S 384a-4,5) as starting from initial negation of the personality aggregates and lasting up to entrance into the syllables of the Intermediate State. It is associated with the Path of Training (*prayoga-mārga*)—according to *Man sñe*, the Stage of Action in Faith (*adhimukti-caryā-bhūmi*) and the Training in Decision about Reality (*tattvanirvedha-prayoga*). In the Prajñāpāramitā doctrine, it has four degrees: those of Heat (*ūṣmagata*), the Climax (*mūrdhagata*), Forbearance (*kṣānti*), and Highest Mundane Natures (*laukika-agra-dharma*).[32] The four easily divide into two groups of two, because Heat and the Climax apply to "non-self of personality", while Forbearance [of Natures] and Highest Mundane Natures apply to "non-self of natures". It is apparent that the "Heart Sūtra" (*Prajñāpāramitāhṛdaya*) is easily interpreted the same way. According to the present writer's translation[33] this Sūtra

29. E. Obermiller, *The Doctrine of Prajñā-pāramitā as exposed in the Abhisamayālaṃkāra of Maitreya*, Reprint from *Acta Orientalia*, Vol. XI (1932), pp. 33-45. The five Paths are *saṃbhāra-mārga, prayoga-mārga, darśana-mārga, bhāvanā-mārga*, and *aśaikṣa-mārga*.

30. *Man sñe* abbreviates the Tibetan title equivalent to *Srisaṃpuṭatantrarājaṭīkāmnāya-manjarī-nāma*, (Tohoku No. 1198), by Ḥjigs-med ḥbyuṅ-gnas sras-pa (*Abhayākara-pāda).

31. Edition of Mithila Institute, p. 135. 15-16.

32. Obermiller (*op. cit.*), pp. 34-37.

33. A Wayman, "The Buddhist 'Not this, not this'," *Philosophy East and West*, XI: 3 (Oct. 1961), especially pages 109-113.

presents three meditations—the first on "non-self of personality", the second and third on "non-self of natures".

Since what is called "generating the mind of Enlightenment" (*bodhicittotpāda*) precedes the *bodhisattva* path, it must be placed in the Path of Training. In his *Lam rim chen mo*, *bodhisattva* section, Tsoṅ-kha-pa thoroughly discusses the two stages called "aspiration mind" (*praṇidhicitta*, *smon sems*) and "progressing mind" (*prasthānacitta*, *ḥjug sems*). The "aspiration mind" is coloured with compassion (*karuṇā*), while the "progressing mind" involves taking the *bodhisattva* vow (*saṃvara*). This vow is associated with the second *abhisaṃbodhi* by Mkhas-grub-rje in his *Fundamentals of the Buddhist Tantras*, Chap. I, through the *mantra*, "*Oṃ bodhicittam utpādayāmi*." In that former section, Tsoṅ-kha-pa quotes Śāntideva's *Bodhicaryāvatāra* VIII, 158: "Therefore, just as you employed your ego (*ahaṃkāra*) in others' *bindu*-s (formed) of semen and menstrual blood, so also devote it to others' (tasmād yathānyadīyeṣu śukraśoṇitabinduṣu / cakartha tvam ahaṃkāraṃ tathānyeṣv api bhāvaya). The "aspiration mind" is parallel with the first aspect (first *abhisaṃbodhi*) and the "progressing mind" is parallel with the second one, as will become clearer by our subsequent observations.

Since the "death" phase is the cause of "birth," the *Pitāputrasamāgamasūtra* may again be cited: "So, great King, a 'first perception' arises having two conditions pertaining to 'birth'—by reason of the 'last perception' as predominant condition (*adhipati-pratyaya*) and by reason of '*karma*' as support condition (*ārambaṇa-pratyaya*)."[34] Otherwise stated, "death" is divided into "Expiration" and "Death vision"[35]—the former being the "last perception" and the latter the "*karma*". In Abhidharma Buddhism, two causes are necessary for a thing to arise—the *hetu*, basic or seed cause; and *pratyaya*, the conditional cause. The phase of "death" covers the first two aspects in both *āgama* passages, the first aspect being the *hetu*—in this case, the predominant condition; the second aspect, the *pratyaya*—in this case, the support condition. In short, both formulations of the five-fold rite begin with symbolic equivalences to death, and this is consistent with the old Upaniṣadic passage, "There was nothing whatsoever here in the beginning. By death indeed was this covered, or by hunger, for hunger is death."[36]

The preceding is more easily related to the 2d *āgama* passage than to the 1st one. In the case of the first two *abhisaṃbodhis*, the "moon" explained (S 381a-5) as the sixteen parts of the *bodhicitta* (hence the sixteen

34. *Op. cit.*, 135, 12-13.
35. A. Wayman, "Climactic Times in Indian Mythology and Religion," *History of Religions*, 4: 2 (Winter 1965), p. 296.
36. S. Radhakrishnan, *The Principal Upaniṣads* (New York, 1953), *Bṛhadāraṇyaka Upaniṣad*, p. 151.

vowels = the sixteen voidnesses) is the *hetu*, in the sense of attaining the realm of the void—the first step in the standard Buddhist Tantric *sādhana*. The red moon (the sun), explained as the thirty-four consonants representing the five elements (*dhātu*: earth, water, fire, wind, space), is the *pratyaya*, in the sense that they are the five goddesses who constitute the objective plenitude. But since the two are the *hetu-vajradhara*, the cause for the *phala-vajradhara*, the comparison is made to father, mother, and son (cf. S 384b-5), to wit: the father releases semen (= *bodhi* = the moon), the mother's menstrual blood wells up with her (is withheld), the two understood in old Indian belief to contribute to the formation of the embryo. Therefore, the "moon" is taken as the "father," the "red moon" as the "mother"; and since these two are the physical condition for the birth, they (i.e., the father emitting semen and the mother holding that "white element" together with her "red element") are—on this symbolic level—also "death."[37]

The 1st *āgama* passage conveys exhortation by mystic song, and is immediately related if we consider another Tantric passage:[38] "Because one experiences the Dharmakāya, joyful, equal to the sky, for only an instant at the time of (1) death, (2) faint, (3) going to sleep, (4) yawning, and (5) coitus." Here, "death" is correlated to the Dharmakāya of the Buddha; and, since (S 387a-6 to 387b-1) there would be no Mahāyāna if the Buddha had remained in the Dharmakāya and had not appeared in the Body of Form (*rūpa-kāya*)—this five-fold rite represents the exhortation for the Buddha as *hetu-vajradhara* to phenomenalize a Nirmāṇakāya for the benefit of sentient beings. In this process (S 383a-4), the first aspect "imagining a man" means the *hetuvajradhara* in union with the consort (= Prajñāpāramitā) producing, as the second aspect, the group of eight goddesses. This is still Symbolical Death, because as yet there is no Saṃbhoga-kāya coordinated with the Intermediate State or Nirmāṇa-kāya coordinated with Birth. Among the group of eight goddesses[39] are the four (S 385a-6) who are the four elements that enable a phenomenal body to be formed; they are a sort of demiurge, secondary creative deities, who by their mystic

37. This involves an archaic symbolism prevalent in Mesopotanian mythology: Erishkigal, Sumerian goddess of death and gloom is in the Nether World as the "birth-giving mother"; cf. Samuel Noah Kramer, ed., *Mythologies of the Ancient World*, A Doubleday Anchor Original (New York, 1961), pp. 107-8. It also involves the world-wide contribution to primitive religion of woman's "blood mysteries", that is, menstrual blood, formation of the embryo by blood, and conversion of blood into mother's milk.

38. A Wayman, "Studies in Yama and Māra," *Indo-Iranian Journal* III: 1 (1959), p. 57.

39. The names of the eight goddesses according to the *Hevajra-tantra* (ed. and tr. by D. Snellgrove) are (his Vol. I, p. 74): Gaurī, Gauri, Vetālī, Ghasmarī, Pukkasī, Savarī, Caṇḍālī, and Ḍombinī. However, Tsoṅ-kha-pa alludes to the names only as "Locanā and so on," obviously employing *Guhyasamāja* traditional terminology, where Locanā, Māmakī, Pāṇḍarā, and Tārā are the four chief goddesses, identified respectively with the elements earth, water, fire, and wind.

TABLE 17

"DEATH" (2 ASPECTS)

	AS "CAUSE OF BIRTH"	SOMEWHERE AN EXPERIENCE (A)	SOMEWHERE AN EXPERIENCE (B)	HETU-VAJRADHARA	DHARMA-KĀYA	PATH OF TRAINING	GENERATING THE *bodhicitta*
1.	Hetu, primary cause	Expiration (last perception)	he (releases semen)	moon (=16 parts of *bodhicitta*)	Hetu-vajradhara in union with Prajñā-pāramitā	"non-self of person (*pudgala*)"	"aspiration mind"
2.	Pratyaya, conditional cause	Death Vision (karma)	she (holds her menstrual blood)	sun (=the 5 elements)	the retinue of eight goddesses	"non-self of natures (*dharma*)"	"progressing mind"

song call forth the "world"—in this case the phenomenal body of the Buddha. See Table 17.

Symbolic Intermediate State

A suggestive example of an "intermediate" statement is when the *Prajñā-pāramitāhṛdayasūtra* remarks: "Taking recourse to the *bodhisattva*'s perfection of insight, one dwells with obscuration of the mental substance (*cittāvaraṇa*). By reason of no obscuration of the mental substance, he is fearless, beyond delusion, with supreme *nirvāṇa*."[40] That is to say, the above statement follows after the mention of meditations on "non-self of personality" and "non-self of natures" and precedes the mention of the Incomparable Enlightenment of the *buddhas*. The order is consistent with what has been set forth previously, namely that the voidness meditation is the preliminary training for the *bodhisattva* path. Therefore, the "Heart Sūtra" is now alluding to the *bodhisattva* path and its culmination, but leaves open the problem of describing this path, as say, with six "perfections" (*pāramitā*) or with ten "stages" (*bhūmi*). Any definite portrayal of the *bodhisattva* path is therefore consistent with the "Heart Sūtra" although not necessarily reflecting the viewpoint of this essence of the Prajñāpāramitā literature. Such is the case with the correspondence now made (S 384b-2,3 quotation from *Man sñe*) of the ten *bodhisattva* stages to the ten lunar-month states (*avasthā*) in the womb, for the given reason that all these stages are attended with obscuration (*sa ḥdi rnams sgrib pa daṅ bcas pa ñid kyi phyir*). In non-tantric Buddhism there is the same teaching, for Vasubandhu says it,[41] and the *Āryasaṃdhinirmocanasūtrasya vyākhyāna* also comments: "The passage, 'so as to perfect those limbs of his, he perfects all the limbs' means: because those ten *bodhisattva* stages are attended with obscuration, they are comparable to the ten periods of the body dwelling in a womb."[42] It appears the correlation was originally made because the *bodhisattva* path, like the intra-uterine months, divide into groups of seven and three; that is, after the seventh stage, the *bodhisattva* is "irreversible" (*avaivartika*), and it was noticed that after the seventh lunar month of pregnancy, an infant can be born alive. However, the tantric division, as will soon be apparent, is not into seven and three, but into two groups of five. Of course the *bodhisattva* gradually eliminates

40. "The Buddhist 'Not this, not this'," p. 113, translation based on the scholarly edition of this *sutra* by F. Max Müller and Bunjiu Nanjio.

41. Vasubandhu's commentary (Toh. 3993) on the *Daśabhumika-sutra*, Derge Tanjur, Mdo-ḥgrel, Ṅi, 112b-1, f.

42. Japanese photo reprint of Kanjur-Tanjur, Vol. 114, p. 314-2-3, ff. (Tohoku No. 5848, commentary on Leḥu dgu-pa). (The passage continues with a reason and illustration).

the "obscuration", so that on the final stages only the most subtle "obscuration" remains.[43]

Accordingly (S 384a-6, ff.), the third path, Path of Vision (*darśana-mārga*), which coincides with the first of the ten *bodhisattva* stages, named Pramuditā, is equivalent to the first *avasthā* in the womb; while the Path of Concentrated Contemplation (*bhāvanā-mārga*), associated with the remaining nine *bodhisattva* stages, is prevalent during the last nine *avasthās*.

Now, the term "Intermediate State" (*antarābhava*) was the topic of lively disagreement by ancient Buddhist schools, some denying that there is such a state.[44] Part of the quarrel may have rested on a different use of the term, because "period between death and rebirth" involves interpretation of "death" and of "rebirth". Sometimes a period of forty-nine days was ascribed to the Intermediate State. As the term is employed in this tantric context, it seems to mean the state that begins when a *gandharva* is headed toward a particular womb—as well as the sojourn in that womb. It follows the second moment of death, which amounts to automatic visions; and precedes the first moment of rebirth occurring with departure from the womb. The *bodhisattva* path of vision may cover this initial movement as well as the first *avasthā*.

As was mentioned previously, "entrance of the *gandharva*" means entrance into the womb. At S 385a-5 Tsoṅ-kha-pa quotes the *Man sñe* for three ways of entrance and supplies further information: (1) "Through the golden portal," also called the Vairocana portal; (2) "Through the mouth" of the mother or of the father and by him transmitted to the mother; (3) "In another way," namely, through the portal of the womb. The third way is asserted (S 385b-1,2) for the ordinary *gandharva* with passion toward either the male or the female. Tsoṅ-kha-pa explains the first way in his *Don-gsal* commentary on the *Guhyasamāja*:

> Moreover, like a man riding a horse—that "perception-master" (*vijñāna-pati*), the "diamond of mind" (*cittavajra*), the Intermediate State Consciousness (*antarābhava-citta*)—along with a very subtle body (**atisukṣma-deha*), rightly straddling that mount of wind, proceeds with great rapidity, and having reached that place in an instant (*kṣaṇa*), a twinkling (*lava*), or a moment (*muhurta*) enters

43. Cf. Obermiller (*op. cit.*), p. 57: "Of these ten Stages the first seven are called the 'impure' and the last three—'the pure' Stages. The reason for such a classification is that on the former the different defiling elements are still existing, whereas on the latter the Bodhisattva has to remove only the most subtle forms of the Obscuration of Ignorance, consisting in the differentiation of subject and object, and of Saṃsāra and Nirvāṇa as two separate entities."

44. André Bareau, *Les Sectes bouddhiques du Petit Véhicule* (Saigon, 1955), p. 283, thesis "Il y a une existence intermédiaire".

> that Vairocana portal. Now, some former lamas, appealing to the passage [in the *Mahāmudrātilaka*] that Vairocana is ordure, explained the anus as the Vairocana portal. This is not tenable, for the citation "in the same way as the Knowledge Being (*jñāna-sattva*)" shows it to be the portal through which the Knowledge Being enters the Symbolic Being (*samaya-sattva*). Hence, in the same way as the Knowledge Being enters through the crown of the head, that ["perception-master"] enters through the crown of the head where is disposed the "diamond of body" (*kāya-vajra*) of Vairocana.[45]

The three ways seems to be ordered as superior, middling, and inferior. The superior way through the golden portal seems indicated for the *gandharva* of the first *āgama* passage. In its explanation (S 383a-2,3) the *gandharva* takes abode in the *bindu-rūpa* (*thig leḥi gzugs*). This is formed from the passionate embrace of the "Father-Mother" (*yab yum*) [aspect No. 1]. Now exhorted by the mystic songs of Locanā and the other goddesses [aspect No. 2], from the *bindu* [into which the *gandharva* has descended] there arise the germ syllables [aspect No. 3) and hand symbols [aspect No. 4], and from these completion as a deity [aspect No. 5]. The last three are the standard three-fold rite (*cho ga gsum*).

Therefore, in both *āgama* passages, the third and fourth aspects constitute the Symbolic Intermediate Stage. Tsoṅ-kha-pa explains that the goddesses exhort the Dharmakāya [of Symbolic Death] to issue the Body of Form for the sake of the candidates. The Dharmakāya, and accordingly any officiant performing this as a rite, is held to think, "Hence, so as to attain that very Samantabhadra, I shall enter this very place," and having made his mind steadfast in that form of the five syllables of the Intermediate State, like a flame he enters the secret lotus of the Prajñā.[46] The next aspect, as mentioned previously form S 385a-1, is the five-pronged thunderbolt. The five syllables are clearly the five as in the Mañjuśrī *sādhana* of our Part I, there imagined to be planted in the five *skandhas*, the latter elsewhere held to arise sequentially in the first five *avasthas* of the womb.[47] Then the five arrows of Mañjuśrī depositing the five knowledges are symbolized here by the five-pronged thunderbolt, and so correspond to the second five *avasthā*-s, held to perfect the five sensory organs. In the case of the Mañjuśrī *sādhana*, this is a case of evocation without exhortation by song. The solution of applying the five arrow names to the five sense objects is possible through Tsoṅ-kha-pa's *Mchan-ḥgrel* on *Pradīpoddyotana*, 7th Chapter, Photo ed., Vol. 158, p. 56-1,2. Here we learn that the *sādhaka*

45. Lhasa Gsuṅ-ḥbum, Cha, "Don Gsal," 32b-3, ff.
46. *Sṅags rim chen mo*, S 387a-4, 5, 6.
47. "Studies in Yama and Māra," (*op. cit.*), p. 72, note 155.

(one realizing the *sādhana*), when reaching "forms" by way of the eye offers the lady Rūpavajrā to the *tathāgata* Vairocana; similarly with the other objects and senses: Sabdavajrā to Ratnasambhava, Gandhavajrā to Amitābha, Rasavajrā to Amoghasiddhi, Sparśa-vajrā to Akṣobhya. This is consistent with the *Pradīpoddyotana* (Mchan-ḥgrel edition), Ibid., p. 55, identification of sense objects with the *tathāgata*-s. Then the correspondences in Table 16 enable us to quickly assign the arrow names accordingly. The only change in order is Akṣobhya's "sexual frenzy" moved from first in the *skandha* series to fifth in the sense-object series, with the others moved up in the same order. But the present order of the arrows is consistent with the story in the *Amarakoṣa* commentary that the fifth arrow (unnamed), here the one named *madana*, succeeded in arousing Śiva sexually, whereas the unfailing arrow in the *Kumārasaṃbhava* version is *saṃmohana*.

Elsewhere, Tsoṅ-kha-pa coordinates the Sambhoga-kāya with the Intermediate State, and the latter with the ten avatāras of Viṣṇu.[48] See Table 18, where the data of this section is summarized. Of course, the five arrows (in terms of their names) can be replaced by the five-pronged thunderbolt, also emblematic of the five *tathāgatas*.

Symbolic Rebirth

Tsoṅ-kha-pa explains at S 386a-3,4 that upon being born as a "son" after the ten stages, there is the Fruitional (*phala-*) Vajradhara, namely the state of manifesting a deity, the Nirmāṇa-kāya. And this is the fifth *bodhisattva* path, called "Stage Beyond Training" (*aśaikṣa-bhūmi*). It is the fifth aspect in both *āgama* passages.

In the case of the first *āgama* passage, the "rebirth" can be interpreted (a) from upwards down, as a passionate emanation of the knowledge of the Dharmakāya, or as an overshadowing of an individual by the *tathāgata* of his family (*kula*); (b) from downwards up, as a deification of the candidate, or as the human *bodhisattva* emerging from the tenth or Dharmameghā stage into the Buddhabhūmi. The second *āgama* passage stresses the method of generating the gods of the *maṇḍala*. In the fifth aspect, the god assumes a concrete attitude, reflecting the repose of the Dharmadhātu, or merges with the external icon.

According to the Siddhānta Commentary by Ḥjam-dbyaṅs bźad-paḥi-rdo-rje, there are three kinds of Nirmāṇa-kāya: (1) "artisan", (2) "of birth", and (3) "of Enlightenment" (*bzo daṅ skye ba byaṅ chub sprul sku gsum*). Citing references, this author explains the "artisan" kind as fashioning for the sake of sentient beings; that "of birth" as the births

48. Cf. *Ibid.*, 70-72, for correspondence of Viṣṇu avatars with stages of womb; and for correspondence of Saṃbhoga-kāya to Intermediate State being, cf. A. Wayman, "Buddhist Genesis and the Tantric Tradition," above.

TABLE 18

"INTERMEDIATE STATE" (2 ASPECTS)

AVASTHĀ IN WOMB	A. SKANDHA PERFECTED	A. DEFILEMENTS TO BE ELIMINATED (SPAŃS PA)	A. GERM SYLLABLE AND COLOR	BODHISATTVA STAGES	VIṢṆU AVATĀRAS
1	vijñāna	hatred	black Hūṃ	Joy (pramuditā)	Fish
2	vedanā	pride	yellow Svā	Immaculate (vimalā)	Tortoise
3	saṃskāra	envy	green Hā	Illuminating (prabhākarī)	Boar
4	saṃjñā	lust	red Āḥ	Blazing (arciṣmatī)	Man-Lion
5	rūpa	delusion	white Oṃ	Unconquerable (sudurjayā)	Dwarf
	B. INDRIYA PERFECTED	B. KNOWABLES TO BE REALIZED (*rtogs pa*)	B. HAND SYMBOL IN CASE OF ARROW NAMES		
6	eyes	forms	dazzle	Facing (abhimukhī)	Paraśu-Rāma
7	ears	sounds	bewitchment	Far-reaching (dūraṃgamā)	The 2d Rāma
8	nose	odors	swoon	Motionless (acalā)	Kṛṣṇa
9	tongue	tastes	unconscious rigidity	Perfect Wisdom (sādhumatī)	Buddha
10	torso (skin)	tangibles	sexual frenzy	Cloud of Doctrine (dharmameghā)	Kalki

depicted in Jātaka stories; and that "of Enlightenment" as the Nirmāṇa-kāya of the Buddha demonstrating, among Twelve Acts, Complete Enlightenment.[49]

The first kind, in further explanation, seems equivalent to hypostasis in chosen individuals, that is, magically manifesting in multiform ways as *śrāvaka*-s, *pratyekabuddha*-s, Indra, Brahmā, etc. So the first of the three kinds is especially applicable to Symbolic Rebirth as the fifth aspect of the rite.

Since the Symbolic Death has been explained above as the cause of Symbolic Birth, it is well to point out a corroboration of this in terms of the "moon (= 16 parts of *bodhicitta*)" of Table 17. Ye-śes-rgyal-mtshan, the Yoṅs-ḥdzin for the Dalai Lama Ḥjam-dpal rgya-mtsho, contains in his Collected Works, Lhasa ed., Vol. Tha (Toh. No. 6016), a commentary on the sixteen Sthaviras, in the course of which (passage beg., f. 160a-3) he refers to various Nirmāṇa-kāya(s) (*sprul sku*) and mentions the *Bkaḥ gdams thig le bcu drug gi sgrub dkyil* ("*Sādhana* and *maṇḍala* of the Bkaḥ-gdams school rite 'sixteen parts of the *bindu*'"). Earlier he states:

> In "final meaning" (*nītārtha*), these sixteen Sthaviras are as said: "The sixteen Sthaviras—concretely the Three Jewels—who are the Arya host of Arhat *nirmita*-s of the Buddha, protecting the Teaching for the sake of the world—provide the grace (*adhiṣṭhāna*) so that the Teaching may long endure." Just as the Buddha was said to have gone to the ultimate of "elimination" (of defilement) and "realization" (of the knowable) so all sixteen Sthaviras have gone to the ultimate of "elimination" and "realization".[50]

Or, as said in the "Heart Sūtra,"—There is Enlightenment. Hail!

Conclusion

It has been a special pleasure for the writer to weave together the above materials, casting some light on Tantric *sādhana*, indicating also some of the non-tantric background of Buddhist tantric ideas—and generally certifying Tsoṅ-kha-pa's tantric reform that requires non-tantric Buddhism as the indispensable preparation for the Tantras.

An incidental conclusion is that the principal message of the Prajñāpāramitā literature is the "Path of Training" of the *bodhisattva*, that is, especially to drill the point that both *pudgala* and *dharma* are *nairātmya*, and then, in the space thus vacated of false views, to arouse the Mind of Enlightenment—consistent with Kamalaśīla's commentary on the

49. The *Grub mthaḥ ḥgrel pa* called *Re ba kun skoṅ*, published at Moussorie (India) under the direction of the Tā bla-ma, Sec. Cha, 50b-51a.

50. Ye-śes-rgyal-mtshan, Vol. Tha, 52b-6, ff.

Vajracchedikā (Tohoku No. 3817), wherein he explains the "Eye of Insight" (*prajñācakṣus*) as "seeing" *pudgala-nairātmya* and *dharma-nairātmya*. Tantric *sādhana* also begins with this "Symbolic Death", referred to as "realization of the void".

The reasonable speculation in Part I that the five arrows may have been based on the *pañcakāmaguṇa* is somewhat borne out by Table 18 in Part II. Much later the arrows were associated with the five *skandhas*, as in Table 16, in connection with the *sādhana* equating these five *skandhas* with the five *tathāgatas*, a feature of the Anuttara-yoga-tantra.

But the writer does not wish to leave this subject, giving the impression that everything "works out" consistently—that the corpus of ancient Buddhism, Prajñāpāramitā and tantric literature—and even non-Buddhist literature—can be "harmonized" by such underlying threads as have been drawn out above. That diverse traditions are involved is an obvious feature, e.g. dividing the ten *avasthā*-s into groups of seven and three, or into two groups of five. Also, the suggestion by E. H. Johnston, *The Buddhacarita*, Part II (Calcutta, 1936), p. 191, n. 16, that Aśvaghoṣa and Kālidāsa (*Kumārasaṃbhava*) have two different traditions about Kāma's attack on Śiva—seems verified by our findings. We may postulate, on the one hand, a tradition of five-fold symbolism, Upaniṣadic (early and later sectarian), Śaivitic, that of Aśvaghoṣa regarding five flowery arrows of Māra = Kāmadeva, followed in the *Amarakoṣa*, and continued in the Buddhist Tantras; and, on the other hand, the single arrow which is a topic in the earliest source, the *Atharva-veda*, continued in Saivitic Purāṇa literature and adopted by Kālidāsa. It is of interest that, according to *Buddhacarita*, xiii, 12, when Māra discharged an arrow at the son of Iḍā, grandson of the moon, he "became *vicitta*", translated by Johnston that he "fell into a frenzy". Johnston apparently interprets the *vi-* as intensive rather than deprivative. This interpretation is certified by *Ibid.* xiii, 16, which depicts Māra as wondering, when his arrow had no effect on the future Buddha, whether the latter was *acitta* or the arrow he had used was not the one which had agitated Śambhu (Śiva). The point is that if Gautama is *acitta* "devoid of thought", his thoughts cannot become enhanced, frenzied, as signified by *vicitta*. And if we associate *citta* with the heart, our Table 16 suggests that Māra's arrow was the one later called *madana* ("sexual frenzy").

This forces us to consider the issue of why in non-tantric Buddhism Gautama is unaffected by Māra's arrow while in the *Guhyasamājatantra* the officiant exhorts Mañjuśrī to pierce five spots of the body with the arrows we have described. It is indeed difficult to imagine, on the basis of our Table 18, the effect on a person who has eliminated hatred, pride, envy, lust, and delusion, of being pierced by the arrows "dazzle", "bewitchment", "swoon", "unconscious rigidity", and "sexual frenzy".

Perhaps these terms have a special meaning gained through "realization" (*rtogs pa*) of the "knowable".

An attempt can be made to suggest the meaning by considering the whole last line in Table 18. Here the 10th *avasthā* in the womb is said to perfect the skin which senses the tangible or touchables; and it is the 10th *Bodhisattva* stage called "Cloud of Doctrine" where *bodhisattva* is a future *buddha*, just as Kalkī is the future avatāra of Viṣṇu. What is the meaning of "sexual frenzy" here as applied to *bodhisattvas* of the 10th stage, Mañjuśrī, etc.? Here a pictorial representation may help convey the point. See the plate 189 of Mañjuśrī the Vajrasattva as Ekavīra ("The Solitary Hero") in Giuseppe Tucci, *Tibetan Painted Scrolls* (Rome, 1949), discussed II, 583, where the phallus is up but hidden. Compare it with "Hermes.—Greek vase painting in the Hamilton Collection," reproduced in C. G. Jung, *Psychology and Alchemy*, Bollingen Series XX (New York, 1953), p. 126, where Hermes is represented only by a head and an erect phallus, both attached to a symbolic post. Then, what is the meaning here of the passion suggested by the Śaivitic *ūrdhva-liṅga*? Starting with the *Atharvaveda* the main spot pierced by love's arrow has been in the heart. So, just as in the "Twenty-one Praises of Tārā," the "upward *liṅga*" is the "thumb" in the heart, marked with the Three Jewels, as seen in the Stūpa-stambha of Amarāvatī (*Bhāratīya Pratik Vidyā*, picture No. 140). In the *Mahāvastu*, the 10th Bodhisattva stage is called *Abhiṣeka* (coronation or initiation), so called in Sanskrit because attended with sprinkling, symbolizing lustration. This is the "heart" meaning of the sprinkled *ūrdhva-liṅga*: the Stūpa-stambha in the heart. Therefore, when Māra's arrow is unsuccessful against the meditating Gautama, it means that a "lower" passion could not be aroused. The ecstatic bliss (*sukha*) associated with lofty *samādhi* attainment could still be present, as suggested by the "firm thunderbolt" (*dṛḍha-vajra*) in the heart, according to the terminology in *Mkhas-grub-rje*'s, Chapter I; and this also suggests a heart location for the "sexual frenzy".

16

RECEIVED TEACHINGS OF TIBET AND ANALYSIS OF THE TANTRIC CANON

I. Outline of the thob yig gsal baḥi me loṅ

A *thob yig* ("manual of what was received") is a work in which the author sets forth the lineages of the various doctrines and practices in which he has become learned or skilled. The East Asiatic Library, University of California, Berkeley, California, possesses a four-volume *thob yig* by the Dzaya-paṇḍita Blo bzaṅ ḥphrin las,[1] entitled *Zab pa daṅ rgya che baḥi dam paḥi chos kyi thob yig gsal baḥi me loṅ*, "The 'Bright-mirror' *thob yig* of the profound and far-reaching illustrious Law". This is a well-printed Peking block-print. The same library also has this author's *Ṅag rnams phyogs su bsgrigs pa*—his minor essays. The latter were quite popular among the Lamas, especially the essay *Ma-ṇiḥi phan yon sogs ston paḥi/byin rlabs myur ḥjug ces bya*, on the celebrated formula *Oṃ maṇi padme hūṃ*, and hence were sometimes separately printed. These are in two volumes in a Peking block-print which has been run off from blocks damaged in part. Both sets were brought to that University by Professor F. D. Lessing. Using the colophon of the *thob yig* and his autobiography

1. In the original printing *Indo-Asian Studies*, Part 1 (1962), the editor, Lokesh Chandra, supplied this note: "For a general idea about *thob yig* also see G. Tucci, *Tibetan Painted Scrolls*, p. 124. It may be noted that a copy of this *thob yig* also exists in the collection of Prof. Dr. Raghu Vira. This work will be printed in the Śatapiṭaka Series in the near future. A short biography of Jayapaṇḍita Blo bzaṅ ḥphrin las and a list of his works is given in Lokesh Chandra, *Eminent Tibetan Polymaths of Mongolia*, introd. p. 18, text p. 10."

among the *ṅag phyogs*, I have already pointed out that he was born *chu pho rta* (1642 A.D.) and was 61 years old when the Sixth Dalai Lama was 19 years old (i.e. in A.D. 1702) and that he may have been the teacher of the Sixth Dalai Lama.[2]

The following outline of the contents of his *thob yig* will serve to illustrate the structure and type of material in such a work. In almost all cases, the biographies have been severely condensed and are replete with religious terms; but as the sources of the author are themselves for the most part unobtainable in Western libraries, it appears desirable to suggest the research possibilities of this compendium. The folio numbers follow the Peking edition; volumes Ka, Kha, Ga, and Ṅa are represented respectively by I, II, III and IV.

The work begins with the usual stanzas of bowing to the great Indian and Tibetan teachers, and acknowledgments to his own teachers.

Chapter (*sarga*) 1, ending I.60a6: Dge baḥi bśes gñen bsten nas thos pa ḥtshol tshul daṅ/raṅ ñid bstan par žugs nas rab byuṅ bsñen rdzogs thob paḥi tshul bśad pa, "Exposition of the method of hearing and search through reliance on a friendly guide (*kalyāṇamitra*); and exposition of the personal method of entering the religious life and receiving ordination through entrance in the teaching".

The chapter title well exemplifies the contents. We may mention also that there is included (f. 5a1, ff.) a general discussion of the Law (*dharma*) and its division into two categories, scripture (T. *luṅ*, S. *āgama*), and higher cognition (T. *rtogs*, S. *adhigama*). Numerous authorities are quoted for this distinction, which in practice is the lineage of promulgation (*bkaḥ*) contrasted with authoritative commentary (*dgoṅs ḥgrel*).

Chapter (*sarga*) 2, ending I.122b1: Thun moṅ baḥi rig gnas rnams la thos bsam gyi bag chags cuṅ zad bžag pa, "A sketch of the traces of hearing (*śrutā*) and pondering (*cintā*) of the common sciences."

The author explains that after one has entered the teaching (as in Chapter 1) he studies sciences (*vidyāsthāna*) of two kinds, common sciences (*thun moṅ baḥi rig paḥi gnas*, S. *sādhāraṇa-vidyāsthāna*) and uncommon science (*thun moṅ ma yin paḥi rig paḥi gnas*, S. *asādhāraṇa-vidyāsthāna*). The first kind is the subject of this chapter. Many legends are given to account for the origin of the sciences. The ones in this chapter are for the most part accessible in Western sources (through the translations of Tāranātha's and of Bu-ston's History of Buddhism). Lists of teachers are given in each case. The common sciences are grammar, logic, arts, and medicine. The folio numbers will show where the individual sections begin:

I.60b2. *Sgra* (S *śabda*, "grammar"). Sgra has the five appendages or

2. "Studies in Yama and Māra," *Indo-Iranian Journal*, Vol. III (1959), p. 125, note. Beginning this page, I translated his explanations of the three kinds of Yama.

subsidiary topics (*źar byuṅ*) of *sñan dṅags* (S. *kāvya*, "poetic art"), *mṅon brjod* (S. *abhidhāna*, "lexicography"), *sdeb sbyor* (S. *chandas*, "metrics"), *zlos gar* (S. *naṭana*, "drama"), and *dkar rtsis* (S. *jyotis*, "astrology", and *gaṇita*, "astronomy").

I.70a4. *Gtan tshigs* (S. *hetu-vidyā*, "logic").

I.76a2. *Bzo ba* (S. *śilpa*, "the arts").

I.77b2. *Gso ba* (S. *cikitsā*, "medicine"). The inordinate space devoted to this heading is due to the inclusion of tantric rites concerned with medicine.

I.108b6. Sroṅ btsan sgam po. Story of the introduction of the precepts into Tibet during his reign.

Chapter (*sarga*) 3, ending I.174b2: Rgyu mtshan ñid kyi theg paḥi dam paḥi chos la thos bsam gyi bag chags cuṅ zad bžag pa daṅ gžuṅ maḥi luṅ daṅ ḥkhrid thob paḥi tshul bśad pa, "A sketch of the traces of hearing and pondering of the illustrious Law consisting in the causal, or exoteric, vehicle; and exposition of how the textual scriptures and guidance [through them] was obtained."

In beginning his treatment of uncommon science, the author subdivides this into the causal (*rgyu*, S. *hetu*) or exoteric (*mtshan ñid*, S. *lakṣaṇa*),[3] vehicle (*theg pa*. S. *yāna*); and the resultative (*ḥbras bu*, S. *phala*), esoteric (*sṅags*, S. *mantra*), vehicle (*theg pa*). Both are called "inner science" (*naṅ rig*, S. *ādhyātmika-vidyā*); and fundamental (*rtsa bar gyur pa*, S. *mūla-bhūta*) to both is the translated Word (*Bkaḥ ḥgyur* or Kanjur) of the great *muni* (*thub pa chen po*). As can be seen by the chapter title, we are here concerned with only the causal, exoteric, vehicle. The resultative, esoteric, vehicle is treated in chapters 4 through 9. The translated Word is treated in chapters 10 and 11. Our present chapter in turn divides the treatment of *luṅ* (S. *āgama*, "scripture"), beginning I.122b3; and of *ḥkhrid* (S. *nayana*, "guidance"), meaning a guided tour through the scriptures, beginning I.171b4. The first subdivision occupies most of the chapter and is devoted chiefly to biographies, which also mention works and lineages.

I.123a2.	Biography of Maitreya-nātha.	
I.125b4.	,,	Asaṅga.
I.130a3.	,,	Vasubandhu.
I.134a3.	,,	Guṇaprabha.
I.136b3.	,,	Nāgārjuna.
I.138b1.	,,	Āryadeva.

3. The expression *lakṣaṇayāna* is literally "vehicle of the characteristic(s)". Here "characteristics" may well mean "characteristics of Buddhism" and be a usage drawn from Asaṅga's *Yogācārabhūmi*, as I suggested in "The Rules of Debate according to Asaṅga," *Journal of the American Oriental Society*, Vol. 78 (Jan.-March, 1958), p. 35. The Tibetans may also have adopted this term with the implication that the highest vehicle is "without characteristics."

I.141b2. Biography of Haribhadra.
I.144a1. „ Diṅnāga.
I.145b2. „ Dharmakīrti.
I.148a3. „ Candragomin.
I.151a1. „ Śākyaprabha.
I.151b2. „ Dharmarakṣita.

I.152b5. History of the six texts of the Bkaḥ gdams pa school, i.e. the *Mahāyānasūtrālaṃkāra*, the *Bodhisattvabhūmi*, the *Śikṣāsamuccaya*, the *Bodhisattvacaryāvatāra*, the *Jātakamālā*, and the *Udānavarga*. In the course of this he gives the biography of Śāntideva.

I.162b3. The *chos chuṅ brgya rtsa* (a centenary of minor works) concerned with the teaching of Atīśa. 103 commentaries listed with translators. This is the collection called *Jo-boḥi chos chuṅ* (Tohoku Kanjur-Tanjur Catalog nos. 4465-4567).

The six texts of the Bkaḥ gdams pa, and the *chos chuṅ brgya rtsa*, are the exoteric *āgama* introduced by the reformer Atīśa, who arrived in Tibet in the year 1042.

I.169a5. Biography of Śākyaśrī, who arrived in Tibet in the year 1204 (*śin pho byi*).

I.171b4. The second subdivision of the chapter, devoted to *ḥkhrid*, or guidance. Here we learn that the exoteric guidance is comprehensively given in two works by Tsoṅ kha pa, his *Lam rim chen mo* and *Lam rim chuṅ ṅu*—respectively, the stages of the path (full version), and the same (compressed version). These, in turn, each incorporate two guidance lineages called *rgya chen spyod* (ample practice), headed by the Bodhisattva Maitreya; and *zab mo lta* (profound doctrine), headed by the Bodhisattva Mañjughoṣa.

Chapter (*sarga*) 4, ending I.297a5 (and concluding Volume I): Zur bkaḥi rjes gnaṅ gi skor thob paḥi tshul bśad pa, "Exposition of how the cycle of 'permission' (*anujñā*) in the specialized promulgations was obtained."

In the resultative, esoteric vehicle which now begins, there is a division into specialized promulgations (*zur bkaḥ*), general promulgation (*spyi bkaḥ*), and the abstruse cycle of associated collected works of Lamas, analyzing the concepts of *sūtra* and *tantra* (*žar byuṅ bla maḥi gsuṅ ḥbum sogs mdo sṅags tha sñad so sor dbye dkaḥ baḥi skor*). The present chapter is concerned with the first category, namely specialized promulgations; and is devoted only to the subsection of the *anujñā* ("permission" to invoke the deity), which it sets forth in the order in which it was introduced into Tibet. These are further subdivided with an over-all grouping into "permission" in the Kriyā-Tantra, and "permission" in the Anuttara-Yoga-Tantra. The former begins I.174b4; the latter I.249a4. The contents are rich in legends of the main deities worshipped in Tibet, and give the lineage of teachers; or perhaps more appropriately here, "proficients" or "adepts". These are a few of the items:

I.175b4 to 195a6. The 16 Sthaviras, brief biographies, and other matters.
I.221a4 to 231b6. Legend of Tārā.
I.272a2 to 276a3. Legend of the three Yama, called *phyi*, *naṅ*, and *gsaṅ*.

Chapter (*sarga*) 5, ending II.130a5: Zur bkaḥ dbaṅ du ma thob paḥi tshul bśad pa, "Exposition of how numerous initiations (*abhiṣeka*) in specialized promulgations were obtained."

This chapter continued the treatment of specialized promulgations, in the subsection of *abhiṣeka* (*dbaṅ bskur*). This is further divided into *a*. sṅags la ḥjug tshul spyir bśad pa, "General exposition of the methods of entering the *mantra* (vehicle)," that is to say, a general introduction to the concepts of the *tantras*—from beginning of Vol. II to II.14a4; and *b*. bye brag tu rgyud sde so soḥi dbaṅ thob paḥi tshul bśad pa, "Exposition in categories of how the *abhiṣekas* in the various *tantra* divisions were obtained." That is to say, the major divisions of the section are into Kriyā-Tantra, Caryā-Tantra, Yoga-Tantra, and Anuttara-Yoga-Tantra. Under these, there are divisions into different families (*kula*). A few of the topics are as follows: In the Kriyā-Tantra, II.16a3 to 23a5, legend of Amitāyus; 25a5 to 37b3, legend of Avalokiteśvara and his appearance in Tibet; 37b3 to 45b3, legend of Avalokiteśvara in connection with the rite of fasting (*smyuṅ gnas*) in the Kriyā-Tantra. Caryā-Tantra begins 62b5 (only a brief discussion). Yoga-Tantra begins 63a5. Contains the legend of how the Buddha obtained the five *abhisaṃbodhis*, and preached the Yoga Tantras. Anuttara-Yoga-Tantra begins 68a4. General discussion of this branch of the *tantras*, from 68a4 to 74a1. The Anuttara-Yoga-Tantra is divided into Father Tantras and Mother Tantras; the former is treated 74a1 to 98a3, and includes the legends of Vajrapāṇi and Mañjughoṣa in his manifestation as Yamāri. The latter (Mother Tantras) is treated 98a3, ff., and includes f. 98b3 to 110a3, a general discussion of the *Śrī-cakrasaṃvaratantra*. This section, and the chapter, concludes with a discussion of the *Kālacakra* doctrine (115a3 to 128b6).

Chapter (*sarga*) 6, ending II.151a5: Spyi bkaḥi dbaṅ rnams thob paḥi tshul bśad pa, "Exposition of how the initiations (*abhiṣeka*) of the general promulgation were obtained."

This chapter, beginning the major subsection of general promulgation, contains a biography of Abhyākaragupta, and discussion of his work, the *Rdo rje ḥphreṅ*, one of the *skor gsum* (three cycles), that is to say, the *Vajrāvali* (Tohoku 3140), the other two being the *Niṣpannayogāvali* (Tohoku 3141), and the *Jyotirmañjarī* (Tohoku 3142). There is also a biography of the Mahāsiddha Mitra [joki], and list of his work, the *Rdo rje ḥphreṅ* (*Vajrāvali*), comprising the *dkyil ḥkhor drug cu re drug gi dbaṅ*, "*abhiṣekas* of the sixty-six *maṇḍalas*."

Chapter (*sarga*) 7, ending II.259a3: Spyi bkaḥi rjes gnaṅ gi skor thob paḥi tshul bśad pa, "Exposition of how the cycle of 'permission' (*anujñā*) of the general promulgation was obtained."

Here we may especially point out, II.152a6 to 171b2, discussion of the *sādhana* collections in relation to *anujñā* "permission"; II.179a4 to 183a3, description of the Saṃbhoga-kāya in terms of the *ṅes pa lṅa* "the five certainties"; II.183a6 to 251a6, biographies of the 84 Mahā-siddhas (which are numbered in the text). From II.215a6, ff, the author explains that he has summarized the (84) biographies as set forth in the *yig cha* (manual) by the Dge sloṅ Sman grub śes rab; and, without detail, lists several other versions; then, he discusses the text in general, and in connection with *anujñā* "permission".

Concluding the chapter is a brief discussion (f. 257a4, ff.) of guidance (*ḥkhrid*) in the general promulgation.

Chapter (*sarga*) 8, completing Vol. II, and ending III.43a4: Rgya bod kyi mkhas grub sṅon byuṅ bkaḥ gdams pa maṅ poḥi rnam thar daṅ de dag gi gsuṅ ḥbum las luṅ ji ltar thob paḥi tshul bśad pa, "Exposition of numerous biographies of the early learned men of India and Tibet, and of [leading figures of] the Bkaḥ gdams pa; as well as of how the scripture (*āgama*) was obtained from their collected works."

The third division of the resultative, esoteric vehicle, namely, the associated works of Lamas, now begins, and covers chapters 8 and 9. The present chapter covers teachers up to, but not including, Tsoṅ-kha-pa (A.D. 1357-1419). There are lineage lists in almost every case.

II.259a5 to 264b1. Biography of Śāntirakṣita, the 8th century Indian paṇḍit who played a paramount role in early Tibetan Buddhist history, and through whose advice Padmasambhava was invited to Tibet.

II.265b1 to 270b1. Biography of Atīśa, and literature of the Bkaḥ gdams pa school. Atīśa, 11th century Indian paṇḍit, is the most important one of the Indian Buddhist scholars for the later diffusion of Buddhism in Tibet. The Bkaḥ gdams pa school was founded by his chief student (Ḥbrom ston) to hand down Atīśa's oral precepts (*bkaḥ gdams*).

There follow the biographies of Mkhas grub khyuṅ po (II.272b4, ff.), Nag tsho Lotsava (II.274b1, ff.), and Lha bla ma Byaṅ chub ḥod (II.277b5, ff.), outstanding personages of the 11th century. Then, II.278b1 to 283b5, discussion of the *kalyāṇamitras* (friendly guides) of the Bkaḥ gdams pa school. Individual biographies of the outstanding ones of this group follow from II.283b5 to 308a6. II.308a6 to 314b2, biography of Sa skya paṇḍita (A.D. 1182-1251), who was primarily responsible for converting the Mongols to Buddhism. There follow the biographies of immediate predecessors and teachers of Tsoṅ-kha-pa, namely Bu ston rin po che, redactor of the Kanjur and Tanjur (from beginning of Vol. III), Thogs med dpal bzaṅ po (III.14a6, ff.), Sems dpaḥ chen po Dpal ldan ye śes (III.26b1, ff.), Lho brag Nam mkhaḥ rgyal mtshan dpal bzaṅ po (III.26b5, ff.), and Red mdaḥ pa (III.39b2 to 42b5).

Chapter (*sarga*) 9, completing Vol. III, and ending IV.174b4: Rgyal ba Tsoṅ-kha-pa chen po yab sras kyi rtogs brjod daṅ de rnams kyi gsuṅ ḥbum las luṅ ji sñed pa thob paḥi tshul bśad pa, "Exposition of the instructive lives (*avadāna*) of the victorious one, the great Tsoṅ-kha-pa, and of his spiritual sons; as well as of how the scripture was obtained from their collected works."

Chapter 9 is, in effect, a history of the Gelugpa school, founded by Tsoṅ-kha-pa (1357-1419 A.D.), in terms of the lives of its principal figures. The colophon mention of the Sixth Dalai Lama's age as 19 shows that the author finished the work soon after the beginning of the 18th century. Theoretically, the author should include only those teachers in whose lineage he stands. However, apparently by encyclopedic knowledge, he manages to have learned something from almost everyone of importance (at least in the Gelugpa school), and this gives him the opportunity to write up their biographies, even though in many cases it is extremely brief. We shall not itemize the many personages he treats, but restrict ourselves to a few remarks. He treats with greatest amplitude the Dalai Lamas, the Paṇ chen Lamas, and the chief ones among the *yoṅs ḥdzin*, religious teachers of the highly-placed Lamas, has an especially ample treatment of the 1st Paṇ chen Lama Blo bzaṅ chos kyi rgyal mtshan dpal bzaṅ po, III.190b1 to 232a2; and coming up to his own times, gives increasingly greater information in the biographies. Hence, the 17th century, with which he is most familiar, is especially well treated, and he naturally speaks with greatest authority on this period. Understandably, his chief emphasis is religous.

Chapter (*sarga*) 10, ending IV.242b2: Rgyu phar phyin paḥi chos gtso bor ston paḥi mdoḥi skor gyi luṅ thob paḥi tshul bśad, "Exposition of how the scriptures of the cycle of *sūtras* which show principally the teaching of the causal *pāramitā* were obtained."

This and chapter 11 are devoted to the Kanjur (the approximate pronunciation of *bkaḥ ḥgyur*). Recalling the discussion at the outset of chapter 3 concerning the two vehicles, causal and resultative, we see that the author has maintained this distinction to the last, now dividing his treatment of the Kanjur into two chapters on this basis.

He leads up to the main subject matter with the following sections:

IV.175a3 to 187a4, biography of Śākyamuni in terms of the 12 Acts (*mdzad pa bcu gñis*); IV.187a4 to 190a4, how the great Śrāvakas compiled the Word (*Hīnayāna tradition*); IV.190a4 to 190a5, compilation of the Word (*Mahāyāna tradition*); IV.190a6 to 190b3, duration of the Teaching; IV.190b5 to 194b3, important teachers in India and their commentaries; IV. 194b3 to 197a2, diffusion of the Teaching in Tibet.

The *sūtras* which show principally the causal *pāramitā* vehicle fall into four groups:

(1) IV.197a4, ff.: Bkaḥ daṅ po bden bžiḥi chos ḥkhor las byuṅ ba ḥdul ba luṅ, "The *Vinaya-vastu* arising from the first promulgation (*bkaḥ*) which was the Wheel of the Law concerning the Four Truths". In the Tohoku Catalog, nos 1-7.

(2) IV.201a1. ff.: Bar pa mtshan ñid med paḥi chos ḥkhor las byuṅ ba śer phyogs, "The *Prajñā-pāramitā* side arising from the intermediate (promulgation) which was the Wheel of Law concerning lack of characteristics (i.e. the Void, S. *śūnyatā*)." In the Tohoku Catalog, nos. 8-30.

(3) IV.209a2, ff.: Tha ma legs par rnam par phye baḥi chos ḥkhor las byuṅ ba dkon brtsegs daṅ phal chen, "The *Ratnakūṭa* and *Avataṃsaka* arising from the last (promulgation) which was the Wheel of the Law concerning perfect discrimination (i.e. Yoga experience)." In the Tohoku Catalog, nos. 44 (*Avataṃsaka*) and 45-93 (*Ratnakūṭa*).

(4) IV.217b3, ff.: Ḥkhor lo gsum pa ci rigs par gtogs pa sde tshan phyogs gcig tu bsgrigs paḥi mdo maṅ, "The numerous *sūtras* which pertain in some measure to all three Wheels (of the Law), arranged in a single major class." In the Tohoku Catalog, nos. 94-359.

All the works are listed individually with notice of the translators, and listing of the chief names of the lineage going with the particular work. The Kanjur used by the author has few differences with the Derge edition, but the works are not always in the same order. Furthermore, the works with nos. 31-43 in the Tohoku Catalog found in the Derge Kanjur are apparently all translations from Pāli not included in the original plan of the Kanjur and are not discussed by the author.

Chapter (*sarga*) 11, ending IV.289b6: Ḥbras bu rdo rje theg pa gtso bor ston paḥi rgyud kyi skor gyi luṅ thob paḥi tshul bśad pa, "Exposition of how the scriptures of the cycle of *tantras* which show principally the resultative Vajrayāna were obtained."

First (IV.242b4) the author mentions that he will not describe the *Rñiṅ Rgyud* ("The Old Tantras"). Tohoku Catalog nos. 828-844, because *luṅ ma thob* ("their *āgama* was not obtained"), that is to say, he is not the recipient of instruction concerning them handed down from master to disciple. In other words, the mere fact that works have been translated into the Tibetan language gives no one a particular right to expound them, or presume to say he understands them. Even the most prominent authors write authoritatively only in those fields in which they can show they are the link in the chain of teachers. This accounts for the care taken to list the lineage of teachers for the various texts, as well as for the tendency to study only certain works, completely disregarding large sections of the translated canon.

His treatment of the remaining *tantras* undoubtedly follows Bu-ston, who fixed the arrangement in the 14th century, except for a few details, such as the interpolation of one or more later-translated texts. Just as for the *sūtras*, he lists the translators and the lineage. These are the most major categories:

IV.242b6, ff.: Anuttara-Yoga-Tantra (*rnal ḥbyor bla med kyi rgyud*), Tohoku Catalog nos. 360-478.

IV.259a3, ff.: Yoga-Tqntra (*rnal ḥbyor rgyud*), Tohoku nos. 479-493.

IV.262b2, ff.: Caryā-Tantra (*spyod paḥi rgyud*), Tohoku nos. 494-501.

IV.264b1, ff.: Kriyā-Tantra (*bya baḥi rgyud*), Tohoku nos. 502-827.

There are a few works in the Derge Kanjur not listed by the author.

The whole work concludes with a long colophon, IV.289b2 to 303a.

* * *

II. Analysis of the Tantric section of the Kanjur correlated to Tanjur exegesis

The present analysis of the Kanjur *Rgyud ḥbum* is based on the *Thob yig gsal baḥi me loṅ* by the Dzaya-paṇḍita Blo bzaṅ ḥphrin las.[4] The correlation to the Tanjur exegesis is made with the help of Palmyr Cordier's *Catalogue du Fonds Tibétain de la Bibliothèque Nationale*, Vols. II and III (Paris, 1949 and 1915), along with his Leḥu numbers.[5] All numbers of works are references to *A Complete Catalogue of the Tibetan Buddhist Canons* (published by the Tohoku Imperial University, Sendai, Japan, 1934). The latter is a catalog of the Derge edition of the Kanjur and Tanjur, but presumably every library which possesses a Kanjur and

4. Cf. my preceding "Outline of the Thob yig gsal baḥi me loṅ." Prof. G. Tucci in *Tibetan Painted Scrolls* (Rome, 1949), pp. 261-263, presents the minute systemization, but the Blo bzaṅ ḥphrin las work was more convenient to me at the time the study was made—in fact, early summer, 1953, according to the typescript from which the present article is prepared with corrections according to my present knowledge.

5. The two volumes are Cordier's index to the Tanjur. His tragic death at the outset of the First World War prevented his completion of the projected Vol. I devoted to alphabetical indexes. This part was finished by Marcelle Lalou in her *Répertoire du Tanjur d'après le Catalogue de P. Cordier* (Paris, 1933). By Leḥu numbers is meant the data in Cordier's Vol. III, pp. 537-550. It should also be mentioned that my correlation to the Tanjur does not exhaust all the Tanjur Tantric entries, particularly in Cordier's catalog, but fairly well accounts for the numbers in the *Rgyud ḥgrel* section of the Derge Tanjur, as catalogued at the Tohoku University.

Tanjur of whatever edition would have this catalog because it is the only one so far for both a Kanjur and Tanjur.

The Kanjur classification of the *Rgyud ḥbum* was finally set by Bu-ston (1290-1364 A.D.) in four groups—Anuttara-Yoga-Tantra, Yoga-Tantra, Caryā Tantra, and Kriyā-Tantra. A separate group called the *Rñiṅ rgyud* (Tohoku catalog nos. 828-844) comprises the old Tantras considered genuine but whose *āgama* (descent through master and disciple) had been broken or at least was not available to Bu-ston.

	Derge Kanjur (Toh. Cat. nos.)	Derge Tanjur (Toh. Cat. nos).
A. Anuttara-Yoga-Tantra		
1. Neither Father nor Mother.[6]		
Mañjuśrī-nama-saṇgīti[7] (Cordier, Leḥu 12)[8]	360	1395-1400, 2090-2121
Kālacakra (Cordier, Leḥu)[9]	361-365	1346-1394
2. Mother Tantras, under seven groupings,		
a. Ston pa, through g. Vajradhāra.[10]		
a. Ston pa (*deśaka).		
Sarvabuddhasamayoga (Cordier, Leḥu 8)	366-367	1659-1682
b. Heruka (i.e. Akṣobhya), in five classes.		
(1) *Saṃvara* (Cordier, Leḥu 2)	368-415	1401-1606[11]
(2) *Hevajra* (Cordier, Leḥu 3)	417-423	1180-1345[12]

6. Tsoṅ-kha-pa did not admit this category; for him, the *Kālacakra* is a Mother Tantra. His views are summarized by his disciple Mkhas grub rje in the *Rgyud sde spyi rnam*, which Prof. F. D. Lessing and I have translated. It was my work on Mkhas grub rje's text that originally inspired the research embodied in the present article.

7. This work is in a class by itself, because it has a set of commentaries as an Anuttara-Yoga-Tantra, and another set as a Yoga-Tantra (therefore see also the Yoga-Tantra section).

8. Cordier's Leḥu 12 covers only the numbers 2090-2121, which are located immediately after the Father Vairocana *Yamāri* Tantric exegesis and are followed by the Father Padma-kula *Bhagavadekajaṭā* Tantric exegesis. It can be assumed that nos. 2090-2121 are commentaries in the Father Vairocana Tantric tradition. On the other hand, nos. 1395-1400 are included in Cordier's Leḥu 1 as *Kālacakra* commentaries.

9. Cordier's Leḥu 1 also includes nos. 1395-1400, as pointed in note 5.

10. The intention is to list the Tantras under the Buddha (Tathāgata, Jina) being emphasized. The first category (Ston pa) deals with all the Buddhas equally, and so strictly speaking does not constitute an individual Tantric family. The remaining six groups then correspond, and in the same order, to the six of the Father Tantras. The sixfold group can be increased to seven by dividing the Vajradhara family into causal (*hetu-*) and fruitional (*phala-*) Vajradhara. In such a case, the causal Vajradhara is called Vajrasattva.

11. The numbers 1401-1540 and 1541-1606 roughly correspond to Cordier's division into Yab skor and Yum skor, respectively.

12. Yab skor, nos. 1180-1304; Yum skor, nos. 1305-1320; Gur skor, 1321-1330; Thig skor, 1331-1345.

	Derge Kanjur (Toh. Cat. nos.)	*Derge Tanjur* (Toh. Cat. nos.)
(3) *Buddhakapāla* (Cordier, Leḥu 7)	424	1652-1657
(4) *Mahāmāyā* (Cordier, Leḥu 5)	425	1622-1648
(5) *Ārali* (Cordier, Leḥu 7, last item)	426-427	1658
c. Vairocana.		
Catuḥpīṭha (Cordier, Leḥu 4)	428-430	1607-1621
Caṇḍamahāroṣaṇa, *Krodharāja*, *Acala* (in Cordier, Leḥu 24)	431-434	1782-1783
d. Rdo rje ñi ma (Vajraprabhā, i.e. Ratnasaṃbhava).		
Vajrāmṛta (Cordier, Leḥu 6)	435	1649-1651
e. Padma gar dbaṅ (Padmanarteśvara, i.e. Amitābha). (In Cordier, Leḥu 9).		
Lokanatha	436	1750-1751
Tārā-Kurukullā	437	—
f. Rta mchog (Paramāśva, i.e. Amoghasiddhi). (In Cordier, Leḥu 9).		
Namastāre ekaviṃśati[13]	438	1683-1744[14]
Vajrakīlaya	439	—
Mahākāla	440[15]	1752-1781
g. Vajradhara.		
Yathālabdhakhasama	441	—
3. Father Tantras, under six groupings, a. Akṣobhya, through f. Vajradhara.		
a. Akṣobhya.		
Guhyasamāja (Cordier, Leḥu 10).	442-451[16]	1784-1917
Vajrapāṇi (Cordier, Leḥu 14)	454-464[17]	2147-2216
b. Vairocana		
Yamāri (Cordier, Leḥu 11)	467-475, 478	1918-2089
c. Ratna-kula (lacking).		
d. Padma-kula.		

13. This is an extract from no. 726, 3rd chapter, listed among the Kriyā-Tantras. That work is the most important one among the Tantras of the Mother of the Padma kula. Its Sanskrit title: *Sarvatathāgatamātṛtārāviśvakarmabhava-tantra*.

14. Since the twenty-one forms of Tārā represent all the moods of the World Mother, the different forms undoubtedly take care of the bulk of these commentaries. However, it is possible that some of the numbers constitute commentaries on *Tārā-Kurukullā* under e. above. Furthermore, the general works nos. 1745-1749 may have been placed immediately after the Tārā commentaries as generalities pertaining to those foregoing works.

15. And possibly also no. 416.

16. And possibly also nos. 452-453.

17. And possibly also no. 465.

	Derge Kanjur (Toh. Cat. nos.)	Derge Tanjur (Toh. Cat. nos.)
Bhagavadekajaṭā (Cordier, Leḥu 13).	476	2122-2146
e. Karma-kula (lacking).		
f. Vajradhara.		
Candraguhyatilaka	477	—
The Tanjur has moreover a section on generalities of the Anuttary-yoga-tantra, including the mystic songs of the Mahāsiddhas (Cordier, Leḥu 15).		2217-2500
B. Yoga-Tantra		
1. The *mūla-tantra.*		
Tattvasaṃgraha, in four sections (*dum bu*).[18]	479	
2. Explanatory (*ākhya*) Tantras.		
Vajraśekhara, chiefly *thabs* (*upāya*).	480	
Paramādya, chiefly *śes rab* (*prajñā*).	487-488	
Others, chiefly *śes rab*:		
Vajramaṇḍalālaṃkāra, *Guhyālaṃkāravyūha* and *Guhyamaṇitilaka*.	490, 492-493	
Māyājāla[19]	466	
Commentaries on the *mūla* and explanatory Tantras (Cordier, Leḥu 17)		2501-2531
Mañjuśrī-nāma-saṃgīti, as an explanatory Tantra (Cordier, Leḥu 17)	360	2532-2622
3. *Cha mthun* Tantras.[20]		
Sarvarahasya, explanatory (*thabs*) of 1st section (Tathāgata-kula)	481	
Trailokyavijaya, explanatory (*thabs*) of 2nd section (Vajra-kula)	482	
Others, explanatory from *thabs* standpoint	483-486	
Prajñāpāramitānayaśatapañcaśatikā, and *Pañcaviṃśatikāprajñāpāramitāmukha*, explanatory from *śes rab* standpoint[21]	489, 491	

18. The four sections represent five Buddha families compressed into four groups. This Tantra is also first of the ones showing chiefly *thabs* (*upāya*).

19. The Māyājāla was not included by the Dzaya-paṇḍita under the Yoga-Tantra, but its commentaries (nos. 2513-2514) are among the commentaries on the *mūla* and explanatory Tantras. The work itself is located among the Anuttara-yoga-Tantras in the Derge Kanjur, suggesting that its status was a matter of dispute among the Lamas.

20. A *Cha mthun* Tantra is one with materials arranged to go specifically with one or more sections of the basic Tantra. Explanatory Tantras that are not *Cha mthun* develop various topics of the basic Tantra without regard to the sectional divisions.

21. In particular, no. 491 goes with no. 490.

	Derge Kanjur (Toh. Cat. nos.)	Derge Tanjur (Toh. Cat. nos.)
Moreover, no. 488, above, can also be considered a *Cha mthun* Tantra for no. 487; and no. 487 can be considered a *Cha mthun* Tantra for the *mūlatantra*, no. 479.		
Commentaries on the *Cha mthun* or *Ḥphros pa* Tantras (Cordier, Leḥu 18)		2623-2661
C. Caryā-Tantra		
1. Tathāgata-kula.		
Mahāvairocana[22]	494	
Acala-kalpa	495	
Commentaries on the Tathāgata-kula Tantras (Cordier, Leḥu 19)		2662-2669
2. Padma-kula (lacking).		
3. Vajra-kula.		
Vajrapāṇy-abhiṣeka	496	—
Aṣṭadevī-dhāraṇī	497	—
Others:	498-501	—
D. Kriyā-Tantra[23] (Cordier, Leḥu 20)		(2670-3139)
1. Tathāgata-kula.		
a. Tantras of the Lord (*gtso bo*)	502-542	2694-2697, 3130-3139
b. Tantras of the Master (*bdag po*)	543-552	2674, 2701-2719
c. Tantras of the Mother (*yum*):		
Prajñāpāramitā (the *Aṣṭaśataka* and *Kauśika*)	553-554	—
Suvarṇaprabhāsottama	555-557	—
Pañcarakṣā	558-563	2690-2693, 3117-3129
Mārīcī	564-566	—
Others:	567-589	—
d. Tantras of the Uṣṇīṣa	590-603	2688-2689, 3068-3116

22. Apparently the last chapter is taken as an Uttara tantra (*phyi ma rgyud*).

23. As in the Caryā-Tantra there are three *lokottara* families, Tathāgata, Padma, and Vajra. In addition there are three *laukika* families, Maṇi, Pañcaka, and Laukika. Included among the Kriyā-Tantra are works of a general character (nos. 805-808) which give basic material that can be used by the higher Tantras (Caryā, etc.) as well. Finally, there is a division, often extracts from other works, of Pariṇāma and Praṇidhāna.

	Derge Kanjur (Toh. Cat. nos.)	Derge Tanjur (Toh. Cat. nos.)
e. Tantras of Wrathful Deities (*khro bo*):		
Tantras of Male Wrathful Deities (*khro bo*)	604-611	(?) 3052
Tantras of Female Wrathful Deities (*khro mo*)	612-613	—
f. Tantras of Messengers (*pho ña*)	614-630	
Tantras of Male and Female Obedient Ones (*bkaḥ ñan pho mo*) auxiliary to the Messengers	631-633	3059-3065
g. Bodhisattvas belonging to the family	634-644	—
h. Gods, etc. of the Pure Abode	645-673	—
2. Padma-kula.		
a. Tantras of the Lord	674-680	2698-2700
b. Tantras of the Master	681-723	2720-2864
c. Tantras of the Mother	724-732	— [24]
d. Tantras of the Wrathful Deities, Male and Female	733-736	3053-3058
e. Tantras of Obedient Ones, Male and Female	737-742	—
3. Vajra-kula.		
a. Tantras of the Lord	743	—
b. Tantras of the Master	744, 756 746-751	2675-2687, 2865-3049
c. Tantras of the Mother	752	—
d. Tantras of Wrathful Deities, Male and Female	753-755	—
e. Tantras of Male and Female Messengers and Obedient Ones	757-763	3050-3051
4. Worldly Families.		
a. Nor can (Maṇi)	764-771[25]	—
b. Lṅas rtsen (Pañcaka)	772	—
c. Ḥjig rten pa (Laukika)	773-804	—
5. General Kriyā-Tantra.		
Subāhuparipṛcchā	805	2671-2673
Sāmānyavidhīnām guhya-tantra	806	—
Susiddhi	807	3066

24. While no commentaries on the Mother of the Padma-kula are included in Cordier, Leḥu 20, the Sādhana collection nos. 3645-3704 includes a large block of Tārā commentaries (nos. 3666-3696) which are probably Kriyā-Tantra works for the most part. Certainly the ones by Candragomin are Kriyā-Tantra.

25. However, nos. 766-767 are really one work in two *brtag pa* called *sṅa* and *phyi*.

	Derge Kanjur (Toh. Cat. nos.)	*Derge Tanjur* (Toh. Cat. nos.)
Dhyānottarapaṭalakrama	808	2670
6. *Yoṅs su bsṅo* and *Smon lam*.		
a. Yoṅs su bsṅo (*pariṇāma*).	809-810	—
b. Smon lam (*praṇidhāna*)	811-827	—

The above ends the analysis of the Kanjur *Rgyud ḥbum* correlated to Tanjur exegesis. In addition the Tanjur has a section of generalities pertaining to all four Tantras.

	Derge Tanjur (Toh. Cat. nos.)
Cordier, Leḥu 21:	
1. General on all four Tantras.	
The *Vajrāvali*, *Niṣpannayogāvali*, and *Jyotirmañjarī*, by Abhayākaragupta	3140-3142
2. Sādhana collections.	
a. Pa-tshab sgrub thabs brgya rtsa	3143-3304
b. Ba-ri sgrub thabs brgya rtsa	3306-3399
c. Sgrub thabs rgya mtsho	3400-3644
d. Lha so so sna tshogs kyi sgrub thabs	3645-3704
3. Preparation of maṇḍala.	3705-3706
Cordier, Leḥu 22:	
1. Distinctions among the 3 Yānas and 4 Tantras	3707-3720
2. Samaya and saṃvara (pledges and vows)	3721-3729
3. Cycle of Dharmapāla, Vasudeva, etc.	3730-3755
Cordier, Leḥu 23:	
Miscellaneous, *cho ga*, etc.	3756-3785
Cordier, Leḥu 24:	
Later translations.[26] In Derge Tanjur:	3305

26. Most of these translations are not included in the Derge Kanjur. When they are, they have been incorporated in earlier sections, except for the one work now mentioned, no. 3305, which the Derge edition places between the Pa-tshab and Ba-ri *sādhana* collections. The title, *Vajrācāryakriyāsamuccaya*, gives no clue to the placement. It is a large work devoted, according to the title, to the duties of the Tantric Hierophant (*vajrācārya*) who explains the Tantras, initiates others, and so on.

INDEX

INDEX*

* For convenience of use and relevance to this work, which is mainly based on original sources and terms, this index features the same, with Western titles and articles omitted. Western names are given only if persons have contributed to these Buddhist tantra materials or are cited more than once. Commentaries are grouped when possible: "& comm." means, along with commentaries; "incl. X" means, including entries for X: "also Y" means, see Y for separate listing.